Therapist Performance
Under Pressure

Therapist Performance Under Pressure

Negotiating Emotion, Difference, and Rupture

J. CHRISTOPHER MURAN

CATHERINE F. EUBANKS

AMERICAN PSYCHOLOGICAL ASSOCIATION
Washington, DC

Published by
American Psychological Association
750 First Street, NE
Washington, DC 20002
https://www.apa.org

Order Department
https://www.apa.org/pubs/books
order@apa.org

In the U.K., Europe, Africa, and the Middle East, copies may be ordered from Eurospan
https://www.eurospanbookstore.com/apa
info@eurospangroup.com

Typeset in Meridien and Ortodoxa by Circle Graphics, Inc., Reisterstown, MD

Printer: Sheridan Books, Chelsea, MI
Cover Designer: Beth Schlenoff, Bethesda, MD

Library of Congress Cataloging-in-Publication Data

Names: Muran, J. Christopher, author. | Eubanks, Catherine F., author. |
   American Psychological Association, issuing body.
Title: Therapist performance under pressure : negotiating emotion,
   difference, and rupture / J. Christopher Muran and Catherine F. Eubanks.
Description: Washington, DC : American Psychological Association, [2020] |
   Includes bibliographical references and index.
Identifiers: LCCN 2019050268 (print) | LCCN 2019050269 (ebook) |
   ISBN 9781433831911 (paperback) | ISBN 9781433831928 (ebook)
Subjects: MESH: Psychotherapeutic Processes | Psychotherapy—methods |
   Professional-Patient Relations | Emotions
Classification: LCC RC480.5 (print) | LCC RC480.5 (ebook) | NLM WM 420 |
   DDC 616.89/14—dc23
LC record available at https://lccn.loc.gov/2019050268
LC ebook record available at https://lccn.loc.gov/2019050269

http://dx.doi.org/10.1037/0000182-000

Printed in the United States of America

10 9 8 7 6 5 4 3 2 1

To Jeremy
"You'll Never Walk Alone"
—OSCAR HAMMERSTEIN II

CONTENTS

Preface: Positioning the Authors ix

Introduction: Pressure in the Therapeutic Relationship 3

1. The Science of Performance Under Pressure **13**

    Naturalistic Decision Making *14*

    Counterfactual Thinking *15*

    Implicit Bias *17*

    Affect Effect *17*

    Clinical Judgment *18*

    Stress Response *20*

    Self-Focus *21*

    Emotion Regulation *21*

    Resilience *23*

    Deliberate Practice *24*

    Reflective Practice *25*

    Coda *26*

2. The Science of the Therapist Under Pressure **29**

    Why Do We Need a Strong Alliance? *30*

    What Gets in the Way of a Strong Alliance? *30*

    How Do Therapists' Personal Difficulties Contribute to Problems

      in the Alliance? *31*

    How Do Therapists Contribute to Negative Process? *33*

    What Are Alliance Ruptures? *37*

    What Do We Know About Rupture Repair? *41*

    Case Example: Immediate and Exploratory Resolution Approaches *47*

    Coda *49*

3. From Emotion to Rupture   **51**

Emotion: From Basic to Complex   52

Emotion: From Generation to Regulation   54

Emotion: From Multiplicity to Intersubjectivity   56

Emotion: From Rupture to Repair   67

Coda   70

4. From Emotion to Repair   **73**

Emotion: From Communication to Metacommunication   73

Emotion: From Patient to Therapist   82

Coda   101

5. A Way to Therapist Training   **103**

Other Supervision and Training Models   104

Supervisors as Responsive Models and Secure Bases   105

Alliance-Focused Training: Helping Therapists Regulate Emotions
  and Negotiate Ruptures   106

Coda   126

6. A Way to Therapist Self-Care   **129**

Some Basic Attitudes   129

Some Useful Strategies   135

Coda   142

Conclusion: In the Pressure Cooker   143

What We Know We Know About Clinical Judgment, Alliance, and Training   145

What We Know We Don't Know About Rupture, Intervention, and Training   146

What We Don't Know We Don't Know About Emotion Regulation   147

Appendix: The Rupture Resolution Rating System   149

References   191

Index   223

About the Authors   233

PREFACE: POSITIONING THE AUTHORS

Over the past 30 years or so, we have seen a marked shift in academia toward providing more autobiographical insight (see N. K. Miller, 1991, for an early call in this regard). Accordingly, here we would like to "get personal" and provide some context to our respective approaches to the subject that we address in this book.

PERSONAL NOTES FROM THE AUTHORS

J. Christopher Muran

For 3 decades, I have been studying "ruptures" in the therapeutic alliance. *Ruptures* are disagreements in the collaboration between patient and therapist, deteriorations in their emotional bond, and breakdowns in the negotiation of their respective needs—as well as their respective identities (Muran, 2019; Safran & Muran, 2000). This focus was founded on the research demonstrating the predictive validity of the alliance (Flückiger, Del Re, Wampold, & Horvath, 2019), with the ultimate aim of providing more insight for the clinician on how the alliance functions, especially when things go awry, which we have demonstrated is quite often (Eubanks, Muran, & Safran, 2019). I began this professional journey in 1989, when Jeremy Safran hired me as his postdoctoral fellow at the Clarke Institute of Psychiatry, University of Toronto. A year later, I took on directorship of the Psychotherapy Research Program at Beth Israel Medical Center (now Mount Sinai Beth Israel) and invited Jeremy to be a principal consultant. Our collaboration flourished with numerous initiatives (supported in part by grants from the National Institute of Mental Health). Our work attempted to integrate principles from the psychoanalytic, cognitive-behavioral, and humanistic traditions, including findings from contemporary research on cognition and emotion. Arnold Winston and Lisa Samstag played critical roles in our efforts to study ruptures and their relevance for improving treatment success. Over the past 12 years, Catherine Eubanks (with her interest in therapist experience and development) became pivotal in helping us refine our approach to training therapists to resolve ruptures, and she helped me to further my thinking and focus on helping therapists negotiate difficult moments marked by rupture and manage their emotions under pressure.

During this time, my wife, Elisa, and I had a son, Andy, and I found myself spending every free moment with him, playing the role of father–coach. By this, I mean beyond the usual responsibilities and challenges of being a father, I also tried to coach him in his various athletic pursuits—something that is *not* typically recommended (and by and large, I would agree with this). I comanaged his Little League and travel soccer teams, and I coached him on the U.S. Squash junior circuit. Coaching him in squash was a unique challenge: In this individual sport, you can coach the player between games, and often Andy was facing a player coached by a paid professional who had a world ranking. My own background was that I captained varsity tennis and squash in college (a culmination of my junior years in competition), but whatever success I had was part of another era and modest by today's standards. Trying to help your son between games, in the heat of the moment, is no small feat: We had exchanges that no father and son should have; we also had brilliant moments (and I'm happy, proud, and relieved to say that Andy was recruited by and became a highly ranked college athlete at Cornell University—and most important, we have remained very close).

At some point, these father-and-son experiences struck me as remarkably comparable to experiences I had in training therapists to negotiate their emotions and skills in the face of rupture events. My reading of the developing literature on performance science only reinforced this recognition. My professional path intersected with my personal path. Some might wonder why it took me so long to realize this, why I kept them separate or thought they were. (The answer, like many things, is complicated.) This book is a product of this intersection.

Catherine F. Eubanks

When Chris invited me to join him on this book project, I accepted eagerly. I cannot lay claim to the kind of athletic career Chris had—though mine did have enough of an impact on me that I still experience an anxious anticipation when I smell fresh-cut spring grass and can almost feel the high school track under my feet as I wait for the starter pistol to fire.

I began collaborating with Chris and Jeremy more than 12 years ago, and in that time I have developed a deep appreciation for their approach to understanding alliance ruptures. In many ways, it feels as if I "fell into" this work.

Thanks to the wise and impactful teaching of my mentor, Marv Goldfried, I was introduced to Chris and Jeremy's theoretical and empirical contributions to the psychotherapy literature during graduate school. I then had the opportunity of being supervised by Chris during my clinical internship at Beth Israel. I enjoyed working with Chris, so when he invited me to stay on in a postdoctoral fellowship, I agreed; I began collaborating with him and Jeremy on alliance research, and essentially never left.

Looking back, I hope that my path to a career as an alliance rupture researcher was not simply inertia on my part but rather that I found something that resonates with me. Chris and Jeremy approached alliance ruptures and therapist performance under pressure in a way that felt different and, dare I say, therapeutic for me. Befitting my upbringing as a young woman from the American South, I entered this research collaboration well acquainted with an idea of "grace under pressure" as the appearance of seamless perfection. Chris and Jeremy introduced me to something radically different: the idea that our clinical misfires have the potential to be transformational, that a therapy with ruptures might end up yielding a better outcome than a seamlessly smooth one, that we can admit and own our vulnerability with curiosity and compassion rather than being paralyzed by shame. This is a different way of thinking about grace under pressure—not grace as ladylike perfection but more akin to the kind of grace I hear about on Sunday mornings.

I have spent a lot of time in church pews as well as in classrooms, research labs, and therapy offices, and before I studied psychology, I studied theology. Like Chris, I find that two paths in my life intersect in this work. Alliance ruptures are too awkward to be described as graceful, but perhaps can be seen as full of grace. Chris's and Jeremy's work challenges me to risk making my patient and myself uncomfortable and to dare to have faith in the therapeutic process. I am learning to savor the surprises that come my way when I risk exploring a rupture and seeing what new things can unfold. Grace under pressure is a gift.

ACKNOWLEDGMENTS

We first acknowledge Susan Reynolds of American Psychological Association (APA) Books, who asked me (JCM) at a Society for Psychotherapy Research meeting in Brisbane, Australia, back in 2013, "What are you thinking about these days that excites you?" I was hesitant to say at first, but eventually I expressed my interest in marrying the performance science and psychotherapy research literatures (as just described). I remember adding that I was not ready to undertake this and not sure the excitement I felt wasn't just a passing fancy. "Ask me again in a couple years," I suggested with a smile. And Susan did. Our next conversation was still marked by some hesitancy about taking on what seemed to me a massive undertaking, to which she responded, "What you need is a really good collaborator." Of course! Enter CFE, with whom I had been working swimmingly for some time and with whom I shared a deep interest in the therapist side of the therapeutic alliance equation. In her gentle and prescient manner, Susan brought this project to fruition.

In addition to the indelible influence of Jeremy Safran, we also acknowledge our many other mentors and colleagues, especially Jacques Barber, Louis Castonguay, Marv Goldfried, Elizabeth Ochoa, Lisa Wallner Samstag, and Arnold Winston, without whom our thinking and writing would not be what it is. We are very grateful to Mount Sinai Beth Israel (and the National Institute of Mental Health, in part) for supporting our research program. There are also the many new colleagues (academic and administrative) at Derner (Adelphi University) and Ferkauf (Yeshiva University). We would be remiss not to recognize our students who questioned us and our patients who challenged us: They taught us so much. Finally, we express our gratitude to our respective families for their inspiration and support. Thank you all!

Therapist Performance
Under Pressure

Introduction

Pressure in the Therapeutic Relationship

All real living is meeting.

—MARTIN BUBER

I (JCM) had just called down to the reception desk, saying they could let my next appointment come upstairs for our session, when the phone rang. It was another patient who was in a paranoid panic. She had a suspicion or delusion that her former boyfriend was working for the CIA, and she was convinced he was now stalking her. She was freaked out and needed to talk to me. She was calling from nearby—and she conveyed she had gotten a gun to protect herself. I was a doctoral student in my third year of training. I had only a couple minutes before my next appointment would walk through the door. I don't remember what I said to my patient on the phone, but I was able to get off the phone just before I heard a knock on my door. My next patient was a young man close to my age. He dutifully took a seat across from me and pronounced, "I'm having a panic attack." My mind was still racing with thoughts and feelings about my patient *nearby with a gun*. I looked up at my patient in front of me and impulsively replied, "Give me a moment while I get over mine"—at which he broke out laughing, and I joined in. Our shared laugh quickly diffused our respective states of anxiety. My response wasn't driven by any carefully formulated treatment plan or deliberate thought, but it was an invaluable lesson about the role of therapist emotion.

http://dx.doi.org/10.1037/0000182-001
Therapist Performance Under Pressure: Negotiating Emotion, Difference, and Rupture,
by J. C. Muran and C. F. Eubanks

Every therapist has experienced moments of pressure, even those marked by bursts of emotion, such as a surge of anxiety when a patient threatens to self-harm, a flash of irritation when a patient is condescending or critical, a pang of hopelessness when nothing seems to be working, or even a more sustained experience, such as a struggle to remain alert while a patient drones on and on and on. Therapists have to perform under pressure every day. The aim of this book is to provide a practical guide for therapists to negotiate the difficult emotional challenges that they frequently face in psychotherapy. In this book, we draw on the performance science literature, including findings from the cognitive and emotion sciences, to provide us with a fresh lens through which to view the psychotherapy literature on therapists' performance under emotional duress. We review the empirical literature on therapist negative emotion, negative interpersonal process in the therapy session, and ruptures in the alliance between therapist and patient. We aim to approach these topics from a pragmatic, integrative stance that will be relevant and relatable for therapists of various theoretical orientations and professional backgrounds.

We consider therapists' negotiation of their own experience of intense or challenging emotional states—from basic to self-conscious emotions, such as anxiety and panic, anger and hate, sadness and despair, embarrassment and shame, guilt and self-doubt, and pride and hubris, as well as other emotional challenges such as boredom and neglect, love and seduction, and misempathy and overidentification. The consideration of each state includes clinical examinations of the processes involved in emotion regulation and alliance rupture resolution. We define strategies for self-care and training based on the empirical evidence. In addition, we highlight case examples from our own clinical experiences to illustrate how we addressed emotional experience and alliance ruptures in our own work.[1] Our ultimate objective is to facilitate therapists' abilities to negotiate these experiences for therapeutic gain.

We also discuss the Rupture Resolution Rating System (3RS; Eubanks, Muran, & Safran, 2015), a useful tool for assessing alliance ruptures and strategies to repair them. The entire 3RS manual is available in the appendix of this book.

BACKGROUND AND JUSTIFICATION

The field of psychotherapy has not always acknowledged the emotional and interpersonal challenges that therapeutic work can pose for the individual therapist. In fact, in many ways our field has promulgated a myth that therapists are uniform dispensers of treatments: If one underwent behavior therapy or psychoanalysis, one received it regardless of who delivered it. More

---

[1]The case examples are based on actual experiences, so we have taken the proper steps to disguise the identities of our patients to maintain their confidentiality.

than 50 years ago, Donald Kiesler (1966) eloquently argued against this seemingly widespread notion that all therapists are the same. "The therapy" equaled "the therapist"—a perspective that persists today as suggested by the *New York Post* headline "How to Figure Out Which Therapy Is Right for You" (Laneri, 2016). It is akin to the notion that if one asks for a latte at a Starbucks, one gets the same latte—no matter which Starbucks barista one goes to (a key to the company's success).

Where did this idea of therapist uniformity come from? In psychoanalysis, there has long been the notion that the *analyzed analyst* could have all confounding countertransference expunged and could be totally objective—a blank screen for patient transferences or projections—and perfectly capable of implementing a single agreed-upon technique. The notion continues today in the *manualized therapist* (largely though not exclusively promoted by the cognitive-behavioral tradition), who is expected to conduct (or to be trained to conduct) an operationalized treatment protocol in a uniform manner. To some extent, the randomized controlled trial as the gold standard for evaluating the efficacy of an intervention has promoted the possibility of uniformity with its emphasis on operationalization and replicability, but to be fair there has always been a belief that training can produce some kind of uniformity. Maybe the only difference is a shift in emphasis from the promise of personal analysis to that of manual adherence.

In the past decade or so, we have witnessed an increasing interest in the development and measurement of *core competencies* in many fields, including clinical psychology, as evidenced by the "guidelines and principles" (now defined as "standards") by the American Psychological Association's Office of Program Consultation and Accreditation. In the same vein, we have also seen a number of recent considerations of *expertise* in psychotherapy (Hatcher, 2015; Tracey, Wampold, Lichtenberg, & Goodyear, 2014). It is interesting to note the parallel interest in *mastery* across disciplines (see D. Epstein, 2014; Gladwell, 2008). Although these ideas are notably controversial and complex, they highlight the orientation of the field of psychotherapy—and the implicit pursuit of perfection. Not surprising, this pursuit has been linked to the measurement of treatment outcome and the sobering body of research regarding treatment failure rates, which become more alarming when one includes premature termination (Lambert, 2010, 2013).

The unfortunate consequence of such efforts is the depersonalization of the clinician. The relational turn in psychotherapies (an integrative movement that aimed to bridge the *interpersonal* with the *intrapersonal*) has challenged this with the introduction and careful consideration of the therapist's subjectivity, personality, and emotionality (see Aron, 1996; Mitchell, 1988; Ogden, 1994; Wachtel, 2008)—an appreciation that has expanded across theoretical orientations (Muran, 2001c, 2007a; see also L. S. Greenberg & Paivio, 1997; Guidano & Liotti, 1983; Safran, 1998, for further transtheoretical considerations—cognitive and humanistic). Accordingly, the therapeutic relationship has become more figural to the change process and understood as a cauldron of desires and emotions contributed to by both patient and therapist. The turn was toward greater mutuality and intimacy—and to recognizing a new relational (Safran & Muran, 2000) or corrective emotional (Alexander & French, 1946) experience in the context of the therapeutic relationship.

The seeds of this movement were sown in the early contributions of Sándor Ferenczi (1932/1988) with regard to *empathic reciprocity* and Harry Stack Sullivan (1953) with regard to *reciprocal emotion* in the psychotherapeutic encounter. And various threads of thought are associated with it, including *social constructionism* (the recognition that meanings are developed in dialogue with others rather than separately within each individual; see Gadamer, 1960/1975) and relatedly *intersubjectivity* (the consideration of subject–subject relations in contrast to subject–object relations in human communication; see Habermas, 1971, and see Buber, 1923/1958, for his comparable "interhuman" perspective). The feminist impulse, which recognized and privileged the personal from the "I" of subjective experience (see Dinnerstein, 1976), is another major thread drawn in consideration of the psychotherapy process as an "intersubjective negotiation" (J. Benjamin, 1990; Pizer, 1998), in which patients and therapists are continuously negotiating their respective subjectivities—that is, their respective wishes about how they will work together (at a more explicit level), as well as their identities and desires to be mutually recognized (at a more implicit level).

The relational movement has been supported in part by considerable research demonstrating that not only are the nature and quality of the therapeutic relationship strong predictors of treatment success (Muran & Barber, 2010; Norcross & Lambert, 2019a) but therapists' individual differences may be an even stronger predictor (Wampold & Imel, 2015). In other words, (a) some therapists are consistently more helpful than others, (b) differences in therapist ability seem to be more important than type of psychotherapy, and (c) the more helpful therapists appear better able to facilitate the development and management of an alliance. This movement has also been supported by research on interpersonal complementarity (Kiesler, 1996) and by emotional communication (Tronick, 2007) that demonstrates the interactional nature of behavior and emotion. The empirical literature in psychotherapy suggests that developing therapist skills in negotiating the alliance may be a worthwhile way to redress psychotherapy failure rates (Eubanks, Muran, & Safran, 2018, 2019; Muran, 2019).

In our own work, we have identified *ruptures* in the alliance as both critical risk factors for failure and opportunities for therapists to improve outcomes. We have defined these events as marking the increased tension or conflict between the respective desires or needs of the patient and therapist (Safran & Muran, 2000). They indicate a breakdown in purposeful collaboration and a deterioration in the emotional bond between patient and therapist. Research has demonstrated that patients and therapists (whether in psychodynamic or cognitive behavior therapy) report ruptures in up to 50% of their sessions, whereas observers report them in as many as 30% to 100%; rupture frequency has been linked to negative process and treatment failure, and their resolution to treatment completion and success. Other research has shown that ruptures pose significant emotional challenges to therapists, who too often engage in iatrogenic activities to manage or avoid them (Eubanks, Muran, & Safran, 2018, 2019).

There is increasing research on strategies to develop therapists' abilities to negotiate these ubiquitous challenges. Our own efforts in this regard have concentrated on developing therapists' emotion regulation skills, such as mindfulness and emotion labeling in relation to the other, and shown promising results, specifically decreasing negative process, such as hostility and control, and increasing positive process, such as expressiveness and affirmation (see Muran, 2019; Muran, Safran, & Eubanks-Carter, 2010; Muran, Safran, Eubanks, & Gorman, 2018). Research also links ruptures to the notion of microaggressions from the multicultural literature (e.g., Chang & Berk, 2009; Hook, Davis, Owen, & DeBlaere, 2017), suggesting that rupture resolution training has relevance for developing cultural competence. Now there is a developing literature regarding the notion of cultural humility (Hook, Davis, Owen, & DeBlaere, 2017), which promotes an open orientation to the other (sensibility oriented rather than knowledge based) and is in line with such notions as *allocentricity* (Schachtel, 1959), *beginner's mind* (S. Suzuki, 1970), and *courting surprise* (D. B. Stern, 1997), as well as the intersubjective and interhuman perspectives just presented.

Emotion regulation has been defined as the capacity to alter the trajectory of emotions and to tolerate intense emotions, including negative states such as anxiety, anger, and sadness (Gross, 1998; Gross & Thompson, 2007). It can involve various cognitive (reappraisal, distraction, suppression, distancing, and labeling) and behavioral (practice-based and exposure-based) strategies and has implications for communication and performance. Emotion (and affect) regulation has received significant attention with regard to patient personality and dysregulatory disorders (Fonagy, Gergely, Jurist, & Target, 2002; Linehan, 1993a) but much less so with regard to the therapist—and specifically therapist performance under pressure (and negotiation of ruptures). There is a growing body of research on performance under pressure in other disciplines and contexts, specifically investigating the cognitive and emotion science of such performance and examining strategies to promote emotion regulation, which can contribute to advancing performance science for the psychotherapist (e.g., see reviews by Beilock, 2010; Johnston & Olson, 2015; Kahneman, 2011).

In our research on rupture resolution and on how therapists can effectively negotiate negative emotions, we developed and evaluated a stage-process model (Eubanks, Muran, & Safran, 2018, 2019; Muran, 2019; Safran & Muran, 1996, 2000) that confirmed the effect of metacommunication—that is, communication by both therapist and patient about the communication process in which they are engaged. This technical principle involves therapists and patients putting words to their emotional experience and thus promoting emotion regulation for both. We have also demonstrated a positive effect of training therapists with regard to this stage-process model and technical principle: Our research suggests that the movement to a more expressive position by both therapists and patients has therapeutic implications for rupture resolution and treatment outcome (Muran et al., 2018; Muran, Safran, Samstag, & Winston, 2005). We consider this movement as bringing intersubjective negotiation into relief and making *mutual recognition* more possible—that is, an intimate interhuman meeting between therapist and patient, a new relational experience for both.

CONCEPTION OF THE BOOK

As expressed in our preface, the conception of this book was based on professional and personal experiences. From our professional experiences in practice, research, and training, we have come to appreciate that therapists vary in their abilities to negotiate their relationships with patients, and this variability can be attributed to many factors: personal, familial, and cultural. You can see this variability by trait (across cases) and by state (within each case). We have devoted considerable time and effort to studying this variability, and in recent years we have concentrated on training therapists to better negotiate the emotional challenges they face in relation to their patients. From our personal experiences, we have come to appreciate the trials and tribulations involved in our various pursuits, which has made us recognize the challenges that are common to performance in many contexts. We have also come to appreciate that, for a variety of reasons, there is much to learn from other disciplines. As suggested by the ancient Indian parable of the blind men who each touch and describe a different aspect of an elephant from their limited perspective, there are multiple perspectives with equal truth claims; bringing them together increases the possibility of describing a more complete truth. Therefore, we should always be careful to study a topic with some regard for other worlds and eras. This book was conceptualized as one such effort that aims to integrate various sciences on performance, including and promoting that which concerns psychotherapy.

STRUCTURE OF THE BOOK

With this introduction, we characterize the therapeutic relationship as a cauldron of emotions that poses significant challenges for therapists, which we describe as alliance ruptures—breakdowns in collaboration and deteriorations in relatedness. Accordingly, therapists invariably face pressure to perform and to negotiate these critical events. In this regard, we propose careful consideration and integration of the science on performance, cognition, and emotion to advance our understanding and approach to psychotherapy. We suggest an intersubjective and interhuman perspective founded on formulations from other disciplines and on findings from our own psychotherapy research program.

Chapter 1. The Science of Performance Under Pressure

We begin with a review of the science on decision making and judgment. We consider cognitive research on the various heuristics and biases that facilitate and interfere with our abilities to navigate ambiguity. Here we review the foundational work on naturalistic decision making (G. A. Klein, 1998) and counterfactual thinking (Kahneman, 2011) and outline the paths to mastery and pitfalls to failure. With regard to heuristics, we highlight overconfidence (Kahneman, 2011) and implicit bias (Greenwald & Banaji, 2017) as particularly pernicious and recommend greater humility and reflection in clinical practice. We examine the research on stress and its effect on attention, memory, appraisal, and judgment (Staal, 2004) and acknowledge the complex relationship of stress to performance, depending on the task and context. Then we turn to the role of emotion in performance—with particular attention to emotion regulation (Gross, 1998; Gross & Thompson, 2007), including its role in adapting to adversity and developing resilience (Bonanno, 2004). We also present the literature on deliberate practice and reflective practice (Ericsson & Pool, 2016; Schön, 1983) toward maximizing performance, which is integral to our later consideration of professional development.

Chapter 2. The Science of the Therapist Under Pressure

One of the most consistent findings in psychotherapy research literature is that the alliance between therapist and patient predicts treatment outcome (Flückiger, Del Re, Wampold, & Horvath, 2018). In Chapter 2, we review the research on how therapists fare in challenging clinical situations, with a focus on what therapists need to do to maintain strong alliances with their patients. We note factors that can contribute to therapist burnout, and we review the research literature on how therapists' difficulties managing their blind spots can contribute to problems in the alliance, with specific attention to countertransference (J. A. Hayes, Gelso, Goldberg, & Kivlighan, 2018), therapist attachment style (Strauss & Petrowski, 2017), and therapist microaggressions (Hook et al., 2017). We explore key findings from research on how therapists can contribute to negative process in therapy (e.g., Strupp, 1998), and the importance of therapists' skills under pressure (Anderson, Crowley, Himawan, Holmberg, & Uhlin, 2016). We then turn our focus to the research on alliance ruptures (Eubanks et al., 2018), with particular attention to our own program (see Muran, 2002, 2019; Muran et al., 2009; Muran et al., 2018; Muran et al., 2005; Safran & Muran, 1996; Safran, Muran, Samstag, & Winston, 2005). We provide an operational definition of ruptures as specific patient behaviors or communications, highlight our stage-process model of rupture resolution processes supported by task-analytic and other research, and present findings that aim to sensitize clinicians to critical interpersonal markers of rupture and possible trajectories of repair or resolution.

Chapter 3. From Emotion to Rupture

In recent years, we have witnessed an explosion in the study of emotion and a marked shift in emphasis on emotion in psychotherapy. We introduce current considerations from emotion researchers (Barrett, Lewis, & Haviland-Jones, 2016) that conceptualize emotion as state and process, basic and complex, and personal and interpersonal. We present a contemporary perspective of the research that basic emotions should be understood as componential and constructed (Barrett, 2017); that is, a basic emotion such as anger may have multiple systems and response tendencies that are constructed from previous experience and social influence. This perspective oriented toward the complex, from the intrapersonal to the interpersonal, leads to consideration of the interaction between emotions and emotion regulation (Gross, 2014a). We review the research on emotion regulation and then integrate the literature on multiplicity and intersubjectivity. We define emotion with regard to self schemas and self states and how these interact with those of another, how they reflect implicit needs for agency and communion, and how the negotiation of these needs relates to confrontation and withdrawal ruptures (Muran, 2001a, 2007b). We return to the concept of rupture; introduce its consideration in terms of therapist interpersonal markers; and then further our conceptualization as expressions of dissociative disconnections, interpersonal transformations, affective misattunements, vicious circles, and power dynamics in the process of intersubjective negotiation (J. Benjamin, 1990; Pizer, 1998). Both Chapters 3 and 4 represent a culmination of decades of clinical experience and advice. They synthesize some of the most important points from our previously published works and significantly update them to provide a fresh perspective on how to address emotional ruptures and repair them.

Chapter 4. From Emotion to Repair

We consider the principle of metacommunication (i.e., communication about the communication process) with fundamental features as a rupture resolution strategy that promotes emotion regulation and mutual recognition in the therapeutic relationship (Kiesler, 1988; Safran & Muran, 2000). In earlier chapters, we present various interpersonal markers (patient and therapist communications) of rupture: In Chapter 4, we introduce intrapersonal markers with regard to therapist emotions or internal experience. We present various basic to self-conscious emotions that therapists experience and provide clinical illustrations for each that demonstrate the principle of metacommunication and possible pathways toward regulation and recognition. Specifically, we consider (a) basic emotions, such as anxiety and panic, anger and hate, sadness and despair; (b) self-conscious emotions, such as embarrassment and shame, guilt and self-doubt, pride and hubris; and (c) other emotional challenges, such as boredom and neglect, love and seduction, and misempathy and overidentification. We present brief vignettes with the understanding that emotional experience is complex and idiosyncratic and with the aim to illustrate *regulation-in-action* and *recognition-in-action*.

Chapter 5. A Way to Therapist Training

Historically, the literature on training has been limited, especially compared with the literature on practice and with regard to empirical support (Hill & Knox, 2013). In recent years, however, there has been much more attention given to this subject. In Chapter 5, we review several models of supervision (Falender & Shafranske, 2017; Hill, 2020; Ladany, Friedlander, & Nelson, 2016) and the literature on supervisory responsiveness (e.g., Friedlander, 2015). We concentrate on the presentation of our training program that was developed with support from the National Institute of Mental Health (Eubanks et al., 2015; Muran et al., 2010, 2018). The program targets emotion regulation as the essential therapist skill and implements principles and strategies consistent with those described with regard to deliberate and reflective practice (Ericsson & Pool, 2016; Schön, 1983). We highlight the program's training principles: (a) recognizing the relational context, (b) emphasizing self-exploration, (c) establishing an experiential focus, (d) practicing in simulated conditions and under pressure, (e) being responsive, and (f) practicing what you preach. We describe the program's training strategies: (a) didactic training on various theoretical lenses, evidence-based stage-process models, and process coding schemes, plus feedback through video analyses; (b) experiential training through mindfulness meditation and awareness exercises. We discuss the supervisory alliance and ruptures within it. We conclude with a presentation of a supervision illustration, specifically the application of an experiential or awareness exercise.

Chapter 6. A Way to Therapist Self-Care

Emotion regulation is also at the heart of our consideration of therapist self-care. We review relevant literature on self-care and self-development (see Bennett-Levy, 2019; Norcross & VandenBos, 2018) and draw from the performance science literature (covered in Chapter 1). We present recommendations for therapists to care for themselves and manage the emotional pressures and stress of psychotherapy. Specifically, we identify certain attitudes that we consider necessary for self-care: (a) maintaining humility, (b) cultivating compassion, (c) courting curiosity, (d) being patient, and (e) balancing with positivity. We also suggest a number of strategies: (a) mindfulness exercises (before sessions), (b) emotion journal (after sessions), (c) audio/video review (between sessions), (d) critical inquiry (search for contrary data; read about probability theory, cognitive heuristics/implicit biases, and negative process), (e) practice under pressure (awareness-oriented role-plays), and (f) a competence constellation—a network of colleagues who provide guidance and support.

Conclusion: In the Pressure Cooker

Tennis great Billie Jean King famously noted, "Pressure is a privilege." Drawing on this quote (a good example of reappraisal and reframing that can emotionally regulate), in our conclusion chapter we return to our consideration of the emotional pressure inherent in the therapeutic relationship, and we elaborate on our narrative to normalize the experience of the negative emotions covered in this book and to emphasize the importance of embracing them for therapeutic gain. We have identified emotion regulation as an essential therapist skill with significant interpersonal implications, namely, for facilitating mutual regulation and mutual recognition—an intimate, interhuman meeting of the minds. We close by providing some definition to *what we know we know* and *what we know we don't know*, plus some speculation about *what we don't know we don't know* regarding therapist performance under pressure.

AIM OF THE BOOK

As fans have come to recognize when a team manager in baseball calls for a closer, the outcome is not always certain—not all closers are the same. Not every closer can deliver under pressure like New York Yankee great and Hall of Famer Mariano Rivera. And not always did the great Mariano deliver. Similarly, therapists vary in their abilities (both between and within) to negotiate experiences of intense emotions. By bringing together the performance literature and the psychotherapy literature in an accessible and engaging way, we aim to provide therapists with both conceptual and practical tools to help them mind and mine their own emotional experiences in high-pressure psychotherapy situations so that they too can perform with greater success under pressure.

Our target audience includes clinicians-in-training (graduate and postgraduate students in the range of mental health disciplines) during their academic education and practicum supervision, as well as more experienced clinicians who wish to reconsider and refine their approach to the ubiquitous experience of emotional stress, identity difference, and alliance rupture.

1

The Science of Performance Under Pressure

Be like water . . . and you shall find a way around or through.

—BRUCE LEE

A good deal of evidence exists regarding the efficacy and effectiveness of psychotherapy (Lambert, 2013; Wampold & Imel, 2015), and now a body of evidence demonstrates that the quality of the psychotherapy varies by the therapist (Baldwin & Imel, 2013; Wampold & Imel, 2015). As Donald Kiesler (1966) seminally argued more than 50 years ago with his "uniformity myth," not all therapists are the same, even if the psychotherapy is manualized or the training uniform. Some therapists indeed perform better than others—that is, some therapists achieve better outcomes. These findings on therapist effects have led to some consideration of what constitutes competence or expertise (e.g., Castonguay & Hill, 2017) and how complex it is to define and measure expertise in psychotherapy (Tracey et al., 2014).

Evidence also shows that some therapists are better at developing a working alliance (Baldwin, Wampold, & Imel, 2007; Del Re, Flückiger, Horvath, Symonds, & Wampold, 2012; Dinger, Strack, Leichsenring, Wilmers, & Schauenburg, 2008), one of the most predictive variables of treatment success in psychotherapy (Flückiger et al., 2018). These findings were foundational to our own efforts to develop therapist abilities to more effectively negotiate challenges in the therapeutic alliance (Muran, Safran, Eubanks, & Gorman, 2018).

http://dx.doi.org/10.1037/0000182-002
Therapist Performance Under Pressure: Negotiating Emotion, Difference, and Rupture,
by J. C. Muran and C. F. Eubanks

Given all this, we thought it would be useful to take a careful look at the performance science literature, especially with regard to performance under stress or pressure. To define stress itself has also been challenging, as there have been many definitions as well as associations to many different constructs (Tepas & Price, 2001). However, one seminal view of stress is its conceptualization as an interaction among perceived demand, perceived ability to cope, and perceived importance of being able to cope with the demand (McGrath, 1970). Thus, stress is not seen as simply a mismatch between demand and ability but rather one's perception of these two elements plus the desire to meet the demand. Relatedly, pressure is defined as a situation in which one perceives that something desirous, something at stake, is dependent on the outcome of one's performance (Weisinger & Pawliw-Fry, 2015). Again, perception and desire are at the heart of the experience. Often stress and performance are used interchangeably, and perhaps this is justified by the shared emphasis on perception and desire. Our aim in this chapter is to highlight some of the critical findings and principles from the performance science literature that we consider especially important to advancing our understanding of therapist choices and actions under stress and pressure in psychotherapy.

NATURALISTIC DECISION MAKING

A number of studies on decision making in natural settings have focused on defining intuitive expertise, beginning with early research on chess masters (Chase & Simon, 1973; de Groot, 1946/1978) and including subsequent research on fire commanders (G. A. Klein, Calderwood, & Clinton-Cirocco, 1986), aviation personnel (Hutton, Thordsen, & Mogford, 1997; G. A. Klein & Thordsen, 1991; Stokes, Kemper, & Marsh, 1992), and military officers in the field (Collyer & Malecki, 1998; G. A. Klein, 1998), as well as nurses on intensive care units (Crandall & Getchell-Reiter, 1993). From this research tradition, important principles have been defined and developed with regard to how decisions are made under complex and stressful conditions. For example, from his seminal research on chess masters, Adriaan de Groot (1946/1978) introduced the notion of *progressive deepening*, which describes how so-called experts proceed to identify a single plausible option drawn from a repertoire of patterns based on previous experience: If necessary, the option is modified to fit the situation and to find an acceptable course of action; if the option does not fit the situation, then and only then is another option pursued. This has been repeatedly observed in other studies (see G. A. Klein, 1998). Another noteworthy finding is Herbert Simon's (1957) notion of *satisficing*, which refers to looking for the first workable option rather than trying to find the best possible option.

The naturalistic tradition has yielded several models of the decision-making process (see Lipshitz, 1993, for a review). The most prominent and what is the primary protocol derived from this tradition is the recognition-primed decision model (RPD; G. A. Klein, 1993; see G. A. Klein, 1998, for a review of research). There are variations in the present form of RPD, but essentially the model involves a blend of intuition and analysis (see Newell, Lagnado, & Shanks, 2007, for more detail). The intuitive part includes *pattern matching*, how people form patterns from previous experience—patterns that highlight relevant cues, predict expected outcomes, identify possible goals, and suggest a typical course of action. The analytic part includes using a deliberate process of *mental simulation* to imagine how a situation would play out given the context of the current situation. RPD demonstrates the principles of progressive deepening and satisficing as just described.

As psychotherapists accrue clinical experience, RPD can prove useful: For example, clinicians can more quickly identify patterns in their patients' behaviors or relationships and predict likely outcomes that can inform their choice of interventions. However, research suggests that RPD can also lead to clinical errors and misinterpretations, particularly when psychotherapists are under stress. Research on naturalistic decision making, especially RPD, took off with support from the U.S. Navy (following the 1988 USS *Vincennes* catastrophe, in which the naval cruiser mistakenly shot down a commercial airliner), the results of which are described in the Tactical Decision Making Under Stress Project (Cannon-Bowers & Salas, 1998), as well as evidenced in the U.S. Army Field Manual on Command and Control (FM 101-5; 1997) and the NASA report *Stress, Cognition, and Human Performance* (Staal, 2004). The official report on the USS *Vincennes* incident (Fogarty, 1988; see also Collyer & Malecki, 1998) concluded that an unfortunate series of events resulted in undue stress and consequential "task fixation"—a fulfillment of a scenario based on misinterpretation of the data (viz. the commercial airline was associated with hostile and threatening encounters).

COUNTERFACTUAL THINKING

Counterfactual thinking refers to any thinking that is contrary to the facts (Roese, 1997) and is rooted in the research tradition on heuristics and biases, notably exemplified by the work of Amos Tversky and Daniel Kahneman (1974). Heuristics and biases are simple mental rules, shortcuts, and orientations that people use to form judgments and make decisions, especially under uncertain conditions. Tversky and Kahneman demonstrated three examples that underlie a wide range of intuitive judgments. Specifically, in complex situations people tend to rely on a limited number of heuristic principles; the most frequently applied include *representativeness* (the assessment of probability that Object A or Event A belongs to Category B), *availability* (the ease with which one can think of an instance that will support the probability of an event occurring), and *anchoring* (the initial value either presented or formulated by the judge serves as an orienting point for subsequent decisions). Although the focus in this tradition has been on how these heuristics lead to error, a number of researchers have argued that they can and should also be seen as adaptive and good enough to serve most situations (e.g., Gigerenzer, 1996).

In his most recent book, *Thinking, Fast and Slow*, Kahneman (2011) discussed how we have a two system way of thinking: System 1 is the intuitive way—fast, implicit, unconscious processing (e.g., automatic reaction to a stimulus)—where we spend most of our time, and System 2 is the analytic way—slow, explicit, conscious processing (e.g., deliberate planning of an action)—which is activated when something is posed to us that violates the model of the world that System 1 maintains. Both systems rely on heuristics and biases that can lead to errors in judgment. In this discussion, Kahneman described the phenomenon of how we jump to conclusions based on limited information, how we "focus on existing evidence and ignore absent evidence" (p. 104). His abbreviation for this phenomenon is WYSIATI: "what you see is all there is." He elaborated that when we make decisions, we tend to primarily deal with *known knowns* (what has already been observed), to rarely consider *known unknowns* (what one knows to be relevant but has no information about), and to be completely oblivious to the possibility of *unknown unknowns* (unknown phenomena of unknown relevance). As a result, System 1 creates a coherent story, which System 2 in turn converts into a deep-rooted belief.

Kahneman (2011) highlighted specific judgment errors that can result from System 1 thinking and WYSIATI. Many of these are intersecting and derivatives of the heuristics originally observed with Tversky, demonstrated in subsequent research efforts: (a) law of small numbers (the tendency to draw conclusions on a few data points), (b) antistatistics bias (the tendency to incorrectly estimate the occurrence of events from random chance or regression to the mean), (c) illusion of understanding (the tendency to interpret actions and intentions as simple and coherent manifestations of general propensities or personality traits—the "narrative fallacy" phenomenon), (d) hindsight bias (the tendency to reconstruct a story around past events—the "I-knew-it-all-along" bias), (e) confirmation bias (the tendency to focus on limited evidence to confirm an existing perspective), (f) anchoring effect (the tendency for a selected reference point—the anchor or frame—to have a disproportionate impact on the decision made), (g) overoptimism (the tendency to formulate plans that overestimate benefits and underestimate costs—to be loss-averse), (h) competitor neglect (the tendency to ignore the presence and ability of competition), and (i) overconfidence effect (the tendency to think or to have the illusion that we have substantial knowledge and control—again the underestimation of complexity and chance). Overconfidence is considered by Kahneman as perhaps the most insidious of these biases. How often do we as psychotherapists commit such errors—and very confidently try to organize an experience according to a particular theory, especially as a result of ambiguity or stress?

IMPLICIT BIAS

Any discussion of heuristics and biases must also consider implicit biases and their effect on behavior or performance. First introduced by Anthony Greenwald and Mahzarin Banaji (1995, 2017), *implicit biases* refer to unconscious features of prejudiced judgment and social behavior, automatic attribution of particular qualities to a member of a certain social or cultural group, based on implicit attitudes (an evaluative disposition not understood by the person) or implicit stereotypes (mental associations between a social group or category and a trait). These are understood as developing from interaction with other people and exposure to media—a product of social learning, a cultural consequence. The biases are widely considered to have a profound influence on our choices and actions. For example, there are disturbing demonstrations of the effect of implicit bias in various contexts, including its impact on decisions and behaviors by health care professionals that result in lower quality of care, including negative interactions as rated by minority patients and external raters (see FitzGerald & Hurst, 2017; Green et al., 2007). Such research raises obvious questions about the effect of implicit biases on the therapeutic alliance.

The development of the Implicit Association Test (IAT; Greenwald, McGhee, & Schwartz, 1998) greatly proliferated research on implicit bias. The IAT is a measure designed to detect the strength of our automatic associations between mental representations of objects or concepts in memory. It does so by observing response latencies in computer-administered categorization tasks. Based on meta-analyses of research including the IAT (Greenwald, Poehlman, Uhlmann, & Banaji, 2009; Oswald, Mitchell, Blanton, Jaccard, & Tetlock, 2013), evidence shows that implicit biases have a significant (though small to moderate) effect on discriminatory behavior, affecting many people and repeatedly the same person (see also Greenwald, Banaji, & Nosek, 2015). Research on implicit bias (including the IAT) suggests that implicit bias can be altered: It can be attenuated when brought to attention, especially if the automatic influence is weak (see Blair, 2002; Greenwald & Banaji, 1995; Nosek, Greenwald, & Banaji, 2007). We should note that the IAT is not without its controversy, specifically with regard to whether it measures alternative constructs such as cultural knowledge or salience of attributes (see Olson & Fazio, 2003).

AFFECT EFFECT

Researchers have come to appreciate the impact of emotion on the decision-making process in different ways (see Grecucci & Sanfey, 2014, for a review). Paul Slovic and colleagues (Slovic, Finucane, Peters, & MacGregor, 2002a, 2002b; Slovic & Peters, 2006), for example, proposed the *affect heuristic*, according to which we let our likes and dislikes determine our beliefs and opinions.

In other words, they demonstrated that our judgments and decisions are guided directly by feelings of liking or disliking, with little deliberation or reasoning. This is a variation or form of *substitution*—that is, when faced with a difficult decision, we often answer or substitute an easier one instead.

In another example of the effect of emotion on decision making, Eduardo Andrade and Daniel Ariely (2009) demonstrated in their research that decisions influenced by an incidental emotion can become the basis for future decisions and thus outlive the original, fleeting, or transient emotion (see also Vohs, Baumeister, & Loewenstein, 2007). We tend to have a poor memory of past emotional states and, in contrast, a good memory for actions we have previously taken: We look at our past behaviors as a guide. If we see ourselves having once made a certain decision, it appears from the research that we assume it was reasonable and so we repeat it—with no memory of the original emotional state: "In general, emotions seem to disappear without a trace" (Ariely, 2011, p. 261). Thus, therapists who are feeling particularly frustrated or anxious might allow that emotion to color how they choose to respond to a particular clinical situation. When therapists encounter a similar situation with another patient, they may look back to their past decision as a good precedent to follow without recognizing how their view of that past encounter was influenced—and perhaps biased—by their emotional state at the time.

In a final noteworthy example, Baumeister, Bratslavsky, Finkenauer, and Vohs (2001) reviewed the research regarding the impact of "bad" or negative events and concluded that bad emotions have a more powerful impact on our behavior than good ones; in fact, "bad is stronger than good" (p. 323). To make their case, they highlighted a great number of studies that demonstrated (a) we have more words for negative emotions, (b) negative emotions result in more thorough and careful cognitive processing, (c) memory or recall is better for negative emotional events, and (d) negative emotions exert a more powerful influence on subsequent emotional states we have than positive ones.

As Kahneman (2011) noted in his most recent book, "Emotion now looms larger in our understanding of intuitive judgments and choices than it did in the past" (p. 12). For psychotherapists, this research suggests a more careful consideration of how emotion (or affect in general)—positive and especially negative—colors our thoughts, stirs other feelings, and shapes our behavior, so we are not mindlessly at its mercy.

CLINICAL JUDGMENT

The fields of psychology and medicine have been investigating clinical judgment since the 1950s. Paul Meehl's (1954, 1960) early work on clinical versus statistical prediction is considered germinal in this tradition. A considerable body of research now demonstrates that "mechanical" judgments (based on actuarial, statistically derived methods of data combination, or formal algorithms) substantially outperform clinical (subjective, informal) judgments in the prediction of behavior—that is, they are more efficient, accurate, and reliable (see Ægisdóttir et al., 2006; Dawes, Faust, & Meehl, 1989; Grove, Zald, Lebow, Snitz, & Nelson, 2000). Despite this well-established research, a survey of 183 clinical psychologists indicated that almost all respondents (98%) applied a form of clinical judgment in practice, and considerably fewer (31%) used a mechanical approach (Vrieze & Grove, 2009).

There has been a fair amount of research on the factors accounting for the error in clinical judgment (primarily founded in medical settings—but easily extrapolated to the psychotherapy situation). Politser (1981), for example, attributed error to cognitive limitations, specifically limited capacities for working memory and attention that result in failures to notice and integrate important information. A number of researchers have identified cultural biases, including illusory correlations between a primary patient characteristic and a secondary ability (Faust, 1986) and halo/horn effects, strong impressions about one aspect of a patient that color the overall judgment (M. Piper, 1979). Not surprising, the work of Kahneman and Tversky on heuristics and biases has been influential in this regard. For example, a clinician's diagnosis can be based more on personal experience (on other cases previously assessed by the clinician) than on actual statistical information (representativeness); after reading literature on some clinical condition (the "recent article" effect), a clinician may be more inclined to see the condition in subsequent clinical evaluations (availability); and a clinician's decision can be unduly influenced by primacy and recency effects in the presentation of information (anchoring; see Bancroft, 1987; Dawes, 1986; Emerick & Hatten, 1974; Oskamp, 1965; Records & Weiss, 1990).

Donald Redelmeier (Redelmeier & Cialdini, 2002; Redelmeier, Ferris, Tu, Hux, & Schull, 2001), who was directly influenced by and collaborated with both Tversky and Kahneman, has been a significant contributor to our understanding of clinical judgment in the medical setting. With a number of colleagues (Redelmeier et al., 2001), he suggested three factors that lead to failures in clinical judgment: (a) intellectual factors (e.g., overconfidence, finite capacity of brain, random chance), (b) lack of checking for errors (e.g., reluctance to change initial opinions, unquestioning self-approval, unawareness of subtle failures), and (c) environmental factors (e.g., impracticality of looking for mistakes, propagation of errors made by others, unawareness of limits of judgment). Subsequently, he also recommended several attitudinal and behavioral strategies or solutions to guard against the possibility of these failures. By attitudinal, he recommended maintaining greater humility. By behavioral, he recommended the use of feedback and follow-up systems; increased supervision and peer review; and training to increase awareness of probability theory, to search for contrary data, and to keep reading the research literature. We demonstrate some application of these recommendations in Chapters 5 and 6 of this volume.

STRESS RESPONSE

The effect of stress on performance is not linear, as indicated by the Yerkes–Dodson (1908) curve demonstrating an optimal level of arousal, and as suggested by Hans Selye's (1975) distinction between positive stress (*eustress*) and negative stress (*distress*): the relevance of perception (i.e., appraising a stressor as a challenge rather than a threat). Nevertheless, there has been a great deal of research on the cognitive costs of stress, specifically with regard to attention, memory, appraisal, and judgment (e.g., Driskell & Salas, 1996). Under stress, for example, there can be shifts and lapses in attention, which can negatively affect performance. There is also a narrowing of attention; in other words, attention appears to channel or tunnel, reducing focus on peripheral information and tasks and concentrating focus on main tasks. This narrowing of attention can result in either enhanced performance or reduced performance, depending on the nature of the task and the situation; for example, if peripheral cues are irrelevant to the main, then performance will be enhanced, and if relevant, then performance suffers (see Staal, 2004, for a review of the research on the effect of stress on attention).

The research literature on the effects of stress on memory consistently demonstrates that working memory capacity can be impaired or "overloaded" as a result. Cognitive load refers to the total amount of mental effort being used in working memory (see Paas & van Merriënboer, 1993; Sweller, 1988). Beilock and Carr (2005) demonstrated that pressure can especially harm performance in individuals high in working memory capacity, specifically reducing its availability for skill execution (see also Beilock & DeCaro, 2007). Skill execution involves a complex interaction of working and procedural memory (see Baddeley, Eysenck, & Anderson, 2009; Colombo & Gold, 2004): Working memory refers to short-term processing of information (encoding and maintenance) immediately presented from the world with information previously stored (retrieval); procedural memory refers to long-term stored information based on procedural learning of complex activities repeated until they become automatic—that is, without much need for conscious control. (This interaction also includes declarative or explicit memory, though this appears more relevant for the development of procedural knowledge, less when it comes to highly practiced performance.)

Stress has also been shown to adversely affect appraisal and judgment. Cognitive appraisal, specifically how we evaluate threat, controllability and predictability, affects performance as would be expected, according to the research: Negative appraisals result in negative outcomes while positive ones appear to reduce subjective distress and to improve objective performance (see Staal, 2004, for a review of research on stress and cognitive appraisal). Judgment and decision making under stress tend to become more rigid, more narrow and repetitive: According to the research, fewer alternative responses or strategies are scanned (Bröder, 2000, 2003; Dougherty & Hunter, 2003; Janis, Defares, & Grossman, 1983; Janis & Mann, 1977; Keinan, 1987; Streufert & Streufert, 1981; Walton & McKersie, 1965; Wright, 1974), and there is more reliance on familiar, well-learned responses regardless of previous response success (Lehner, Seyed-Solorforough, O'Connor, Sak, & Mullin, 1997; Staw, Sandelands, & Dutton, 1981).

As psychotherapists, we should not operate as if we are immune to the impact of stress (whether from our lives in general or our patients in particular) on what we attend to, what we remember, and how we appraise and judge. And as suggested in the previous section on affect effect, stress can evoke emotional states that in turn impact our cognitive processes and behavioral actions.

SELF-FOCUS

By *self-focus*, we mean a form of self-consciousness, a heightened sense of self-awareness or what could be described as hyperreflexivity—more specifically, an increased attention to one's own process of performance. Whether in the face of a patient, a colleague, or a supervisor, this is a common experience for psychotherapists, and maybe especially so because the profession draws and demands a self-reflective disposition. A good deal of research, highlighted by contributions from Baumeister and colleagues (Baumeister, 1984; Baumeister & Showers, 1986; Wallace, Baumeister, & Vohs, 2005), indicates that higher self-focus can disrupt and thus degrade automatic execution of skills that a performer possesses. Other research indicates that the inhibitory effect of self-focus on performance depends on an interaction with other variables, such as personality disposition, audience response, and performance feedback (Heaton & Sigall, 1991; Otten, 2009). In addition, much research has contrasted self-focus and distraction (i.e., drawing performers' attention away from skill) as competing mechanisms of skill failure under performance stress. Distraction theory (Beilock & Carr, 2005) posits that pressure interferes with the ability to use explicit strategies; more specifically, it leads to decreases in available working memory resources and thus negatively affects cognitive performance. Many studies favor self-focus as the explanatory mechanism, but some suggest that distraction plays a role (see Roberts, Jackson, & Grundy, 2019, for a review). As with self-focus, the relationship of distraction to performance is complicated: Much depends on the nature of the task. For example, distraction hinders performance on rule-based tasks (that involve explicit declarative processing and require more working memory) and in contrast helps on information-integration tasks (that involve implicit procedural processing and require less working memory; see Markman, Maddox, & Worthy, 2006). Psychotherapy includes both kinds of tasks.

EMOTION REGULATION

James Gross (1998), the foremost contributor to the study of *emotion regulation*, defined it as involving "the processes by which individuals influence which emotions they have, when they have them, and how they experience and express these emotions" (p. 275). He provided a seminal definition of the core features and essential strategies of emotion regulation (Gross, 2014a). The core features include (a) the activation of a goal to modify an emotion intrinsically (in oneself) or extrinsically (in another); (b) the engagement of the processes responsible for altering the emotion trajectory explicitly (in awareness) or implicitly (out of awareness); and (c) the impact on emotion dynamics or the latency, rise time, magnitude, duration, and offset of emotional responses. Essential strategies include (a) situation selection or modification, which involves avoiding or altering situations that typically stimulate emotion; (b) attentional deployment, which most commonly involves distraction or redirection away from a situation or aspects of it; (c) cognitive reappraisal or change, which involves altering or reframing how one interprets and thus experiences a situation; and (d) response modulation or suppression, which involves any exercise or technique to inhibit an emotion.

The research on the various emotion regulation strategies has largely concentrated on examining (a) the brain mechanisms involved in emotion regulation and (b) the comparative effects of the various strategies. With regard to the former, the research suggests an intricate relationship between the prefrontal cortex and limbic system, with various regions within responsible for different functions and mediations. For emotion regulation, it appears that top-down control is exerted by the prefrontal cortex on the limbic system, what some have described as "the brain's braking system" (Johnston & Olson, 2015; Lieberman, 2009). More specifically, the research has demonstrated that cognitive reappraisal increases activity in the prefrontal and cingulate regions implicated in cognitive control and decreases activity in structures such as the amygdala, insula, and striatum, which are implicated in emotion generation (Ochsner, Bunge, Gross, & Gabrieli, 2002; Ochsner & Gross, 2008; Ochsner, Silvers, & Buhle, 2012).

With regard to comparisons of the various regulation strategies, the research has found cognitive reappraisal, expressive suppression, and attentional distraction to be effective, with reappraisal significantly more effective than the other two in most studies—that is, showing more reduction on subjective ratings of emotion and objective measures of physiological arousal and amygdala activity, as well as faster prefrontal activation (see Goldin, McRae, Ramel, & Gross, 2008; Gross, 1998; Kanske, Heissler, Schonfelder, Bongers, & Wessa, 2011; McRae et al., 2010; Webb, Schweiger Gallo, Miles, Gollwitzer, & Sheeran, 2012). Gross and John (2003) also found that the use of regulation strategies varied markedly among individuals but that the greater the use of reappraisal, the better the mental health of the individual. In a study that compared reappraisal and acceptance (a condition likened to mindfulness) with regard to a negative memory as stimulus, acceptance resulted in less subjective distress and amygdala activity (Gross & John, 2003). In another series of studies, spontaneous or self-initiated distancing (i.e., the ability to view one's thoughts as constructions, also likened to mindfulness) while reflecting on negative memories was shown to predict less emotional and physiological reactivity and to have both short-term and long-term benefits (Ayduk & Kross, 2010; Kross & Ayduk, 2008). Finally, certain studies looking at affect labeling (i.e., putting words to feelings; what Barrett, 2017, described as *granularity*) found it to be effective in reducing skin conductance and amygdala activity, with one study comparing it to reappraisal and distraction and demonstrating greater effect (Kircanski, Lieberman, & Craske, 2012; Lieberman et al., 2007).

Many (maybe most) models of psychotherapy involve interventions that explicitly or implicitly target emotion regulation in the patient (one reason why it is receiving increasing consideration as a transdiagnostic process in the clinical literature; e.g., Aldao, Gee, De Los Reyes, & Seager, 2016; Aldao, Nolen-Hoeksema, & Schweizer, 2010). We discuss emotion regulation further in Chapters 3 and 4 with regard to therapist experience.

RESILIENCE

Related to emotion regulation, *resilience* refers to the process of adapting successfully to disturbances (adversity, trauma, pressure, or stress) that threaten an individual's growth and function. The study of resilience can be traced to the work of developmental psychologists, most notably Norman Garmezy and Emmy Werner (Masten, Best, & Garmezy, 1990; Werner, 1989), who observed in their longitudinal research projects how individuals thrive in the face of adversity—that is, how people adapt to environmental threats. Resilient individuals have been shown to have developed various coping strategies to effectively navigate negative experiences or crises. These coping strategies include the emotion regulation strategies just described (Gross, 2014a), as well as the use of optimistic attitudes and positive emotionality to counter negativity (Seligman & Csikszentmihalyi, 2014).

George Bonanno (2004) introduced a theory of resilience founded on an observation that we all possess the same fundamental stress-response system with varying abilities to apply it. He has also argued that one of the central elements of resilience is perception—that is, events are not traumatic unless we perceive them as such. In other words, trauma is not inherent in a negative event but rather resides in our psychological construal or cognitive appraisal of it, which is consistent with the literature on emotion regulation. In a study in the wake of 9/11, Bonanno, Papa, Lalande, Westphal, and Coifman (2004) demonstrated that college students who were more able to flexibly regulate their emotions (e.g., to express or suppress as the situation demanded) demonstrated better mental health—in other words, better adjustment to college.

Related to resilience is the notion of *grit* developed by Angela Duckworth (2016). She defines grit as a trait of perseverance, which is the steadfast pursuit of a task, mission, or journey in spite of obstacles, discouragement, or distraction. Grit enables an individual to persevere in accomplishing a goal despite obstacles over an extended period. In research on two samples of adults ($N = 1,545$ and $N = 690$), she and her colleagues demonstrated that grit has incremental predictive validity of success over intelligence and conscientiousness. Duckworth and colleagues argued that the achievement of difficult goals entails not only talent but also the sustained and focused application of talent over time (Duckworth, Peterson, Matthews, & Kelly, 2007, p. 1087). In a recent meta-analytic review of grit based on 88 studies ($N = 66,807$: Credé, Tynan, & Harms, 2017), however, Duckworth's suggestion of grit as a higher order structure was not confirmed, raising questions about its construct validity and explanatory value (beyond conscientiousness and perseverance).

There is evidence that resilience in the form of positive construal can be taught. In his study of emotion regulation, Kevin Ochsner (see Ochsner, 2004; Ochsner & Gross, 2005) demonstrated that you can teach individuals to reframe their initial negative response to a stimulus in positive terms and thus change their experience to it—with lasting effects. In a similar vein, Martin Seligman (2000, 2002; Seligman & Csikszentmihalyi, 2000; Seligman, Steen, Park, & Peterson, 2005) found that training individuals to change their explanatory styles (from internal to external, from global to specific, and from permanent to impermanent) made them less prone to depression and promoted psychological well-being and greater resilience. These efforts have important implications for training therapists and the promise of developing therapists' abilities to regulate their own emotions in the face of challenging clinical situations.

DELIBERATE PRACTICE

Anders Ericsson (Ericsson, Krampe, & Tesch-Römer, 1993; Ericsson & Pool, 2016; Ericsson, Roring, & Nandagopal, 2007) introduced the notion of *deliberate practice* to describe the process toward expertise or mastery in human performance. His research began with detailed analyses of acquired exceptional memory performance and then extended to studies of superior performance in such domains as medicine, music, chess, and sports. Generally, deliberate practice has been portrayed as high concentration practice beyond one's comfort zone. Specifically, it has been described as a well-defined practice regimen that (a) is based on effective techniques, (b) requires full cognitive commitment, (c) stretches the individual beyond current abilities, (d) involves expert monitoring and self-monitoring, and (e) produces effective mental representations (of critical tasks).

The notion of practice beyond one's comfort zone can be traced to Lev Vygotsky's (1930/1980) concept of the zone of proximal development (ZPD), which has been described as the difference between what one can do with help and what one cannot do. In other words, ZPD is the area of learning in which one needs the assistance of another with a higher skill set in order to accomplish a task. The concept was developed further by David Wood, Jerome Bruner, and Gail Ross (1976) with the notion of *scaffolding*—the structure of "support points" for performing an action, the guidance received from another more competent to permit work within the ZPD. It has been argued and illustrated that assigning the most difficult tasks an individual can do with scaffolding can lead to the greatest gains in learning (Wass & Golding, 2014).

Others have contributed to this perspective with emphasis on the importance of "practicing under pressure." Sian Beilock (2010; Beilock & Carr, 2001, 2005; Beilock & Gray, 2007; DeCaro, Thomas, Albert, & Beilock, 2011) has studied the deleterious effect of pressure on academic and athletic performance (i.e., "choking" in a competitive situation) and has advocated for training in conditions where pressure is simulated. Raôul Oudejans (2008; Oudejans & Pijpers, 2009) has also demonstrated that practicing under anxiety can prevent degradation or choking in expert perceptual-motor performance. Training exercises involving increased pressure can acclimatize performance to the specific processes accompanying anxiety.

In Chapters 5 and 6, we present our training program that incorporates many of the recommendations associated with deliberate practice, especially developing mental representations, applying empirically supported techniques, and using scaffolding to support practicing in simulated pressure situations that put the individual just beyond his or her comfort zone.

REFLECTIVE PRACTICE

Donald Schön (1983) was a prominent voice in developing the notion of *reflective practice*, which refers to the ability to reflect on one's actions so as to engage in a process of continuous learning. In his study of various professions, including psychotherapy, he introduced the concepts of *reflection-on-action* (reflecting on an action after the fact) and *reflection-in-action* (reflecting while doing) to describe the integration of theory and practice, the cyclic pattern of experience, and the conscious application of lessons learned from experience. His work built on John Dewey's (1933/1998) earlier exploration of the relationship among experience, interaction, and reflection. Dewey considered reflection to stem from doubt, which brings about a way of thinking that frames situations as problems. For Schön, professional development involves doubting and viewing one's actions with a critical lens, through which one carefully evaluates and plans until doubts are resolved.

Over the years, many models of reflective practice have been developed that highlight the concept of experiential learning: the transformation of information based on experience into knowledge, the continuous application of this knowledge to new situations (creating new experiences), and the cyclical process of reapplication and revision. These models have brought more detail and resonance to Schön's conceptualization, though most share an orientation on reflection as retrospective (i.e., reflection-on-action). Two noteworthy ones were advanced by Graham Gibbs (1988) and Christopher Johns (1995), which not only provided more definition regarding reflection as a cyclical process but also introduced emotion (i.e., what was felt or emotionally experienced with the description of what happened) into the equation (before evaluation and analysis).

Contemporary perspectives on reflective practice have also put forward a model that defines it as a synthesis of reflection, self-awareness, and critical thinking (see Eby, 2000). In this regard, Linda Finlay (2002, 2003, 2008) introduced the concept of *reflexivity*, defined as "a more immediate and dynamic process which involves continuing *self*-awareness" (2008, p. 6, italics in original). Finlay proposed five intersecting variants of reflexivity: introspection (solitary self-dialogue and probe of personal meanings and emotions), intersubjective reflection (focus on relational context and negotiated nature of practice encounters), mutual collaboration (participatory, dialogic approach to reflection as conversation), social critique (of wider discursive, social, and political context), and ironic deconstruction (of discursive practices). Her revision of reflective practice took a feminist turn with a greater emphasis on subjective and relational considerations.

Our training program, described in Chapters 5 and 6, especially aims to promote reflection-in-action. It includes strategies specifically designed to increase reflection on process—intrapersonal and interpersonal—having therapists articulate their experience (what they see and feel) as it unfolds and in relation to their patients, which also results in regulation of their emotions. Consistent with Finlay's reflexivity, it has an intersubjective and dialogic orientation.

CODA

What the Research Says About Decision Making and Judgment

The decision making process involves a blend of intuition (pattern-matching from previous experience) and analysis (mental simulation regarding whether a pattern would fit a given context). The selection of a pattern may first be determined by a workable option and then modified or substituted for another to fit the situation. Decision making is shaped by heuristics and prejudicial shortcuts or biases, including implicit biases, particularly in uncertain conditions. It has also been shown to be colored by emotion, especially negative emotions. A considerable amount of research regarding error in clinical judgment is consistent with this literature. As a result, greater humility in attitude is recommended, given that overconfidence has been identified as prevalent and pernicious, as well as systematic feedback on performance and continuous education on evidence and probability.

What the Research Says About the Impact of Pressure on Performance

Pressure, beyond the stress of uncertainty, has been found to narrow attention (for better or worse, depending on the task), overload working memory capacity, and adversely affect appraisal and judgment. Evidence suggests that pressure can result in self-focus or distraction, both of which can inhibit performance. Much depends on the nature of the task, and much can be moderated by other variables, including the presence of another person. Emotion regulation has been identified as an important variable in resilience and performance under pressure, with certain strategies shown to be effective, especially those involving distancing or acceptance and affect labeling (conditions that can be likened to mindfulness).

What the Research Says About Adaptation and Development

Certain evidence shows that resilience can be developed by training in emotion regulation strategies. In addition, research on training suggests practicing evidence-based techniques, with full cognitive commitment and under pressure (i.e., beyond one's comfort zone) but with adequate support and safety and with expert monitoring and self-monitoring or feedback. The objective of such training is to produce pattern recognition abilities or mental representations that facilitate implementation of an effective course of action. This research has been described as deliberate practice. There is also research on reflective practice, which has promoted the value of both reflection-on-action (reflecting on an action after the fact) and reflection-in-action (reflecting while doing) in the process of continuous learning.

2

The Science of the Therapist Under Pressure

No pressure, no diamond.

—THOMAS CARLYLE

Therapy can present many moments of pressure for therapists: moments when a therapist feels confused, or frustrated, or stuck, and must wrestle with these feelings while trying to remain composed, attentive, and connected to a patient. For example, in a survey of psychologists, Pope and Tabachnick (1993) found that more than 80% reported experiencing a negative emotion like anxiety or anger toward their patients. In a study of 132 patients, Dalenberg (2004) found that more than 60% reported that their therapist had been angry with them. Therapists have to navigate the pressures of trying to help patients who are struggling with challenges such as suicidality, self-harm, addiction, trauma, and despair; they may find themselves working with patients who are ambivalent about or, in the case of court-mandated treatment, perhaps even opposed to the idea of being in therapy. In addition, many therapists face pressure from managed care or employers to take on increased workloads without a commensurate increase in support or compensation.

As we presented in Chapter 1, pressure can negatively impact performance. Pressure can lead us to become more rigid and narrow in our thinking and to overrely on heuristics and biases. This can negatively impact our abilities to do a thorough assessment and develop a comprehensive case conceptualization; to recognize when we need a consultation, supervision, or feedback; and to

http://dx.doi.org/10.1037/0000182-003
Therapist Performance Under Pressure: Negotiating Emotion, Difference, and Rupture,
by J. C. Muran and C. F. Eubanks

choose and skillfully implement optimal interventions tailored to each patient. In addition, pressure can negatively impact our ability to build and maintain a strong relationship with our patients. Norcross and VandenBos (2018) suggested that the therapeutic relationship holds a unique place in clinical work: "It is, at once, the most significant source of pleasure and displeasure in psychotherapy" (p. 51). Given the importance of the therapeutic relationship across treatment modalities, we have chosen to focus our attention in this chapter on how pressure impacts the therapeutic relationship—more specifically, the alliance between therapist and patient.

WHY DO WE NEED A STRONG ALLIANCE?

First, we need to establish why it is so important for therapists to navigate pressure in a clinical situation such that they maintain a strong alliance with their patients. The working or therapeutic alliance is usually defined in terms of the therapist's and patient's abilities to agree on the goals of therapy, collaborate on the tasks of therapy, and maintain an affective bond (Bordin, 1979). The importance of the alliance is one of the most reliable and consistent findings in the psychotherapy research literature. A recent meta-analysis of almost 300 studies involving more than 30,000 patients found that the quality of the alliance is positively associated with treatment outcome, with a moderate effect size (Flückiger, Del Re, Wampold, & Horvath, 2018). This finding remained robust across different alliance measures, different points of view (patient, therapist, or observer), different treatment approaches, different patient characteristics, and different countries.

Therapeutic approaches differ with respect to how much emphasis they place on the alliance, with some making it a central focus (e.g., Safran & Muran, 2000) and others regarding it as a necessary but insufficient condition that permits the use of therapeutic techniques that produce change (e.g., J. S. Beck, 2011). To the best of our knowledge, most (if not all) therapeutic approaches regard the alliance as important and a "good enough" alliance as essential: If there is no agreement, no collaboration, and no bond of mutual trust and respect, the work of therapy cannot take place.

WHAT GETS IN THE WAY OF A STRONG ALLIANCE?

Research literature points to some factors that can get in the way of building and maintaining a strong alliance and working effectively with patients. Undoubtedly, certain patients can be particularly challenging and create a higher level of stress for clinicians; prolonged occupational stress can result in the emotional exhaustion, cynicism, and reduced sense of accomplishment that characterize burnout (Maslach, Schaufeli, & Leiter, 2001). For example, using a large naturalistic data set of 119 therapists and more than 10,000 patients, Saxon and Barkham (2012) found that therapists with a caseload including a higher percentage of patients at risk of harming themselves or others achieved poorer outcomes, not only with the at-risk patients but with all of their patients. The authors speculated that working with high-risk patients contributed to therapist burnout, which adversely impacted the therapists' ability to work effectively across their caseload. The researchers found support for the negative impact of therapist burnout in another study, based on a sample of 49 therapists and more than 2,000 patients (Delgadillo, Saxon, & Barkham, 2018): Delgadillo et al. (2018) found that higher therapist burnout was significantly associated with poorer patient outcomes on measures of anxiety and depression.

Stressful job situations can contribute to burnout and less effective performance, but so can issues in the therapist's personal life. In one study using a naturalistic outpatient sample, therapists' reports of feeling more burdened in their personal lives were negatively associated with patient-reported alliance development over time (Nissen-Lie, Havik, Høglend, Monsen, & Rønnestad, 2013). Of interest, therapist burden was not related to therapists' ratings of the alliance, which may indicate that therapists were not aware of how their personal burdens were impacting their ability to collaborate and build a bond with their patients. As the authors observed, these findings suggest that it can be difficult for therapists to keep struggles in their personal lives from impacting their work in the therapy office. Patients may be particularly sensitive to therapists' experiences of distress, which therapists may unknowingly communicate to patients through the therapists' in-session behaviors.

HOW DO THERAPISTS' PERSONAL DIFFICULTIES CONTRIBUTE TO PROBLEMS IN THE ALLIANCE?

The idea that therapists' personal issues can affect their ability to work effectively with patients is not new. We are probably most familiar with thinking of this phenomenon in terms of countertransference. The field has defined countertransference in various ways, but increasingly, most empirical studies of countertransference have conceptualized the construct in terms of a therapist's unresolved conflicts being triggered by a characteristic of the patient (J. A. Hayes, Gelso, Goldberg, & Kivlighan, 2018). Therapist countertransference reactions can take the form of feeling anxious and avoiding and withdrawing from personally threatening patient material or meeting one's own needs by excessively nurturing patients. Therapists may have a distorted or inaccurate recall of what a patient said in a session, or they may experience somatic reactions such as sleepiness or headaches. A meta-analysis of the countertransference literature found that more frequent countertransference reactions are associated with worse patient outcome (J. A. Hayes et al., 2018).

Therapists' abilities to successfully manage their countertransference reactions have most commonly been operationalized with the Countertransference Factors Inventory (CFI; Van Wagoner, Gelso, Hayes, & Diemer, 1991), a supervisor-rated measure that focuses on therapist qualities of self-insight, self-integration (as manifested by recognition of interpersonal boundaries), empathy, anxiety management, and conceptualization ability. Research with the CFI has found that therapists' abilities to manage their countertransference reactions are associated with better treatment outcome (J. A. Hayes et al., 2018). This finding suggests that therapists who are aware of and able to understand their emotional reactions to a patient, to identify with the patient's experience, and to draw on theory to contextualize the patient's behavior are better able to help their patients make treatment gains.

Several studies have found that engaging in negative countertransference behavior may be a particular risk for therapists with insecure attachment styles (Ligiéro & Gelso, 2002; A. Martin, Buchheim, Berger, & Strauss, 2007; Mohr, Gelso, & Hill, 2005; Rubino, Barker, Roth, & Fearon, 2000). According to Bowlby's (1988) conceptualization of attachment theory, we develop inner working models of relationships based on early experiences with significant caregivers. These models inform our expectations for ourselves and others we relate to over the course of our lives. Individuals who develop secure attachment styles display cooperative behaviors and flexible coping strategies under stress, whereas individuals with insecure attachment styles may be distant and distrustful (dismissing attachment) or demanding and dependent (preoccupied attachment) in relationships (Strauss & Petrowski, 2017).

As one might expect, research suggests that therapists with secure attachment styles have better alliances with their patients (Schauenburg et al., 2010). Therapist security may be particularly important when working with more challenging patients: One study found that secure therapist attachment was associated with better outcome for patients who had higher levels of impairment (Schauenburg et al., 2010). Therapists with insecure attachment styles tend to have weaker alliances and report more problems in therapy (Black, Hardy, Turpin, & Parry, 2005; Dinger, Strack, Sachsse, & Schauenburg, 2009) and tend to display less attuned behaviors in session (Talia, Muzi, Lingiardi, & Taubner, 2018). Patients working with therapists with insecure attachments are more likely to describe their attachment to the therapist as insecure (Petrowski, Pokorny, Nowacki, & Buchheim, 2013). This finding suggests that insecurely attached therapists are vulnerable to the therapeutic situation activating their attachment-related concerns, which might hinder their ability to form a good working relationship with their patient (Strauss & Petrowski, 2017). For example, a therapist with a dismissing attachment style might maintain a cool distance from patients, whereas a therapist with a preoccupied attachment style might self-disclose excessively about his or her personal life. By contrast, a therapist with a secure attachment style might be better at flexibly negotiating distance and closeness based on the patient's needs, rather than the therapist's.

Countertransference reactions and attachment-related concerns can be thought of as therapist blind spots that can contribute to problems in our working relationships with our patients. There is a small but growing research literature on another type of therapist blind spot: biases that lead therapists to commit microaggressions, conceptualized as direct and indirect disrespectful, insulting, dismissive communications about an individual's cultural group (Hook, Davis, Owen, & DeBlaere, 2017). Patient ratings of microaggressions related to patient gender (Owen, Tao, & Rodolfa, 2010) and race or ethnicity (Owen, Tao, Imel, Wampold, & Rodolfa, 2014) have been linked to lower alliance ratings. In a survey of lesbian, gay, and bisexual patients, 21% reported that their therapist was either dismissive of their sexual orientation or viewed it as a problem (Kelley, 2015). Microaggressions can range from explicitly prejudiced comments to invalidations, such as assuming that patients are heterosexual unless and until they tell you otherwise.

HOW DO THERAPISTS CONTRIBUTE TO NEGATIVE PROCESS?

We have identified evidence that therapists' own difficulties—in the form of problematic countertransference reactions, attachment insecurity, and biases—can negatively impact their abilities to work effectively with patients. In this section, we consider negative process.

In her review of qualitative studies, Clara Hill (2010) described qualitative efforts that have demonstrated the complexity of negative process, including patients' reluctance to disclose negative feelings; the difficulty for therapists to recognize these feelings; and, even if aware, the challenge for therapists to address these feelings (Fuller & Hill, 1985; Hill, Thompson, Cogar, & Denman, 1993; Hill et al., 2003; J. Martin, Martin, Meyer, & Slemon, 1986; J. Martin, Martin, & Slemon, 1987; Regan & Hill, 1992; Rennie, 1994). Here we examine research findings that shed light on how therapists can contribute to negative process, which increases the likelihood of poor treatment outcome.

Some of the most important studies on negative process in psychotherapy were the Vanderbilt studies conducted by Hans Strupp and colleagues (Strupp, 1998). With the first Vanderbilt study, Strupp and colleagues were interested in the role of specific therapeutic interventions versus common factors—that is, elements of healing relationships such as empathy that are presumed to be common across treatments. To investigate, Strupp compared professional therapists, who had training in specific interventions, with college professors, who were sought after for their advice and would presumably have access to only the common factors. Male college students who had difficulties with depression, anxiety, or shyness were randomly assigned to either a professional therapist or a professor and received two sessions each week, up to 25 sessions. The researchers found no significant differences in outcome between the two groups (Strupp & Hadley, 1979) and concluded that the question of specific versus common factors was the wrong question. To better understand what therapists do that contributes to outcome, Strupp and colleagues focused on the cases seen by professional therapists in the study. They conducted post hoc comparisons of good and poor outcome patients who were seen by the same therapists (Strupp, 1980a, 1980b, 1980c, 1980d). They observed negative behaviors by the therapists that interfered with the therapists' ability to form a good working alliance, such as a lack of empathy when working with patients who were less motivated or less receptive to the therapist's approach. In his discussion of one such comparison, Strupp (1980d) concluded the following:

> Thus, major deterrents to the formation of a good working alliance are not only the patient's characterological distortions and maladaptive defenses but—at least equally important—the therapist's personal reactions. . . . Traditionally these reactions have been considered under the heading of countertransference. It is becoming increasingly clear, however, that this conception is too narrow. The plain fact is that *any therapist—indeed any human being—cannot remain immune from negative (angry) reactions to the suppressed and repressed rage regularly encountered in patients with moderate to severe disturbances.* (p. 953; italics in original)

Strupp (1980d) observed that therapists in his sample tended to respond to challenging patients with what he described as "counterhostility that not uncommonly took the form of coldness, distancing, and other forms of rejection" (p. 954). This hostility on the part of the therapist contributed to poor alliances, dropout from treatment, and poor treatment outcome. Strupp (1980d) emphasized that this phenomenon was not unique to a subset of "bad" therapists: "In our study we failed to encounter a single instance in which a difficult patient's hostility and negativism were successfully confronted or resolved" (p. 954).

A more recent research study on therapist reactions supports Strupp's contention that the problem of negative therapist reactions to patients is widespread and important. Westra, Aviram, Connors, Kertes, and Ahmed (2012) examined therapists' reactions to patients in a sample of 30 patients receiving eight sessions of cognitive behavior therapy (CBT) for generalized anxiety disorder. They found that when therapists had certain negative reactions to patients early in treatment, such as the therapist feeling that he or she was in a power struggle with the patient or feeling drained, helpless, guilty, and frustrated, patients were likely to display higher levels of resistance behaviors (such as ignoring or disagreeing with the therapist) later in treatment. By contrast, when therapists reported positive reactions such as liking, enjoying, and feeling attached to patients, their patients had lower levels of resistance at midtreatment and evidenced reductions in resistance across the early stage of treatment. These findings suggest that therapists' own personal reactions to patients may impact their ability to respond effectively to patient resistance and that negative therapist reactions may worsen patient resistance.

The clinical importance of these findings is underscored by another study from the same data set: Button, Westra, Hara, and Aviram (2015) found that patient resistance was a significant predictor of poor treatment outcome. Of additional concern is the possibility that therapists may not only have difficulty managing patient resistance but also lack awareness of it. In another study drawing on a different sample of patients with generalized anxiety disorder receiving CBT, Westra and colleagues (Hara et al., 2015) found that observers appeared to be better than therapists at detecting resistant behaviors that impacted clinical outcomes. Compared with therapist ratings, observer ratings were more predictive of patient perceptions of the therapeutic alliance, patient compliance with homework assignments, and treatment outcome. The tunnel vision and the self-focus that can arise under pressure may interfere with therapists' abilities to remain sensitively attuned to their patients' experience in therapy.

Based on the findings of the first Vanderbilt study, Strupp and colleagues sought to address therapists' difficulties with responding effectively to negative patient reactions by developing a treatment manual and a training program (Strupp & Binder, 1984). In the Vanderbilt II study, they examined the impact of the training on treatment process and outcome in a sample of 16 experienced therapists who each treated several patients (Strupp, 1993). Strupp and colleagues found that contrary to their hopes, the training did not improve therapists' abilities to manage interpersonal processes within the therapeutic relationship. Rather, they found an *increase* in negative process, specifically an increase in therapist hostility and in complex communications in which the therapist conveyed mixed messages (e.g., communicating both friendliness and hostility or both approach and avoidance; Henry, Strupp, Butler, Schacht, & Binder, 1993). The researchers also found that negative process was related to worse treatment outcome (Najavits & Strupp, 1994).

Why didn't the training work? One possible explanation is suggested by a series of analyses that Strupp and his colleagues conducted using therapists' ratings of how they treated themselves (Henry, Schacht, Strupp, Butler, & Binder, 1993). Therapists who reported that they treated themselves in negative ways (e.g., self-indicting and oppressing) demonstrated the greatest adherence to the training and were linked to the increases in negative process that resulted from the training. By contrast, therapists who treated themselves in a more positive and nurturing way showed decreases in negative process after training. These findings are consistent with the research findings on performance under pressure: Judgment and decision making under stress often become more rigid and narrow. When therapists experience pressure in a clinical situation—which could be generated or exacerbated by their own inner critic—they may become more adherent to a treatment protocol in a way that ends up being unhelpful for the patient. Additional research offers more support for this idea. Studies of both cognitive therapy (Castonguay, Goldfried, Wiser, Raue, & Hayes, 1996) and psychodynamic therapy (W. E. Piper, Azim, Joyce, & McCallum, 1991; W. E. Piper et al., 1999; Schut et al., 2005) have found evidence that some therapists respond to a difficult interaction with a patient by increasing their adherence to their theoretical model— for example, cognitive therapists increase their challenging of the patient's distorted cognitions, and psychodynamic therapists make more transference interpretations—and this type of arguably rigid adherence in the context of a strained patient–therapist relationship has been linked with poor outcome and dropout from therapy. It is not hard to imagine how frustrating it would be for a patient who is feeling misunderstood by the therapist or dissatisfied with the treatment to realize that the therapist's response is to double down on their approach instead of pausing and creating space to hear the patient's concerns.

Therapists differed in their response to the training offered in the Vanderbilt II study, which points to how therapists' personal characteristics can moderate therapists' responses to challenging clinical situations. This observation contributed to a line of research on therapist facilitative interpersonal skills. Drawing on case examples from the Vanderbilt studies, Anderson, Patterson, and Weis (2007) developed a performance task (Facilitative Interpersonal Skills) to measure therapists' abilities to respond to challenging interpersonal situations in therapy. With this task, therapists respond verbally to brief video clips based on patients from the Vanderbilt studies. Therapists' responses are recorded and then coded using an observer-based measure of skills such as empathy, warmth, verbal fluency, and the ability to build and maintain a strong alliance. This task can be stressful for therapists: Not only are they asked to respond to a difficult clinical situation, but they are under pressure to quickly come up with a response that they know will be recorded and evaluated. Hence, to perform well on the task, therapists must not only possess good interpersonal skills but also be able to demonstrate these skills under pressure.

Studies using the Facilitative Interpersonal Skills task have found links between performance on the task and treatment outcome (Anderson, McClintock, Himawan, Song, & Patterson, 2016; Anderson, Ogles, Patterson, Lambert, & Vermeersch, 2009). One particularly striking finding is from a study that was partly modeled after the Vanderbilt I study comparing therapists and college professors: Participants were randomly assigned to attend seven sessions with either psychology graduate student therapists or graduate students in other disciplines who had not received therapy training (Anderson, Crowley, Himawan, Holmberg, & Uhlin, 2016). The researchers found that therapists' facilitative interpersonal skills predicted alliance ratings and change on most outcome measures. There were no significant differences between the psychology students and the students from other disciplines. This finding suggests that what mattered was not whether a therapist had received training in psychotherapy but rather whether the therapist could respond empathically and skillfully to challenging clinical situations.

Findings from another study provide more support for this idea of the importance of therapists' skills under pressure. Schöttke, Flückiger, Goldberg, Eversmann, and Lange (2017) showed therapy trainees a 15-minute film clip of a provocative therapy intervention and then observed the trainees as they engaged in a group discussion. The researchers found that trainees' abilities to communicate in the discussion with clarity, respect, warmth, and empathy predicted their outcome with their patients over a 5-year period.

WHAT ARE ALLIANCE RUPTURES?

The literatures on therapists' personal difficulties and on negative process point to ways in which therapists can struggle to build and maintain good working alliances with their patients, particularly in challenging clinical situations. We now turn to a literature that directly focuses on moments of tension and strain in the therapeutic relationship: the literature on alliance ruptures.

Drawing on Bordin's (1979) tripartite conceptualization of the alliance, ruptures can be characterized as disagreements between patients and therapists on the goals of treatment, failure to collaborate on the tasks of treatment, and/or a strain in the emotional bond. Although the word *rupture* connotes a sudden or dramatic break, we have found it useful to also view subtle tensions and misattunements as markers of rupture and to draw on related constructs such as countertransference to inform our understanding of ruptures. By paying close attention to early signs of potential rupture, clinicians can find opportunities to intervene before the therapeutic relationship reaches a breaking point. Research on ruptures suggests that this is important; for example, one study found that experiencing more intense ruptures, as reported by both patients and therapists, was associated with a worse outcome on measures of patients' interpersonal functioning and that a failure to resolve these ruptures predicted premature dropout from treatment (Muran et al., 2009). Research also suggests that ruptures are not a clinical problem that is solely the concern of mediocre therapists or particularly challenging patients: In the study just cited, around 33% of patients and 50% of therapists reported that they experienced difficulties in the therapeutic relationship early in treatment (Muran et al., 2009). Studies using observer-based measures of ruptures often report even higher frequencies—from 33% to 100% of sessions (see Eubanks, Muran, & Safran, 2018, 2019).

In our work, we have found it useful to distinguish between two types of ruptures: withdrawal and confrontation ruptures (Safran & Muran, 2000; Samstag, Muran, & Safran, 2004; see Exhibit 2.1). We have defined withdrawal ruptures as movements *away* from an other, including efforts toward isolation

---

EXHIBIT 2.1

Alliance Ruptures

Withdrawal ruptures
- Movements <u>away</u> from other or self
- Efforts toward *isolation* or *appeasement*
- Pursuits of *communion* at the expense of *agency*

Confrontation ruptures
- Movements <u>against</u> other
- Efforts toward *aggression* or *control*
- Pursuits of *agency* at the expense of *communion*

or attempts to deny an aspect of the self—such as stifling a desire—in order to appease the other. These movements away are efforts to protect an attachment: Take the example of the child who learns to be quiet around a domineering parent in order to maintain some connection and avoid rejection. We have defined confrontation ruptures as movements *against* an other, including movements toward aggression or control. Another way of thinking about withdrawal and confrontation is in terms of the ongoing negotiation between the patient and therapist in terms of what they wish for or need from each other. In a withdrawal rupture, the patient sacrifices or compromises his or her need for *agency* in an effort to maintain a relationship (the need for *communion*) with the therapist. For example, the patient may disagree with what the therapist is saying, but rather than state this directly, the patient changes the topic for fear that direct expression would endanger the therapeutic relationship. In a confrontation rupture, the patient is trying to preserve or defend his or her agency by moving against the therapist, at the expense of communion and collaborating well with the therapist. We should also note that ruptures can present as complex combinations of both withdrawal and confrontation markers, as patients wrestle with their own ambivalence or concerns about their needs and fears around agency and communion.

In describing types of withdrawal and confrontation ruptures, we draw on an observer-based measure of ruptures that we have developed—the Rupture Resolution Rating System (3RS)—to provide specific examples (Eubanks, Lubitz, Muran, & Safran, 2019; Eubanks, Muran, & Safran, 2015; see also the appendix). In confrontation ruptures, the patient moves against the therapist and/or the work of therapy. This could take the form of behaviors such as criticizing or complaining about the therapist, the activities or parameters of the treatment, or the patient's lack of progress. Additional examples of confrontation ruptures include rejecting the therapist's efforts to intervene, defending oneself against perceived criticism by the therapist, or attempting to control or pressure the therapist. In withdrawal ruptures, the patient moves away from the therapist or the work of therapy. This could take the form of avoidant behaviors such as the patient denying his or her true feelings about how treatment is going, giving minimal responses to the therapist's questions, shifting the topic or telling stories in an effort to avoid the topic at hand, speaking in a vague or intellectualized manner, being overly appeasing and deferential, or pulling away from the therapist via a self-critical and hopeless stance. Additional descriptions and examples of these markers of ruptures are provided in Table 2.1. In a recent study using the 3RS to code ruptures in early sessions of CBT, we found that the frequency of confrontation ruptures predicted premature dropout from treatment (Eubanks, Lubitz, et al., 2019).

In this discussion of withdrawal and confrontation ruptures, we are describing ruptures in terms of patient behaviors. However, we believe that ruptures are dyadic phenomena that are coconstructed by both patient and therapist (Safran & Muran, 2000), and we have long emphasized the importance of therapists attending to their internal experience during ruptures (see Chapter 3). Therapists' contributions to ruptures have been recognized in some

TABLE 2.1. Alliance Rupture Markers From the Rupture Resolution Rating System

Withdrawal rupture markers and examples	
Denial	The patient withdraws from the therapist and/or the work of therapy by denying a feeling state that is manifestly evident, or denying the importance of interpersonal relationships or events that seem important and relevant to the work of therapy.
	Therapist: Are you OK? You look upset.
	Patient: It's nothing, I'm fine.
Minimal response	The patient withdraws from the therapist and/or the work of therapy by going silent or by giving minimal responses to questions or statements that are intended to initiate or continue discussion.
	Therapist: That sounds really difficult. How did it make you feel?
	Patient: *(Shrugs)*
Abstract communication	The patient avoids the therapist and/or the work of therapy by using vague or abstract language.
	Therapist: How did you feel when she turned you down?
	Patient: It really made me reflect on how my relationship with her is an example of the rise of transactional interactions in society today. I think she and I are both really impacted by that.
Avoidant storytelling and/or shifting topic	The patient tells stories and/or shifts the topic in a manner that functions to avoid the therapist and/or the work of therapy.
	Therapist: I think we really need to talk about our goals. I'm concerned that we aren't really on the same page. Would you be willing to talk about this?
	Patient: You know, that reminds me of something that happened at work the other day. We were working on this project—oh, I have to tell you about this project, it's really interesting . . .
Deferential and appeasing	The patient withdraws from the therapist and/or the work of therapy by being overly compliant and submitting to the therapist in a deferential manner.
	Therapist: I think for homework you should focus on tracking your thoughts and feelings around asking your boss for a raise.
	Patient *(Sitting very stiffly, looking uncomfortable)*: That sounds like a good idea. Yes, absolutely.
Content/affect split	The patient withdraws from the therapist and/or the work of therapy by exhibiting affect that does not match the content of his or her narrative.
	Therapist: It's hard for you to tell me about those sad feelings.
	Patient *(A bright, forced smile)*: Yes, it's not easy to talk about. *(Patient chuckles nervously.)*

(continues)

TABLE 2.1. Alliance Rupture Markers From the Rupture Resolution Rating System (*Continued*)

Withdrawal rupture markers and examples

Self-criticism and/or hopelessness	The patient withdraws from the therapist and/or the work of therapy by becoming absorbed in a depressive process of self-criticism and/or hopelessness that seems to shut out the therapist and to close off any possibility that the therapist or the treatment can help the patient.
	Therapist: That sounds important. Can you tell me more about that?
	Patient: *(Sighs)* What's the point? It's not going to make me feel better.

Confrontation rupture markers and examples

Complaints/concerns about the therapist	The patient expresses negative feelings or concerns about the therapist.
	Patient: I can see I'm not going to get anything useful out of you.
Patient rejects therapist intervention	The patient rejects or dismisses the therapist's intervention.
	Therapist: When did your insomnia begin?
	Patient: What difference does that make? That's irrelevant.
Complaints/concerns about the activities of therapy	The patient expresses dissatisfaction, discomfort, or disagreement with specific tasks of therapy such as homework assignments, empty chair exercises, or exposure.
	Patient: I really don't understand what you're asking me to do on these thought records. I don't see the point of them at all.
Complaints/concerns about the parameters of therapy	The patient expresses complaints or concerns about the parameters of treatment, such as appointment times, session length, or frequency, or about completing questionnaires.
	Patient: Once a week is not enough time to address all my problems!
Complaints/concerns about progress in therapy	The patient expresses complaints, concerns, or doubts about the progress that can be made or has been made in therapy.
	Patient: I've been coming here for four weeks now, and I really can't think of anything that has changed. Maybe this has all been a waste of time.
Patient defends self against therapist	The patient defends their own thoughts, feelings, or behavior against what they perceive to be the therapist's criticism or judgment.
	Therapist: A lot of things have changed for you.
	Patient: But I think it's normal for people to change. I'm going through a transitional period. It doesn't mean that I'm unstable!
Efforts to control/ pressure therapist	The patient attempts to control the therapist and/or the session, or the patient puts pressure on the therapist to fix the patient's problems quickly.
	Patient: I want to know how this therapy works. Tell me how it's going to help me with my problems. And none of that fancy therapist talk; I want a direct answer.

Note. Data from Eubanks, Muran, and Safran (2015).

research on alliance ruptures, such as the Collaborative Interactions Scale (Colli & Lingiardi, 2009), an observer-based measure that assesses both patients' and therapists' positive and negative contributions to the alliance, as well as the System for Observing Family Therapy Alliances (Friedlander et al., 2006), which includes negative alliance-related behaviors of both patients and therapists in family therapy. In our own research program, we are interested in drawing more attention to how therapists contribute to the development and maintenance of ruptures by engaging in withdrawal and confrontation behaviors themselves (see Eubanks, 2019, for an example of applying 3RS markers to both patient and therapist behaviors). For example, therapists may withdraw by becoming passive in the session or by engaging in intellectualized digressions that move away from the patient's presenting concerns. Or therapists may engage in confrontation ruptures by criticizing the patient or being overly controlling of the session. Our preliminary efforts to examine the therapist's role suggest that therapist contributions to ruptures in an early therapy session, as rated by observers, predict premature dropout from therapy (Eubanks, Lubitz, et al., 2019).

WHAT DO WE KNOW ABOUT RUPTURE REPAIR?

Although alliance ruptures can contribute to poor patient outcome or dropout, a meta-analytic review of 11 studies found that repair or resolution of ruptures were quite prevalent (from 15% to 80% of cases) and significantly predictive of improved patient outcome (see Eubanks et al., 2018; Eubanks, Muran, & Safran, 2019). These studies included treatments from various orientations. A striking example from this literature is a study of 79 patients who received either CBT or psychodynamic-interpersonal therapy for depression (Stiles et al., 2004). The researchers found that patients with repaired ruptures—identified based on changes in patients' self-reported alliance scores—attained, on average, greater improvement in therapy than patients who did not experience ruptures. This is a provocative finding: Ruptures may spell doom for a case if they are not adequately addressed, but if they are handled well, they can contribute to patient improvement. What can therapists do to facilitate this kind of rupture resolution? How can therapists respond to the pressure of a rupture in a way that contributes to better outcome rather than making the rupture worse?

In our research program, our efforts to better understand the resolution process were grounded in a series of task analyses, studies in which a model of rupture resolution was constructed and then progressively refined based on empirical data (Safran & Muran, 1996; Safran, Crocker, McMain, & Murray, 1990; Safran, Muran, & Samstag, 1994). Safran and Muran (1996) developed a four-part stage-process model of rupture resolution with the aim of sensitizing therapists to the critical processes and pathways involved. In Stage 1, the therapist recognizes and addresses the rupture by drawing the patient's attention to it. In Stage 2, the patient and therapist collaboratively explore the negative feelings associated with the rupture. This process can become uncomfortable for the patient, who may try to avoid further exploration. If this happens, the therapist pivots to Stage 3, in which he or she draws the patient's attention to the patient's avoidance maneuvers and explores them. In the final stage, the therapist and patient focus on clarifying the patient's core relational need that underlies the initial rupture. Figure 2.1 provides an illustration of this stage-process model.

In withdrawal ruptures, the process usually involves moving from exploring the patient's efforts to avoid directly engaging with the therapist to recognizing and helping the patient more clearly assert what the patient really needs from the therapist: a progression to *agency*. In confrontation ruptures, the process of exploring the rupture would typically involve moving from exploring the patient's expressed anger toward the therapist to identifying feelings of disappointment with the therapist and then to contacting the patient's underlying vulnerability and recognizing the need to be nurtured: a progression to *communion*. The four stages of the rupture resolution model should be understood as a heuristic that facilitates the development of a *mental representation* of rupture resolution. In reality, repairing a rupture often involves cycling between these stages multiple times, and the process may extend across multiple therapy sessions. Efforts to resolve one rupture may lead to another rupture; for example, a therapist's initial attempt to draw attention to a rupture (e.g., "I feel that there is some distance between us") may cause the patient to feel criticized (e.g., "Are you saying that I'm doing something wrong?"), and the therapist will need to recognize and address this new rupture. It is important that the therapist move flexibly to where the patient is rather than rigidly adhere to one resolution strategy or plan (Safran & Muran, 2000). If the therapist is focused on repairing an initial rupture, while the patient is actually upset about a subsequent rupture, the therapist's misdirected efforts at repair may only serve to strengthen the patient's sense of being misunderstood or disconnected from the therapist.

The hope is that this exploration will not only help the dyad to work together toward a greater understanding of the rupture but also shed light on how the patient understands and experiences themselves in relationships. In other words, by exploring this particular relational event, the patient will gain greater awareness of how the patient navigates other relationships as well (Safran & Muran, 2000). By exploring a patient's complaints about the therapist, a therapist may help a highly critical patient become more aware of how their hostility pushes others away, leaving them alone in their contempt. By encouraging a patient to directly assert what is needed, a therapist may help a deferential patient recognize how the patient's prior efforts at appeasement successfully kept the peace, but at the price of the patient's needs for true recognition and intimacy. The therapist may make such links explicit by pointing out parallels between the therapeutic interaction and patterns in the patient's interpersonal relationships. However, it is important that therapists not move too quickly to make these links. As we noted, therapists can focus too much on transference interpretations, particularly when feeling

FIGURE 2.1. Safran and Muran's (1996) Stage-Process Model of Rupture Resolution

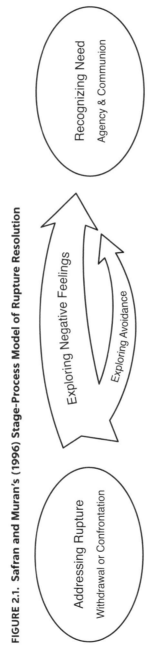

Note. Version designed by Rachel Small, 2019.

anxious (e.g., W. E. Piper et al., 1991, 1999). Moving away from exploring the patient's experience in the here and now—perhaps because of the therapist's own anxiety—can lead the therapist to miss the opportunity for a richer understanding of the patient's experience and a more powerful, in vivo exploration of the patient's relational schemas. It is much more impactful to become aware of how one is moving away or against the therapist *in this very moment* than to make those connections about relationships in the past or outside of the room.

Several other research groups have also developed models of rupture resolution based on task analyses. Similar to the model just described, some of these models regard the starting point of rupture resolution as the therapist acknowledging the rupture and exploring it collaboratively with the patient; these include studies of rupture repair in interpersonal psychodynamic therapy with patients who are depressed (Agnew, Harper, Shapiro, & Barkham, 1994), cognitive analytic therapy with patients with borderline personality disorder (Bennett, Parry, & Ryle, 2006; Daly, Llewelyn, McDougall, & Chanen, 2010), and emotion-focused therapy with couples (Swank & Wittenborn, 2013). However, task analyses of CBT for depression (Aspland, Llewelyn, Hardy, Barkham, & Stiles, 2008) and CBT for borderline personality disorder (Cash, Hardy, Kellett, & Parry, 2014) concluded that therapists did not need to explicitly acknowledge a rupture. Rather, they described how therapists can resolve ruptures by changing the topic of discussion or the task in which the patient and therapist were engaged in a way that is responsive to the patient's needs or concerns.

Whether or not a therapist explicitly acknowledges a rupture, it seems important for the therapist to have some internal recognition that a rupture is occurring in order to be best positioned to address it. Several research studies found evidence suggesting that therapist recognition of a rupture is related to subsequent improvements in alliance or outcome (e.g., Atzil-Slonim et al., 2015; Chen, Atzil-Slonim, Bar-Kalifa, Hasson-Ohayon, & Refaeli, 2018; Rubel, Zilcha-Mano, Feils-Klaus, & Lutz, 2018; Zilcha-Mano, Snyder, & Silberschatz, 2017).

Once a therapist recognizes that a rupture is occurring, the therapist has multiple response options. First and foremost, we argue that part of building and maintaining a good alliance is the therapist consistently approaching the patient with empathy, validation, and curiosity. The therapist never presumes that he or she has all the answers; the therapist respects the patient's unique perspective and appreciates that the work of therapy always involves a collaboration between patient and therapist. The therapist brings a "skillful tentativeness" (see Safran & Muran, 2000; see also Muran, Safran, & Eubanks-Carter, 2010) to interactions with the patient; the therapist is seeking greater understanding and clarification of the patient's experience. As this should always be taking place, with some ruptures, the therapist may simply maintain this position, continue to validate the patient, and try to understand their concerns, and that may suffice to repair the rupture. This is represented as the first potential path in Figure 2.2.

FIGURE 2.2. Strategies for Alliance-Building and Rupture Repair or Resolution

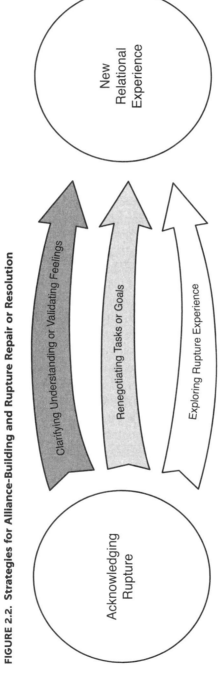

Note. Version designed by Rachel Small, 2019.

The second and third potential paths in Figure 2.2 represent what we have described as *immediate* and *exploratory* resolution strategies (Eubanks et al., 2018). Immediate strategies are efforts to promptly address a rupture and get treatment back on track, such as strategies involving renegotiating tasks or goals, as indicated in the second path in Figure 2.2. For example, if a patient objects to a therapy task, the therapist might address the patient's concerns by offering more explanation of the rationale for the task, or the therapist could change the task, as suggested by the task analytic studies of CBT. A therapist might choose an immediate strategy if it is very early in treatment and they do not feel the bond is strong enough yet for an in-depth exploration of the rupture. A therapist might try to initiate an exploration of a rupture and find that the patient is not willing to collaborate on such a discussion at this point; shifting the topic from the rupture back to the patient's presenting concerns might be an effective way to keep the patient engaged until a more propitious moment for exploration arises. Or if the patient is in great distress, the therapist might choose an immediate strategy to prioritize getting back to specific therapy techniques aimed at alleviating the patient's symptoms.

Exploratory strategies involve shifting the focus of the session toward exploring the rupture experience (the third path in Figure 2.2), consistent with the type of exploration described in Safran and Muran's (1996) stage-process model. For example, the therapist could invite the patient to share his or her thoughts and feelings about the impasse. The therapist could disclose his or her own experience of the therapeutic relationship and acknowledge how he or she has contributed to the difficulties they are experiencing. A therapist might choose to use exploratory strategies when they reach an impasse so great that it is impossible to move forward with therapy without taking time to fully address the alliance rupture. A therapist might also choose an exploratory approach if he or she has a sense that what is unfolding between the therapist and patient is related to the patient's key interpersonal difficulties and is therefore important to explore further.

Although our research program has focused on the exploratory approach to rupture resolution, it is important to emphasize that both immediate and exploratory approaches can be useful and that even the "simplest" approach can have a powerful impact on a patient, providing a new relational experience. We have noted how the process of exploring a rupture can be a powerful corrective experience for patients (Christian, Safran, & Muran, 2012). A patient might find it a unique opportunity to talk about and work through an interpersonal conflict with an empathic person; this may be in stark contrast to the patient's other interpersonal experiences and provide a powerful challenge to the patient's assumptions about what is possible in an interpersonal relationship. Other forms of resolving ruptures can also provide a corrective experience. For example, a patient complains about a homework assignment, and the therapist agrees to change the assignment in a flexible and nondefensive manner. The therapist may not link this directly to the patient's underlying interpersonal problems, but nevertheless it may be profoundly impactful for a patient who is not accustomed to being heard and validated.

CASE EXAMPLE: IMMEDIATE AND EXPLORATORY RESOLUTION APPROACHES

To further illustrate how a therapist might employ immediate and exploratory resolution approaches, I (CFE) present an experience with one of my patients. We had been working together for a while, and I had become accustomed to her tendency to tell and retell the story of her life—revisiting why she had made certain life decisions and trying to understand how she had ended up in an unsatisfying marriage and a dead-end job. Initially I had listened with the assumption that she was telling me this story to communicate content that I needed to know and understand. However, as I realized she was telling the same story over and over, with no change or movement in the narrative, and I could not see how it was benefitting our work, I began to shift my focus to the process. I started interrupting her when she began her story and asked her why she was telling me this story again at this moment. Sometimes she agreed that she was going off on a ruminative tangent (like the 3RS withdrawal rupture marker of avoidant storytelling) and thanked me for refocusing her (the immediate resolution strategy of redirecting the patient). Other times she told me that there was a reason she was telling me the story now and would note a new detail and explain why she felt this was important. This would shift my view of her story from an effort to withdraw to an effort to engage and enrich our work.

But then came a session when she spoke about relationships with various people in her life, and I heard the familiar complaints differently: as an endless string of one "poor me" after another, blaming everyone in her life for all her problems. I experienced her as more intense than usual, as aggrieved and indignant. I don't know if the increase in intensity lay in how she expressed herself or in how I received it that particular day—or most likely an interaction between the two—but I found myself trying to interject more with questions and observations, anything to break up the tired narrative. As she continued, I became acutely aware that nothing that I was saying was penetrating, as if we were speaking different languages. When she complained about a request her boss had made of her—something that I perceived as appropriate and part of her job description—and she said that her boss was being "cruel," I suddenly had the overwhelming sense that I could not complete this session. The session was infuriatingly pointless because she was not listening to me and was not open to anything I was saying. Either I would have to walk out of the room, or I would have to ask her to leave.

I was taken aback by my visceral reaction. I knew that I had to say something to tolerate staying in my chair: "I feel like we are having two separate conversations here. There is a wall between us, and we aren't really communicating with each other."

My effort to draw attention to what was happening between us (the exploratory strategy of disclosing my internal experience of the patient–therapist interaction) got her attention. She stopped her narrative and asked me what I meant. I shared my reaction to her calling her boss "cruel"—my sense that she was being unfair to him, that he was asking something reasonable. I revealed my thought that one reason she had been having so many problems at work was that she thought the job was beneath her.

I was blunt and forthright, and she responded in kind: "You are being so direct with me right now. You're usually so gentle. We've been talking about my work problems for a long time. Why didn't you say this before?"

Now I felt both defensive and self-critical: Why had I been holding back so much for so long? At the same time, was *I* now being cruel? I tried to continue exploring what was happening between us by disclosing more of my experience: "I think I didn't really put it all together until just now. I think when we started working together, I couldn't figure out what was going on for you at work, and it took time for me to form an opinion." A moment from our prior session suddenly came to my mind: "I'm remembering right now something you said in our last session, that you are a grown woman and you can take it. I have to take responsibility for the fact that I haven't been treating you like a grown woman. I've been holding back, feeling like I need to protect you, and to protect us. But you *are* a grown woman, and I need to show you that respect and be honest with you." She was looking closely at me with an intense focus, and I was concerned about how she was receiving my effort to acknowledge my contribution to the rupture. I returned to a focus on what was happening between us in this moment (the exploratory strategy of inviting the patient to discuss thoughts or feelings about the therapist or therapy): "How is this, to hear me say this?"

Her face softened, and her response surprised me: "It reminds me of my mother. She would do this sometimes; she would give me a kick in the seat of the pants when I needed it. Thank you for being honest with me. It means a lot."

By exploring what was happening between us, we were able to change what I experienced as a moment of profound disconnection into a moment in which we were genuine with each other, and I think we both felt seen and heard by the other. This does not mean that our interpersonal difficulties were completely resolved. My patient continued to be prone to avoidant storytelling, and speaking honestly about what was going on between us was not easy. For example, in the next session, she spoke more about her mother than usual and expressed some criticism of her mother, and I used the exploratory strategy of linking the rupture to larger interpersonal patterns in the patient's other relationships to try to explore how her criticism of her mother might be related to her concerns about me and my ability to help her. In that session, through a mixture of moving against (confrontation markers such as *patient rejects therapist intervention*) and moving away (withdrawal markers such as *denial, shifting topic, avoidant storytelling* and being *deferential and appeasing*), she adeptly outmaneuvered my attempts to facilitate an exploration of what she wanted and needed from me. The challenge for me was to keep moving with her: to stay close to the process and my experience of it, remembering what I had learned about my tendency to be overprotective of her and the potential value of being more direct, without becoming rigidly fixed in that position. Our rupture resolution process was not one moment in time but rather an ongoing negotiation between both our desires to protect our connection while respecting our needs to be heard and seen by each other.

CODA

Challenges Therapists Face in the Alliance

Therapists can have difficulty building and maintaining strong working alliances with patients when the therapist is under pressure. The stress of working with high-risk patients, issues in the therapist's personal life, struggles with countertransference and insecure attachment, or therapist bias can all hinder therapists' effectiveness. Particularly when working with challenging patients, therapists can be vulnerable to engaging in forms of negative process, such as hostile responses to patient hostility, or overly rigid adherence to therapy protocols.

Alliance Rupture

Based on a meta-analysis of 11 studies, the research indicates that ruptures are quite prevalent: Patients report them approximately one third of the time (early in treatment), therapists half the time, and observers in as much 100% of cases. They are also a demonstrated risk factor for premature termination or poor outcome. We presented an operational definition of rupture distinguishing between withdrawal and confrontation markers (specific patient communications or interpersonal behaviors), furthered by the observer-based 3RS and supported by other measures.

Rupture Repair

Based on the cited meta-analysis, the research indicates that rupture repair is also quite prevalent (up to approximately 80% of cases, per patient report) and significantly predictive of treatment success. Rupture repair or resolution has been defined in different ways; we highlighted both immediate and exploratory strategies. We noted the importance of therapists' abilities to recognize alliance ruptures and to respond nondefensively with curiosity and flexibility. No matter which specific strategy a therapist employs, by maintaining such a stance in the face of a rupture, a therapist can facilitate a new relational or corrective emotional experience for a patient.

3

From Emotion to Rupture

Beauty, Poetry, she is All: once more all in the figure of the other, All except herself.
—SIMONE DE BEAUVOIR (1949/2010)

The etymology of the word *emotion*—from the French word *émouvoir* for "to stir up"—captures the struggle to define its meaning. Despite considerations from many philosophers of diverse cultures, dating back to ancient times (Frevert, 2016), and from psychologists such as William James (see his 1884 article "What Is an Emotion?") in the 19th century, the definition continues to be a challenge fraught with controversy. Since the 1980s, we have witnessed rapid growth in the study of emotion: The most recent edition of the *Handbook of Emotion* (fourth ed.; Barrett, Lewis, & Haviland-Jones, 2016) consists of 50 review chapters that cover the interdisciplinary spectrum—from the philosophical, sociological, biological, developmental, cognitive perspective to perspectives related to personality and health. Since the 1990s, we have witnessed a similar development with regard to emotion regulation: The most recent edition of the *Handbook of Emotion Regulation* (second ed.; Gross, 2014b) consists of 36 review chapters that concern biological bases; cognitive, developmental, and social considerations; and perspectives on personality, psychopathology, and intervention.

Likewise, we have witnessed a significant shift in emphasis on emotion in psychotherapy—from something secondary or epiphenomenal to something central or essential in the change process. For example, in the

http://dx.doi.org/10.1037/0000182-004
Therapist Performance Under Pressure: Negotiating Emotion, Difference, and Rupture,
by J. C. Muran and C. F. Eubanks

cognitive–behavioral tradition, emotion was once construed as a postcognitive phenomenon (A. T. Beck, 1976; Ellis, 1962) before significant reformulations (L. S. Greenberg & Safran, 1987; Guidano & Liotti, 1983) brought emotion front and center and highlighted its integral relationship to core processes. We have seen this turn in psychoanalytic and humanistic psychotherapies as well (e.g., Muran, 2001c; Safran & Greenberg, 1991). With this change has come a proliferation of treatment models[1] in which emotional experiencing and regulation are primary targets of intervention; certain models have gained some degree of empirical support. (See also Peluso & Freund, 2018, for meta-analyses regarding emotional expression in treatment.)

In this chapter, we review the literature on emotion, including conceptualizations that define its functional properties and propositions that define it in basic and complex terms as elemental and multivariate. We highlight a constructionist conceptualization that suggests emotion as pluralistic and idiosyncratic—organized by previous experience and shaped by social influence. We elaborate on this complex conceptualization with a consideration of emotion regulation. We then turn to a consideration of clinical perspectives on multiple selves and intersubjectivity, not only to further this conceptualization but also to justify greater focus on emotion in the therapist. We consider identity politics and revisit the notion of ruptures in the therapeutic relationship. Whereas in Chapter 2 of this volume we concentrated on patient communications or behaviors as interpersonal markers of ruptures, in this discussion we focus on therapist experience of emotions as possible internal or intrapersonal markers of these critical events.

EMOTION: FROM BASIC TO COMPLEX

Emotion is a type of affect, and in contrast to other affects such as mood, temperament, and sensation, emotion can be understood as a state or a process (G. Johnson, 2009). As a state, it has been defined as a type of mental or feeling state, a conscious or subjective experience that interacts with other mental states and is related to certain behaviors and bodily responses. As a process, it has been defined as progressing from stimulus perception and evaluation (including interpretation, judgment, construal, or some other mental representation of the stimulus) to bodily response (including heart rate, skin conductance, facial expression, and behavioral action tendency).

Much has been written about the functional properties of emotion. In this regard, it has long been considered evolutionary and adaptive, beginning with Charles Darwin's (1892/2002) book *The Expression of the Emotions in Man*

---

[1]Affect-phobia therapy (McCullough, 2003), dialectical behavior therapy (Linehan, 1993b), emotion-focused therapy (L. S. Greenberg, 2011), emotion regulation therapy (Mennin & Fresco, 2013), emotional schema therapy (Leahy, 2009; Young, Klosko, & Weishaar, 2003), integrative cognitive-affective therapy for bulimia nervosa (Wonderlich, Peterson, & Smith, 2015), and mentalization-based therapy (Bateman & Fonagy, 2006).

and Animals and including its more contemporary characterization as "an action-oriented form of skillful engagement with the world" (Griffiths & Scarantino, 2005, p. 437). Emotions serve several adaptive functions. First, emotions *inform*: They tell us about our world and where we are in context, help orient us to the environment, and provide meaning. For example, anger indicates violation, fear indicates danger, and sadness indicates loss (Schwarz, 2010). Second, emotions *motivate*: They mobilize the individual through physiological changes and action tendencies to prepare and negotiate with emotion-eliciting events. For example, anger mobilizes us to protect against violation, fear mobilizes us to avoid danger, and sadness mobilizes us to resolve or replace something lost (Salovey, Detweiler-Bedell, Detweiler-Bedell, & Mayer, 2008). Third, emotions *influence*: They influence memory and thought, and they affect decisions we make and actions we take. Research has demonstrated how decisions made based on transient incident emotions can have an enduring impact on future decisions (Andrade & Ariely, 2009; Grecucci & Sanfey, 2014). Fourth, emotions *communicate*: They inform others about our intentions and action tendencies. We read the emotional states of others, especially through vocal, facial, and behavioral expressions; we can empathize and sympathize (Zaki & Ochsner, 2016). Finally, emotions *affect*: They affect the emotions and behaviors of others. Much has been written about emotional contagion and how one's emotion can trigger a similar state in another, such as how anxiety begets anxiety (Hatfield, Cacioppo, & Rapson, 1994).

Emotion has been defined as both basic and complex. By basic, there has been a long-standing view of a select set of discrete, elemental emotions (as seminal examples, see Ekman, 1972; Izard, 1971; Tompkins, 1962; see also R. W. Levenson, 2011). This view consists of six to eight primary emotions organized by positive (e.g., happiness, surprise) and negative (e.g., anger, fear, sadness) dimensions. Complex emotions or variations on these categories are considered the result of combinations or blends of the basic categories, much like the spectrum of colors is formed from the primary colors.

The definition of basic emotions has included the proposition that they are physiologically and behaviorally distinct, but empirical research has challenged this notion and led to reformulations (Barrett et al., 2016; Barrett & Russell, 2015). The research evidence supports neither a unique biological "fingerprint" of an emotion nor dedicated neural circuit or brain region, nor bodily response pattern, nor facial or vocal expression consistently associated with a so-called basic emotion. The functional magnetic resonance imaging research regarding neural activity and emotion does support a core affect founded on the dimensions of arousal and valence (positive and negative), from which emotional experience is constructed.

One reformulation that has gained a great deal of traction involves a constructionist interpretation, prominently promoted by Lisa Feldman Barrett (2017; Russell, 2015; Scarantino, 2015). According to Barrett, emotions are constructed by multiple brain networks, organized by previous experiences and shaped by social influence—both familial and cultural. "In every waking moment, your brain uses past experience, organized as concepts, to guide your actions and give your sensations meaning. When the concepts involved are emotion concepts, your brain constructs instances of emotion" (Barrett, 2017, p. 31). As the research suggests, there are multiple emotion systems (e.g., multiple anger systems) and flexible response tendencies as a rule (e.g., multiple expressive behaviors). This formulation provides for a more nuanced understanding of emotion. Leslie Greenberg and Juan Pascual-Leone (1995, 2001) proposed a dialectical-constructivist perspective that attempts to integrate the notion of basic emotion with a constructivist conceptualization.

The complexity of emotions can also be understood by noting that they consist of multiple dimensions, described as "a syndrome of components" (Barrett & Russell, 2015). These dimensions include (a) phenomenological or subjective experience (what is felt in an emotional state), (b) cognitive processes (from construal to appraisal), (c) expressive and instrumental behaviors (from facial and vocal expressions to action tendencies), and (d) neurological and physiological changes (e.g., Scherer, 2005). Emotions are highly variable on these components, as research evidence indicates (Barrett et al., 2016), which translates into *complexity within emotion* and emotional experience that can be quite idiosyncratic (e.g., Barrett, 2017; Lindquist & Barrett, 2008).

EMOTION: FROM GENERATION TO REGULATION

Another primary source of complexity or variability is due to the interaction between various emotions and emotion regulation (Scarantino, 2015). This translates into *complexity between emotions. Emotion regulation* refers to mental and behavioral processes by which we shape and change the trajectory of our emotions (Gross, 1998): Although it has been distinguished from emotion generation, the relationship between the two is complicated, as emotions are often regulated by the generation of others (Johnston & Olson, 2015).

Leslie Greenberg and colleagues (L. S. Greenberg, 2016; L. S. Greenberg & Paivio, 1997; L. S. Greenberg & Safran, 1987) captured complexity between emotions in terms of various dualities, specifically the distinctions between primary versus secondary and adaptive versus maladaptive emotions. Primary emotions are "fundamental states for which the adaptive value is clear—for example, sadness at loss, anger at violation, and fear at threat" (L. S. Greenberg & Paivio, 1997, p. 38): They organize and motivate the individual for adaptive action. Secondary emotions are developed subsequently, built in relation to primary emotion experiences and comprising a complex integration of cognitive-affective processes that are shaped by social learning: anxious, embarrassed, or hopeless reactions to sadness, anger, or fear. Maladaptive emotions are learned responses that no longer fit a situation that an individual is facing; for example, the individual may have learned that the expression of anger is dangerous and could lead to rejection by a parent, so develops an anxious, avoidant reaction to anger to maintain close attachment. Subsequently, in an abusive adult relationship, the individual experiences anxiety in the face of violation rather than the more appropriate experience of anger that might move them to an adaptive action.

As discussed in Chapter 1 of this volume, Gross (2014a) defined a number of effective regulation strategies, including attentional distraction, expressive suppression, and cognitive reappraisal, and highlighted research demonstrating that reappraisal is more effective than distraction and suppression. More recent research has found affect labeling (which is essentially putting words to feelings—also described in terms of *granularity*), distancing, and acceptance (which is likened to *mindfulness*) to be more effective than reappraisal (see Barrett, 2017, for a review).

Jamil Zaki and Craig Williams (2013) elaborated on Gross's (2014a) definition in their distinction between intrapersonal and interpersonal emotion regulation strategies. They defined the two strategies as existing on a continuum, with the former emphasizing internal processes, such as cognitive reappraisal and expressive suppression, and the latter the presence of another to influence the trajectory of an emotion. They differentiated response-dependent from independent mechanisms (where the response of the other is required vs. when only the presence of the other is needed) and intrinsic from extrinsic strategies (where a person seeks contact with another to regulate their own emotions vs. where a person seeks to regulate another's emotions). In their own effort to organize the research literature, Butler and Randall (2013) proposed an operational definition of *coregulation* (or "social affect regulation"), which consists of "a bidirectional linkage of oscillating emotional channels (subjective experience, expressive behavior, and autonomic physiology) between partners, which contributes to emotional and physiological stability for both partners in a close relationship" (p. 203). Rimé (2009) also provided a critical review of the research on social interdependency in emotion regulation, specifically using the terminology *social sharing of emotion*, or affective states.

These efforts highlighted research on mother–infant face-to-face communication to advance research on emotion regulation in the context of adult relationships. An extensive body of research demonstrates bidirectional dependence in mother–infant interactions, using such terms as *mutual influence, reciprocity, matching, coordination, attunement*, and *synchrony* (see Lewis & Rosenblum, 1974, for early examples). Edward Tronick's (2007; see also Beebe & Lachmann, 2002, 2015) "mutual regulation" model, which has received considerable attention, found that mothers and infants demonstrate self- and other-directed actions toward each other to maintain optimal levels of arousal and engagement. The model describes nonverbal contingencies of signaling and synchrony in the mother–infant interaction. Of interest, it indicates that such interactions are typically "messy"—what is normative is mismatch or misattunement, and the critical process that distinguishes healthier interactions or dyads is the extent that there is *reparation*. This model has been furthered by other "dynamic dyadic systems" research programs that were based on Daniel Stern's (2000) original propositions and have tested how self-processes (each person's behavior in relation to their prior behavior) and interactive processes (in relation to the other person's behavior) coordinate in face-to-face communication. These programs have studied communication modalities such as attention (gaze on and off on the other person's face), facial affect (positive to negative), and vocal affect (positive to negative), and they have uncovered significant self- and interactive contingencies, as well as complicated contingencies between contingencies, such as the finding that one's self-regulation is influenced by the way one coordinates with one's partner (see Beebe et al., 2016). There is also a growing body of research on the neurobiological mechanisms of mother–infant interactions (e.g., Fleming, O'Day, & Kraemer, 1999).

In addition, these reviews highlight other research on related interpersonal processes indicating the effect of emotion from one individual to another, including (a) motivation to help others improve emotional states through *altruism* or *compassion* (Batson, 2011; Goetz, Keltner, & Simon-Thomas, 2010); (b) *emotional transmission* and *contagion*, which involve one person's emotional state affecting another's (Hatfield et al., 1994; Larson & Almeida, 1999); and (c) *social support, stress buffering,* and *emotional modulation,* which refer to the mere presence of another to attenuate negative emotion in the face of stress (e.g., Coan, 2011; Coan, Schaefer, & Davidson, 2006; Diamond & Aspinwall, 2003; Niven, Totterdell, & Holman, 2009; Randall & Bodenmann, 2009; Uchino, 2004; Uchino, Cacioppo, & Kiecolt-Glaser, 1996). These research threads provide further evidence for the complex but intrinsic role of emotion in interpersonal process.

EMOTION: FROM MULTIPLICITY TO INTERSUBJECTIVITY[2]

Understanding emotion complexity and regulation should include a consideration of the idea that each of us comprises multiple selves, a concept founded on the recognition that we live in a world of plurality and changeability, of infinite constructions and reconstructions. Accordingly, the human condition is marked by ever-shifting and ever-expanding realities and identities (see Gergen, 1991, 1994, 2009; Metzinger, 2009; see Muran, 2001a, for a review). Of interest, the notion of multiple selves is not necessarily a new one. In tracing the history of ideas, dating the origin of a line of thought can be a somewhat arbitrary punctuation, but this notion was at least present in various disciplines in the latter part of the 19th century, when James (1890/1981)

---

[2]Portions of this section were adapted from "Contemporary Constructions & Contexts," (pp. 3–44), by J. C. Muran, in *Self-Relations in the Psychotherapy Process,* edited by J. C. Muran, 2001, Washington, DC: American Psychological Association; "A Relational Turn on Thick Description," (pp. 257–274), by J. C. Muran, in *Dialogues on Difference: Studies of Diversity in the Therapeutic Relationship,* edited by J. C. Muran, 2007, Washington, DC: American Psychological Association; and "Reply: The Power of/in Language," (pp. 285–288), by J. C. Muran, in *Dialogues on Difference: Studies of Diversity in the Therapeutic Relationship,* edited by J. C. Muran, 2007, Washington, DC: American Psychological Association.

described the self as "a stream of selves" (see also Nietzsche, 1888/1968; Whitman, 1855/1950). More recently, it is reflected in considerations of the self as the *intersectionality* of various cultural identities (Crenshaw, 2019). In the clinical literature, the idea of multiple selves was sown early on in humanistic psychotherapies, especially those inspired by Carl Rogers (Meador & Rogers, 1979: "[The self] is a fluid and changing process, but at any given moment it is a specific entity," p. 147) and interpersonally oriented psychoanalyses, beginning with Harry Stack Sullivan (1964; "For all I know every human being has as many personalities as he has interpersonal relations," p. 221).[3]

Self Schemas

Many contemporary conceptualizations are founded on a representational formulation of the self (see Muran, 2001a, for a review). As previously presented (Muran, 2001a, 2007b; Muran & Safran, 2002; Safran & Muran, 2000), the self comprises memory stores or knowledge domains that are derived from interpersonal experience and that include internalized self-assessments and expectations regarding other people, which inform the individual how to relate to others. These can be considered self (or relational) schemas that are abstracted on the basis of interactions with attachment figures and others of interpersonal significance in order to increase the likelihood of maintaining a relationship with those figures. Self schemas contain implicit beliefs about self and other—the idea that relationship patterns, the whole and not the isolated elements, are internalized or represented (see Bowlby, 1969; Fairbairn, 1952; Laing, 1972; D. N. Stern, 1985; Sullivan, 1953).

These schemas also contain specific procedural information regarding expectancies and strategies for negotiating needs for self-definition (agency) and relatedness (communion). These oft-cited fundamental motivations drive how individuals relate to their social worlds (see Bakan, 1966; Guisinger & Blatt, 1994): *Self-definition* refers to the need to master, to assert the self, to achieve, and to experience competence and power; *relatedness* refers to the need to cooperate, connect, and closely relate to others. They are considered to have a dialectic relationship to each other, an inherent tension that individuals invariably negotiate in pursuit of fulfilling these needs. Wanting to achieve something can work at odds with wanting to be loved by others. These needs have been shown to vary in emphasis depending on various cultural (including gender) differences (see Diehl, Owen, & Youngblade, 2004).

These schemas represent the multiple discrete experiences of the self. In theory, there may be as many "selves" as there are different interactions in one's life, as Sullivan (1964) originally suggested. This forms the basis for the notion that each individual comprises a unique configuration of selves. The schemas include one's various identities (e.g., those related to gender or race),

---

[3]Both Rogers and Sullivan were greatly influenced by William James, largely through George Herbert Mead (1934).

which are shaped by certain biological constraints (e.g., temperament, physical features) and the familial and cultural experiences of an individual's history. Here the recognition of intersectionality is useful—that "we are all, to some degree, formed by cultural crisscrossing of gender, class, race, sexuality, and religion" (Sullivan, 1964, p. 14) among other characteristics; we move "in and out of borders constructed around coordinates of difference" in a series of identity axes (Awkward, 1995, p. 9; see also Kristeva, 1991, and N. K. Miller, 1991, regarding the identity politics of positionality). Thus, the schemas can be understood as the *foundation for individual differences* (Muran, 2007b).

These schemas should be known as emotional structures (or templates for emotional experience) that are innately given and then elaborated over time through learning into subtle and idiosyncratic variations (Muran, 2001a; Safran & Muran, 2000; see also Leventhal, 1984; Piaget, 1970). From birth, the infant develops memory stores that consist of specific expressive-motor responses, physiological arousal, associated images, and relevant eliciting stimuli. These stores serve a communicative function in that they continually orient the individual to the environment and the environment to the individual. They should also be considered as emergent properties (not representational objects) that involve an interaction of large numbers of simpler elements, a network of units with connections weighted so that activating part of the network will produce an activation pattern that functions like a schema (see Cilliers, 1998; Rumelhart, Smolensky, McClelland, & Hinton, 1986). This consideration captures the complexity of how memories, identities, emotions, and motivations intersect and organize experience.

Self States (Within-Subject Relations)

With the activation of a particular self schema, there is the emergence of a corresponding emotional experience—a particular state of mind or self state (colored by a particular emotion). Self states are the experiential products of the various processes and structures of the self, crystallizations in subjective experience of an underlying schema—put another way, portals to schemas. They may be understood as automatic thoughts or images (in cognitive-behavioral terms) and immediate feeling states such as sadness, fear, or anger. They may be out of awareness but can come into awareness through attention. Different self states can activate different relational schemas, resulting in cycling through different states of mind. The transition points or boundaries among the various self states that each person experiences vary in terms of seamlessness but are often marked by changes such as vocal quality, facial expression, focus and content of verbal reports, or emotional involvement. Indicative of our self-organizing and integral capacities, they are naturally smoothed over, creating the illusory sense of continuity and singular identity, through the process of dissociation. The more conspicuous and abrupt the transitions between self states, however, the more problematic the dissociative process (more on this notion next).

The concept of multiple selves holds that there is no central executive control, in the form of the ego (Mitchell, 1992; see Muran, 2001c). Consciousness is a function of a coalition of different self states. It is thus an emergent product of a self-organizing system. The bifurcation of the psychic system into conscious and unconscious is overly simplified and overly static. That which is conscious is that which is attended to. Attention to different self states in different moments is a function of different stimulus cues, both internal and external. Dissociation is basic to the understanding of multiple selves. It is useful in this regard to make the distinction between dissociation as a "healthy" process of selectively focusing attention and dissociation as an "unhealthy" process resulting from traumatic overload and resulting in severing connections between self schemas (see Bromberg, 1998, 2006). Dissociation is a healthy, adaptive function of the human mind, a basic process that allows individual self states to function optimally and that permits a person to maintain personal continuity, coherence, and integrity of the sense of self. The particular configuration of one's self-experience is always selective. At any time, certain aspects of self-experience are predominant and others not: It is inevitable that certain aspects of self-experience will be out of focal awareness when others are dominant. There is also a systemic direction of attention away from aspects of self-experience associated with anxiety (Sullivan, 1953). In the case of extreme anxiety—dreaded states considered to be potentially dangerous and associated with a traumatic experience—an aspect of the self can be split off and stranded from awareness in an "unhealthy" sense (Davies & Frawley, 1994).

Experiencing and accepting the multiplicity of self is part of the change process. Psychotherapy essentially brings different parts of the self into dialogue with each other through awareness (Muran, 2001a, 2007b). This process is central to contemporary relational perspectives (e.g., Bromberg, 1998, 2006; D. B. Stern, 1997, 2015, Wachtel, 2008, 2014; see also Safran & Muran, 2000). It is consistent with the emotion-focused, process-experiential perspective (see L. S. Greenberg, 2011; L. S. Greenberg, Rice, & Elliott, 1995), which identifies different patient behaviors as markers to guide therapists to invite their patient through two-chair work to dialogue with the different aspects of the self toward creative resolution. There are two marker types called *self-splits*: the conflict split and the interruptive split. The former is when two parts of the self are in conflict—typically between a coercive "should" and adaptive "need." In contrast, the interruptive split involves an interruptive activity against the self—when one part of the self interrupts a second part. In this case, the individual feels cut off or loses contact with a part of the self (integral to the pursuit of one's needs), which can result in a paralyzed state of confusion, helplessness, and hopelessness. This conceptualization of the change process is also consistent with what has been discussed in the third-wave cognitive-behavioral literature, in which (likewise) the emphasis is on how one *relates* to various internal experiences (e.g., S. C. Hayes, Wilson, Gifford, Follette, & Strosahl, 1996; see also Chawla & Ostafin, 2007). Here, the critical marker is defined as *experiential avoidance*, which refers to any attempt to avoid an internal experience, such as thoughts, feelings, or memories. Such attempts are considered to be maintained by negative reinforcement: That is, the avoidance results in short-term relief of discomfort or pain, which in turn increases the probability that the avoidance will continue. Thus, dysfunction is defined by *how* one avoids and *not* by what one avoids.

This perspective has various implications for the psychotherapeutic situation. One is the importance of facilitating patient immediate awareness of their self states. This perspective suggests working in the here and now, drawing attention to self states (with simple questions such as "What's going on for you now?" or observations such as "I notice a trembling in your hands") and to transitions between various states (often marked by vocal, verbal, or gestural shifts, such as the softening of one's voice, the abrupt change of a topic, the emergence of a misplaced smile, or the diverting of one's eyes). It promotes an orientation to what is manifest and to the details of emotional experience (as windows to underlying self schemas)—a respect, even a reverence, for particularity or *granularity* (Barrett, 2017)—basic to a phenomenological sensibility (Husserl, 1931). From a multiple selves perspective, it suggests a process of discovering who within the patient is speaking.

Hannah presented feeling "paralyzed by life." She sat before me [JCM] arms crossed, describing what sounded like a very upsetting experience with her ex-husband. Her description was matter-of-fact, no upset in manner, only in words (what we defined as a content-affect split in Chapter 2, this volume): "So Bill didn't show again to pick up our daughter after school, another excuse, another time I had to ask to leave work earlier than I was supposed to." When I commented, "Sounds pretty upsetting," she just continued, "I hope he comes next time . . ." At some point, I asked, "Can you give me a sense of what's going on for you? It sounds pretty upsetting, but I'm not sure what you're feeling right now." Hannah struggled with this. She revealed some "annoyance" but continued to try to move away; there was a good deal of back-and-forth movement in this regard. My comments appeared to be briefly considered, then dismissed: "I'm just hoping he comes next time." When her movement away from anger was brought to her attention—"I'm not sure how you're taking my wondering about feeling angry"—she began to put words to some fears, including her fear that her anger at her ex would leave her completely alone, and more profoundly her fear that she would fail her daughter. This crystallized her experience of paralysis.

Having patients put words to their immediate experience will have a regulating effect (as suggested by the research previously presented; see Barrett, 2017). In Hannah's case, she was able to recognize and explore the relationship between her frustrations and fears. With such an expansion of awareness also comes an increased sense of responsibility—a greater awareness of how one constructs one's experience. It is at the more molecular level that one can begin to develop a sense of the choices one is making; thus, for one to develop a greater sense of responsibility and agency, one must attend to the details of experience at successive moments of perception and begin to discover the choices one is making on a moment-by-moment basis. For

Hannah, she could begin to see how she would construct her paralysis by stifling her anger (how she was pursuing communion at the expense of agency), which she needed to experience in order to respond with more adaptive action to her ex's violations. Promoting this type of awareness de-automates habitual patterns and helps one experience oneself as an agent in the process of constructing reality rather than as a passive victim of circumstances, which has been argued from an existential point of view to be at the heart of neurotic experience (Basescu, 2009). (In reality, our personal responsibility lies somewhere between active and passive: We both shape and are shaped by our environment ongoingly.)

Self Relations (Between Subjects)

Different self states emerge in different relational contexts (see Muran, 2001a, 2001b). This perspective provides a way of viewing the intersection between interpersonal and intrapersonal realms in therapy in terms of the mutual influence of shifting self states in the patient and therapist. Accordingly, each individual experiences a perpetual cycling between different self states, which in turn evoke complementary self states in the other. As individuals cycle through various self states in an interpersonal encounter, they both influence and are influenced by the various self states of the other; there is continuous emotional communication and regulation, as demonstrated in the mother–infant mutual regulation literature (e.g., Beebe et al., 2016; Tronick, 2007). There are subtle movements and fluctuations in intimacy and varying degrees of relatedness. In the case of Hannah, the therapist often felt confused by her conflict-affect splits and frustrated when he tried to focus on her upset or anger. Much like mood naturally cycles, individuals cycle in degree of contact, approaching and avoiding an other. To some extent, this is dictated by individual pursuits of privacy and intimacy—or put another way, the previously cited needs for self-definition and relatedness.

Another way to understand internal states (and behavioral expressions) in relation to the external world is to consider how the reciprocal relationship in a dyadic interaction is based on the conception that a self schema shapes one's perception of the interpersonal world and leads to cognitive-affective and behavioral processes (e.g., cognitive distortions, security operations, defense mechanisms), which in turn shape the environment in a manner that confirms the schema; thus, a self-perpetuating cycle emerges. Interpersonal theorists have described versions of this perspective, including Edgar Levenson (2005), who suggested that an individual can exert a tremendous pull on another, thus "entrapping" and "transforming" the other. Paul Wachtel (1982) invoked "vicious circles" (Horney, 1950/1991), and Jeremy Safran (1998) referred to a "cognitive-interpersonal cycle" in this regard; Stephen Mitchell (1988) and Jay Greenberg (1995) described this self-perpetuating cycle in terms of a "relational or interactive matrix." Donald Kiesler (1996) similarly suggested that the more restricted one's cognitive and interpersonal repertoire, the more redundant one's patterns of interaction with others, and the more one operates as a closed system. This perspective (and various versions) provides some insight on personality disorder and its persistence.

The interaction of self states between individuals suggests the value of attending to the reciprocal changes of self states in the patient–therapist system during the course of therapy. As previously mentioned, the transitions between self states vary in seamlessness, often objectively marked by observable behavior but also subjectively marked, as Philip Bromberg (1998) noted— that is, these shifts can become apparent in the therapist's experience by a corresponding shift in self state for the therapist. Thus, as certain authors have articulated (Bromberg, 1998; Mitchell, 1992), psychotherapy can be understood as figuring out who is speaking to whom in a given moment—which patient self is communicating to which therapist self (and vice versa). Stuart Pizer (1998) described this process as involving "intersubjective negotiation," whereby patient and therapist ongoingly negotiate what to make of each other. Through dialogue between a patient's dissociated self and a therapist's self, a bridge can be built between that dissociated self and other selves within the patient's self-system. With Hannah, the therapist was able to use his own experience (confusion or frustration) to build a bridge to her angry and fearful selves and to bring her struggle with agency and communion into relief.

Jessica Benjamin's (1988, 1990, 1995) notion of intersubjectivity integrated several perspectives (Buber, 1923/1958; Dinnerstein, 1976; Habermas, 1971; Hegel, 1807/1969; Winnicott, 1965) and provided a comprehensive view of mutual recognition and regulation in the psychotherapeutic situation. One of the central themes in her work follows feminist criticism and challenges the traditional analytic view of the mother as an object to the infant's drives and needs. Benjamin (1990) argued that the child must recognize the mother as a separate subject with her own experiential world, with her own intentions and desires, and that the capacity for such recognition is a developmental achievement. Accordingly, Benjamin (1990) suggested that the aim of the analytic inquiry is such that "where objects were, subjects must be" (p. 34). For her, the developmental achievement of subjective recognition is one that is inconsistently maintained, and the analytic situation must invariably involve a dialectic tension between relating to the other as an object and relating to the other as a subject; the process continually involves the recognition and negation of the other as a separate center of subjectivity (see Muran, 2001a, for a review of various considerations of intersubjectivity in the therapeutic encounter).

Prejudice and Power

The clarification of the patient's self-definition invariably involves more clarification of the therapist's self-definition as well. The idea behind this is essentially twofold: One, we are always embedded in an interpersonal field that exerts a great influence on the emergence of a self state we experience in a given moment (D. B. Stern, 1997; see also Heidegger, 1927/1962). Two, greater self-definition can be achieved only by defining the edges of one self in relation to another self—in this case, the patient in relation to the therapist (Ehrenberg, 1992). In a Hegelian sense, I cannot know myself in isolation; I need another self in order to become aware of my own selfhood (Hegel, 1807/1969). The therapeutic relationship provides a laboratory of sorts in which the subjective and objective aspects of the patient's self can be more sharply or clearly defined in relation to the subjective and objective aspects of the therapist's self. Thus, the therapeutic aim to cultivate mindfulness in patients with respect to the details of their own experience involves therapists becoming mindful of corresponding details of their own experience. This suggests that with every therapeutic encounter, therapists must courageously confront themselves and expand their awareness of themselves in relation to yet another individual (E. Singer, 1965). The therapeutic process should, therefore, *involve change for both participants.*

In this regard, Hans-Georg Gadamer's (1960/1975) dialogic model of understanding seems useful. Gadamer argued that our perception of things is always constrained by our preconceptions or prejudices. We cannot understand anything without reference to them. These preconceptions can be understood as our self schemas, shaped by all our various personal, familial, and cultural experiences. They should not be understood as just limiting factors but rather the ground for all experience, without which new experience is meaningless. Here, one can include the "implicit bias" literature (see Banaji & Greenwald, 2013), according to which the mind is construed as a "difference-seeking machine" that helps one navigate and adapt to the complexities of human relations. Gadamer also suggested that awareness of our prejudices can emerge only (i.e., partially emerge) in dialogue with another, where there is a possibility for "a fusion of horizons"—a moment when a prejudice can be differentiated from its alternative. Thus, understanding becomes an event, not a thing, moving from a static phenomenon to an interactive or interpersonal one.

Defining differences between self and other—bringing respective prejudices into awareness—should be a fundamental task of psychotherapy, regardless of the gender or cultural match between patient and therapist. This should be a given because of the unique nature of the personalities involved in every therapeutic encounter. In cases of obvious mismatch—say, between a male and a female or between an Asian American and a European American—there is the advantage of immediately recognizing a difference (D. B. Stern, 1997). There is also the challenge of "mutual anxiety" because of the explicit difference (Perez Foster, Moskowitz, & Javier, 1996). However, it is important to bear in mind what we see, or think we see, can be at once revealing and concealing of difference. This concept was poignantly portrayed in Ralph Ellison's (1952) *Invisible Man*, which captured the experience of being both recognized to some extent and unrecognized to an even greater extent—an experience that can be applied to people of any race or color in a variety of ways. This is attributable not only to prejudice but also to the nature of attention, which is always a selective process of bringing some things to awareness and keeping other things out of view.

An important part of the negotiation process is the role of the power imbalance in the relationship between patient and therapist. Lewis Aron (1996) described this in terms of the asymmetrical versus mutual dimensions of the therapeutic relationship (see also Burke, 1992). Irwin Hoffman (1998) emphasized that the therapist's gestures toward mutuality, those that are spontaneous and personally responsive, must always be understood in the context of the therapist's assigned role of authority. Jessica Benjamin (1995) suggested that the process toward mutual recognition in psychotherapy is tempered by the patient's investment to not divest the therapist of their authority. The role of authority and power also has a variety of oft-cited implications for different cultural identities (including gender; see Pinderhughes, 1989). As noted by Michel Foucault (1972), it is important to recognize socially assigned conditions of power: When we define someone by some cultural category (and here, *culture* is used in the broadest sense to capture the various gender, sexual, religious, racial, and ethnic identities), we introduce a power inequality: male over female, straight over gay, White over Black, Gentile over Jew. According to Foucault, knowledge (as produced by language) is power to define others, thus power over others.

Gadamer (1960/1975) has been criticized for not fully addressing how inequalities in power can condition dialogue. Another critical theorist, Jürgen Habermas (1979), who wrote extensively on intersubjectivity and recognized the potential to reconcile differences and approximate truth through dialogic consensus, challenged Gadamer on this point. For Habermas, although dialogue does not require an egalitarian relationship, it does require some sort of symmetry and reciprocity. Otherwise, our responses in a given dialogue will be seriously distorted by the concern that what we say may be used against us by a more powerful other. So what does this mean for a therapeutic relationship in which, beyond a mutual dimension of two humans encountering each other, there are potentially *multiple* dimensions of asymmetry, including the power inequalities between therapist and patient, male and female, straight and gay, Gentile and Jew, and so on? Can Gadamer's dialogic model be realistically applied to a complex therapeutic encounter in which there are many power inequalities? Can a fusion of horizons or a meeting of minds ever be achieved in such encounters?

To answer these questions, we think it is important to distinguish between authority assigned by social conditions (as Foucault described) and power integral to the natural course of human relations. With regard to the latter, Jessica Benjamin (1995) invoked Hegel's master–slave dialectic to better understand the intersubjective process. Hegel described the self as requiring the other in order to become aware of its consciousness or existence. He also described an unavoidable conflict between the self's wish for absolute independence and the self's need for recognition by the other. Accordingly, a precarious tension exists, one that we at least initially try to resolve by mastering the other or by submitting to the other. Either position of extremes—master or slave—involves some form of negation, some form of objectification: The former involves objectifying the other and risks isolation; the latter involves being objectified by the other and risks absolute dependency. There is an ongoing struggle to determine who defines the other and who accommodates whom. Ultimately, to recognize its subjectivity, a self must recognize another as a separate subject, and likewise the other must recognize the self as a separate subject. There must be mutual recognition. This is the realization of the intersubjective position.

Jessica Benjamin suggested that Donald Winnicott's (1965) thinking on object use can be considered a version of the Hegelian master–slave dialectic, whereby it is only through seeing the other survive one's destructive attempts (or attempts at negation) that one can see the other as a separate subject. Pizer (1998) developed this perspective further with his notion of intersubjective negotiation. For him, therapists in their interventions and patients in their responses are recurrently saying to each other, "No, you can't make this of me. But you can make that of me" (p. 218). Thus, there are ongoing power plays between patient and therapist: accommodations and refusals to accommodate, which convey to the patient that the world is negotiable and composed of others with separate subjectivities. Returning to Foucault's (1972) treatise, these power plays must also be understood as occurring in the context of therapists' already assigned authority. As Irwin Hoffman (1998) highlighted, the therapists' personal responsivity stands in dialectic relation to their assigned authority—that is, one can be understood only in the context of the other. For a therapist to admit a mistake, for example, is much different than for a patient to do so. These power plays are also modified by other assignments by social conditions—for example, shaped by the gender and sexuality, race and ethnicity, and other power imbued identities of my patient.

We have painted a complex picture of intersubjectivity and the prospect of achieving a meeting of the minds in the therapeutic relationship—of coming to a position where one recognizes another as a separate subject, and likewise feels recognized as such. All the possible power differentials represent potential pitfalls. For Hannah, her struggle to experience agency with communion was complicated by her status as a single working mom and had to be negotiated in the context of working with a male therapist in a more privileged position. How could she feel agentic in such a relationship? This complexity might evoke dread, but as Habermas (1979) has maintained, once there is conversation, there is hope. However complex our positioning, however distorted our communication, each expression holds some possibility of dialogue and further understanding. Moreover, the psychotherapeutic situation can encourage its participants, to the extent there is a shared recognition that the therapeutic relationship can be used as a laboratory of sorts to unpack these complexities and can provide the opportunity for greater awareness for both patient and therapist.

Discovery and Construction

Thus far we have suggested a process of change that emphasizes the discovery of self-experience and expansion of self-awareness in the context of the therapeutic relationship. It is important to recognize, however, that the psychotherapeutic process in a paradoxical sense is not only discovery oriented but also constructive. As Stephen Mitchell (1993) described, self-experience does not simply flow forth without impediment but is channeled by the efforts of the individual to communicate and the other to understand—a basic premise of all intersubjective theories, including various formulations of interpersonal and mutual regulation (or coregulation). Thus, the course it takes is a moment-by-moment coconstruction. For example, the therapist's own experience—and articulation of that, which includes her theoretical orientation (Aron, 1999; Schafer, 1983; Spence, 1982)—has an enormous impact on the patient's experience and articulation. And of course, this is a bidirectional and iterative process.

In a sense, the psychotherapeutic process can be likened to the postmodernist method of deconstruction (Derrida, 1978). The term is a hybrid between destruction and construction and in effect represents an effort to construct by destructing. It suggests the paradoxical idea of tearing something apart while creating something new (Lovlie, 1992). The deconstruction of the self results in a rejection of a substantialized or essentialized conception of self at the center of the world—the death of the modern self—for a relational conception of self, the birth of a postmodern self that exists in intricate relation to others in the world.

For Hannah, it was important for her to see—to discover—her agency in creating her paralysis; the choice points in submitting to another. This had obvious relevance for her relationship with her ex, as well as others in her life. In addition, it had relevance in her relationship with me as her therapist. In response to my comments and questions, my constructive influence on our process, it was also important for her to experience her agency by not submitting to me with simple requests ("Can we reschedule?") or corrections of my observations ("No, that's not quite right"). Inviting her to explore these expressions continued the process of discovery and construction but also promoted difference.

The construction of something different provides the opportunity for new learning, the provision of a new interpersonal experience. This perspective converges in many ways with Franz Alexander's notion of a "corrective emotional experience" (see Alexander & French, 1946), as well as the Mount Zion Group's (Silberschatz, 2013; Weiss, Sampson, & the Mount Zion Psychotherapy Research Group, 1986) view that patients unconsciously submit their therapists to "transference tests" to see whether they will confirm a pathogenic belief. For example, a patient who believes that independence will be punished speaks about quitting therapy, with the hope that the therapist will not react in a controlling fashion. If the therapist passes the test by not confirming the belief, therapeutic progress takes place.

Interpersonal theorists (e.g., Kiesler, 1996; Safran, 1998; Wachtel, 1982) have described this process by indicating that the challenge for therapists is to resist being transformed or pulled by the patient's interpersonal repertoire, to "being caught in a vicious circle or cycle." This concept is consistent with the tradition that originated with Ferenczi (1932/1988), who was the first to suggest that psychotherapy involves the creation of a new or different experience. It should be understood, however, that this is an epiphenomenal change process—one that emerges spontaneously through the process of codiscovery and not one that is deliberately determined (as Alexander originally envisioned). Thus, change is conceptualized as *a process consisting of codiscovery and coconstruction.*

EMOTION: FROM RUPTURE TO REPAIR

Alliance ruptures indicate a breach in the communication process between patient and therapist (Safran & Muran, 1996, 2000, 2006). As introduced in Chapter 2 of this volume, at an explicit level, we defined them as failures to collaborate on the tasks (what are the activities in psychotherapy, including self-reflection, exposure exercises, and skills training) and disagreements about the goals (what are the objectives, including greater insight, symptom reduction, and new behavior), as well as deteriorations in the emotional bond (trust and affection) between patient and therapist. Here we invoke the interdependent dimensions of Bordin's (1979) transtheoretical reformulation. At an implicit level, we defined them as tensions or conflicts between the respective needs or desires of the patient and therapist—as breakdowns in *intersubjective negotiation* (Pizer, 1998). These tensions can be attributed to the dialectics of the need for agency and communion and of the power dynamics inherent in human relations and identity politics of positionality. Ruptures can be understood by the following relational formulations:

- Dissociative disconnections or self-splits: Here we refer to aspects of the self that are split off from awareness because of fear or dread of a painful self state, a form of *experiential avoidance* (S. C. Hayes et al., 1996) that results in *empathic failure* (Kohut, 1984) or feeling disconnected from the other (see Bromberg, 1998; Greenberg et al., 1995; Muran, 2001a, 2001b; Pizer, 1998).

- Affective misattunements, mismatches, or miscoordinations: These refer to literature on mother–infant communication. In empirical analyses, approximately 70% of the time mother and infant are not affectively attuned—not in matched or coordinated states—and approximately 70% of the non-matched states return to a match within 2 seconds—a repair. This research has also shown that repair predicts optimal development, including sense of self-efficacy and capacity to cope (see Beebe & Lachmann, 2002, 2015; Tronick, 2007).

- Interpersonal pulls, transformations, or role-responsiveness: Any individual's interpersonal behavior or pattern of behaviors exerts a pull on the response from another (E. A. Levenson, 1991, 2005; Sandler, 1976; Sullivan, 1953, 1964). The more extreme the behavior, the more extreme the response; the more restrictive the range of behaviors, the more redundant the pattern of interactions. A good deal of circumplex-based research supports this formulation (see L. S. Benjamin, 1993; Constantino, 2000; Horowitz & Strack, 2010; Kiesler, 1996).

- Matrical enactments or vicious circles: Similar to the previous formulation, enactments refer to recurrent patient and therapist interactions, their unwitting participation in an interactive matrix comprising their respective emotional states, interpersonal behaviors, and underlying beliefs (Greenberg, 1995; Mitchell, 1988); they can also be described as *vicious circles* (Horney, 1950/1991) involving two individuals' states and behaviors that continuously reinforce themselves through feedback loops (see Wachtel, 2008).

- Power plays, negations, or objectifications: To become more aware of one's subjectivity or existence, one invariably engages with another in an ongoing struggle fraught with power plays (accommodations and refusals to accommodate)—objectifications of the other and recognitions of the other's subjectivity. Thus negation is normative in human relations, as well as in the therapeutic relationship (see J. Benjamin, 1995; Pizer, 1998). Identity politics of positionality, including the socially assigned authority of the therapist, are factors in these power plays (Muran, 2007b, 2007c). And *microaggressions* (assaults, insults, and invalidations) can be understood as expressions of these power dynamics or differentials (see Sue, 2010).

Ruptures are founded on self schemas (belief systems including procedural operations) that include motivations for self-definition and relatedness. They can be understood as a result of a *dialectical tension* between the pursuits of these motivations. According to our distinction between *withdrawal* and *confrontation* ruptures, withdrawal ruptures are movements away from self (dissociating an aspect of the self to appease the other) or other (avoiding or isolating the self from the other) that promote relatedness at the expense of self-definition. Confrontation ruptures are movements against other (self attacks or controls other) that promote self-definition at the expense of relatedness: They include implicit microaggressions (insults and invalidations) to more explicit attacks or assaults on the other's identity or ability; they also include attempts to coerce or manipulate the other as an object, forcing the other to conform to a role, such as a pseudofriend or even sexual object. Self schemas are shaped in relation to the world (familial, cultural, and social histories) and by the intersection of various identities (gender, sexual, race, ethnicity, and class, to name the most obvious). The interaction of patient and therapist along the axes of these identities, including their various implications for power positions and *dialectical tension* from objectification/subjectification (J. Benjamin, 1995), is integral to how agency and communion are negotiated in the therapeutic relationship—and thus alliance ruptures.

In Chapter 2, we identified withdrawal and confrontation markers by specific patient communications or behaviors—by various patient avoidant operations and aggressive maneuvers—including splits from or denials of emotional experience and complaints about the treatment process or progress. We defined ruptures in terms of what can be observed by the therapist—

markers in an *interpersonal sense*. This approach has resulted in a considerable amount of research demonstrating their prevalence and prediction of treatment failure (see Eubanks, Muran, & Safran, 2019; Muran, 2019, for reviews).

Such markers can also be identified by specific therapist communications or behaviors (also what can be observed; see Exhibit 3.1): For example, therapists can withdraw in silence from confusion or mind-wandering, shift a focus of discussion or pivot to another topic; they can engage in too much or abstract talk (including psychobabble); and they can be overly protective or accommodating. They can also confront patients by insulting, with put-downs or denials of a cultural identity, or by pathologizing them with a critical interpretation (about transference, a dysfunctional attitude or irrational belief) to explain their personality or lack of progress; and therapists can be coercive, forcing a patient to conform to a desire, expectation, or theory, including mismanaging the dimensions of mutuality and asymmetry—that is, emphasizing one at the expense of the other, being too friendly or too clinical. These therapist behaviors can also be used to mark ruptures and alliances at risk.

Ruptures can be marked by emotional experiences that indicate complications in communication. Although relatively less well operationally defined, this is an equally important marker of rupture as suggested by the emotion regulation and intersubjectivity literature reviewed so far. The specific aim of this book is to advance consideration of the therapist emotional responses as rupture markers in an *intrapersonal sense* (what can be felt): Here we have referred to the notion of *felt sense*—an internal awareness of "something" is experienced in the body that has not been consciously thought or

---

EXHIBIT 3.1

Rupture Markers as Therapist Interpersonal Markers

Withdrawal ruptures
- Movements *away* from other or self
- Efforts toward *isolation* or *appeasement*
- Pursuits of *communion* at the expense of *agency*
  Examples
  - Silences (confusion and mind-wandering)
  - Shifts in topics or focus (avoidance)
  - Too much or abstract talk (psychobabble)
  - Overly protective or accommodating

Confrontation ruptures
- Movements *against* other
- Efforts towards *aggression* or *control*
- Pursuits of *agency* at the expense of *communion*
  Examples
  - Pathologizing patient (blaming and belittling)
  - Coercions to conform to a theory or due to empathic failure
  - Microaggressions against cultural identity
  - Coercions regarding mutuality versus asymmetry

verbalized (Gendlin, 1996). We have discussed how the therapeutic relationship should be considered a "laboratory" to explore and the therapist experience as a "compass" to navigate. We have developed a training model with empirical support (Eubanks, Muran, & Safran, 2015; Muran, Safran, & Eubanks-Carter, 2010; Muran, Safran, Eubanks, & Gorman, 2018; see also Chapters 5 and 6, this volume) that emphasizes developing therapist abilities to be more aware and effectively use their internal experience. Nevertheless, more definition regarding therapist emotional experience and regulation seems necessary to advance our understanding of ruptures.

Ruptures represent risk factors for treatment failure, whether measured as patient-report of low alliance and significant shifts or as observer-rated withdrawals or confrontations (Eubanks, Muran, & Safran, 2019; Muran, 2019). They also represent change opportunities: Rupture repair or resolution has been shown to be a change process predictive of overall treatment success (Eubanks, Muran, & Safran, 2019; Muran, 2019). How we understand rupture repair as a change process depends on the various definitions provided thus far. First, building upon Bordin's (1979) formulation, repair can be understood as renegotiating agreement on the tasks and goals between patient and therapist: This process can provide a new relational experience in which the world is seen as more negotiable and others as potentially helpful and trustworthy though different in their own expectations and desires.

Rupture repair can also be understood as a way (a) to build bridges to dissociated selves (Bromberg, 1998; Pizer, 1998), (b) to reattune to the affective state of the other (Beebe & Lachmann, 2002, 2015; Tronick, 2007), (c) to resist interpersonal pulls or transformations (Kiesler, 1996; E. A. Levenson, 2005), (d) to disembed from interactional matrices or unhook from vicious circles (Greenberg, 1995; Wachtel, 2008), and (e) to bring the complex intersection of patient and therapist respective subjectivities and identities into relief (J. Benjamin, 1995; Muran, 2007b, 2007c)—to make the implicit more explicit. In this regard, rupture repair can provide a new relational experience by promoting the possibility of mutual recognition and by resolving various dialectical tensions concerning agency/communion and objectification/subjectification (Muran, 2019). Our research on rupture repair has provided some support for the realization of mutual recognition by demonstrating a movement to a more expressive position on the part of both patient and therapist (Muran, 2019; Muran et al., 2018; Safran & Muran, 1996). The research also suggests that emotion regulation is an important change process for the therapist as well as the patient.

CODA

How We Understand Emotion

Emotional experience can be understood as basic and complex, as personal and interpersonal. It can be understood as an emergent property of identity and motivation. For complexity, we presented its multicomponential nature and its relationship to previous and cultural experiences and to other emotional states within the individual and between individuals: The latter relationship refers to how emotion is regulated and permits consideration of like-minded notions of multiple selves and intersubjectivity. We described emotions as self states that are reflections of self schemas comprising constructed gender and cultural identities or beliefs about self and other, including procedural information about the needs for agency and communion.

How We Understand Rupture

There is a dialectical tension inherent in the pursuit of the needs for agency and communion, which we argue is at the heart of ruptures (breaches in communication) between two individuals (especially with regard to patient and therapist interactions). We define ruptures as breakdowns in intersubjective negotiation, which can be understood in terms of identity and power differentials and described as dissociative disconnections or self splits, misattunements (mismatches or miscoordinations), interpersonal pulls or transformations, enactments or vicious circles, and power plays or negations. Rupture repair can be defined by these formulations and can involve bringing intersubjective negotiation into relief, promoting emotion regulation and mutual recognition.

How We Translate Knowledge to Practice

Practice is oriented toward defining the "details" and "particulars" of emotional experience (toward *granularity*). This requires focusing on both patient and therapist experience—self states—understanding that they emerge and exist in relation to other states in a person and to another person. This focus is understood as a process of discovery and construction and in the context of power differentials as patient and therapist both negotiate needs for agency and communion. Practice implications are furthered in the next chapter.

4

From Emotion to Repair

The measure of a conversation is how much mutual recognition there is in it.
—DYLAN MORAN (TUOHY, 2011, PARA. 18)

In this chapter, we build on our consideration of emotion and rupture in Chapter 3 of this volume and concentrate on therapists' regulation of their own emotions as critical to rupture repair and to promoting the possibility of mutual recognition—how patients and therapists move from objectifying the other to seeing the subjectivity in the other. As a means toward regulation and recognition, we present the principle of metacommunication, which involves the simple but not easy process of putting words to one's experience in collaborative inquiry with the other. Fundamental to this process is the dialogic (or social constructionist) epistemology that truth can be understood only in dialogue with another. In the same vein, ruptures are not only *coconstructed* but also *coresolved*.

EMOTION: FROM COMMUNICATION TO METACOMMUNICATION

As suggested by its early reference as talk therapy or the "talking cure" (Freud & Breuer, 1895), psychotherapy is founded on communication between individuals (typically between a therapist and patient). As communication theorists have long distinguished (Littlejohn, 2002; K. Miller, 2005), it is important

http://dx.doi.org/10.1037/0000182-005
Therapist Performance Under Pressure: Negotiating Emotion, Difference, and Rupture,
by J. C. Muran and C. F. Eubanks

to recognize the difference between *content* (what is said) and *process* (how it is said) in any human communication. From what we have described so far, from the perspectives of interpersonal process, multiples selves, and intersubjectivity, an essential task for therapists is to continuously consider these three questions: What's going on around here? (E. A. Levenson, 2005), Who is speaking to whom? (Bromberg, 1998), and, What do we make of each other? (Pizer, 1998). This task is necessary especially in the context of alliance ruptures and is relevant to addressing emotion regulation for both patient and therapist.

How to do so in this regard—that is, what to do in practical terms—brings us to the technical principle of *metacommunication*. Kiesler (1996) first introduced this principle to the psychotherapy literature and defined it as communication about the communication process *in the interpersonal sense* (i.e., about the two participants in the psychotherapy situation). It is predicated on the idea that we are in constant communication, that all behavior in an interpersonal situation has message value and thus involves communication. This concept was originally discussed in the seminal work on human communication by Watzlawick, Bavelas, and Jackson (1967): "The ability to metacommunicate is not only the condition *sine qua non* of successful communication, but is intimately linked with the enormous problem of awareness of self and others" (p. 53). In previous publications (e.g., Muran & Safran, 2002; Muran, Safran, & Eubanks-Carter, 2010; Safran & Muran, 2000), we elaborated on Kiesler's application by including communication in the *intrapersonal sense*, that is, about the multiple selves within an individual self, specifically focusing on therapists' self-disclosures about their immediate emotional experience.

Metacommunication in general consists of an attempt to step outside of a patient–therapist interaction by treating it as the focus of *collaborative inquiry*.[1] It is best understood as a process, conversation, or dialogue rather than a circumscribed intervention such as a single question or observation. Metacommunication aims to decrease the degree of inference and is grounded in the patient's or therapist's immediate experience of a specific aspect of the therapeutic relationship. This is much like what Edgar Levenson (2005) advised in order "to resist being transformed" by the patient: Instead of offering explanations or conjectures as to the meaning of a current interaction (consistent with traditional applications of transference interpretations), therapists should simply report their own experience of their participation—how it feels to be involved with the patient. It can be likened to more recent considerations of *immediacy*—when therapists "disclose how they are feeling about the patient, themselves in relation to the patient, or about the therapeutic relationship" (Hill, 2004, p. 283).[2]

---

[1]In some respects, what we mean by collaborative inquiry can be likened to *collaborative empiricism* (see Overholser, 2011; Tee & Kazantzis, 2011), but one important distinction is that the former includes the therapist's experience as part of the exploration.
[2]One important distinction is that we are advocating for the specific use of metacommunication in the context of a rupture and in the pursuit of rupture repair.

It is a process that can begin with questions about patients' perceptions of their emotions ("What's happening for you right now?"), about the interpersonal field ("What going on here between us?"), or about their therapist's emotions ("I wonder if you have any thoughts about what's going on for me right now?"). When it comes to such questions, it is important to court surprise, to ask questions to which one does not know the answer: It is a "good" question when the answer comes as a surprise to both patient and therapist (D. B. Stern, 1997). Here, the "beginner's mind" (D. T. Suzuki, 1991) and the Socratic "not knowing" method (Carey & Mullan, 2004) can be helpful. Metacommunication can also include observations about patient emotions ("You seem angry to me right now. Am I reading you right?"), observations about the field ("It seems like we're engaged in a game of cat and mouse. Does that fit with your experience?"), or self-disclosures about one's own emotions ("I'm aware of feeling hesitant to say anything right now"). As just illustrated, it is often important to check if these observations make sense to the patient ("Does that seem fair from your point of view?").

It is important for these interventions to be made in the spirit of "collaborative inquiry." They should be presented with "skillful tentativeness"—with an emphasis on one's own subjectivity and a stance of genuine uncertainty. This is in recognition that therapists' understanding of themselves and their patients is always partial at best, always evolving, and always embedded in the complex interactive matrix within which they exist (Mitchell, 1993; D. B. Stern, 1997). If we become aware at all, it is always in reflection and from another point of view. Metacommunication is the effort to look back at a recently unfolded relational process from another vantage point. But "because we are always caught in the grip of the field, the upshot for clinical purposes is that we face the endless task of trying to see the field and climb out of it—and into another one, for there is nowhere else to go" (D. B. Stern, 1997, p. 158). In other words, process is continuous—endless, for that matter—and we should recognize that we are trying to observe while experiencing; we are trying to move along while still embedded.

Metacommunication is a technical strategy that can promote emotion regulation. It can be understood as a form of "mindfulness in interaction," an attempt to bring immediate awareness to bear on the interactive process as it unfolds, to facilitate distance and acceptance of an emotional experience fraught with negativity and as a result often dissociated or unformulated (Safran & Muran, 2000). Recall the discussion of expanding awareness of patient and therapist self states in Chapter 3 of this volume. Metacommunication aims to engage both patient and therapist to label or put words to their respective (often unformulated) emotions and thus add granularity (as Barrett, 2017, would put it) to their experience. In a sense, the aim is to expand conscious awareness in patients (as well as therapists) with respect to the details of their experience. By invoking mindfulness, we mean to suggest a state of psychological freedom, the curiosity of "a beginner's mind"—a disciplined self-observation that involves a bare attention to our experience of mind and body at successive moments of perception, without attachment to

any particular point of view and without becoming stuck in unconscious prejudices (M. Epstein, 1995; Kabat-Zinn, 1991/2013). In this regard, the aim
takes on the form of a contextualized exploration in the sense of what cultural anthropologist Clifford Geertz (1973, 1983; see also Ryle, 1949/1980)
referred to as a "thick description." Accordingly, therapy involves an intimate process of detailing the complex specifics of patient and therapist
experience—an intimate and infinite process of descending "into detail, past
misleading tags, past the metaphysical types, past the empty similarities to
grasp firmly the essential character of" individuals (Geertz, 1973, p. 53).

Although most clinicians from most orientations would agree with the
importance of this approach, in practice this seems to be lost for a variety of
reasons. In some instances, therapists fail to appreciate what this really means;
in others, therapists' anxieties lead them to assume they are a lot closer "to
the things" (Husserl, 1931) and "to the particular" (E. A. Levenson, 1991)
than they really are. Simply put, therapists' efforts should be directed toward
inviting and orienting patients to look at their immediate experience and
especially calling their attention to the transition points of their experience as
it emerges in the here and now. It is therapeutic, therefore, to increase not
only the patient's retrospective awareness of the intrapersonal or interpersonal patterns, which is increasing awareness of the self-as-object, but also
the patient's immediate awareness of how the patient engages in such patterns, which involves increasing awareness of the self-as-subject in relation to
self-as-object. This process involves increasing one's immediate awareness of
the self as the agent of one's own experience and behavior, of the subjective
processes that mediate the objective patterns.

The notion of *experiencing* (and *focusing*) from Eugene Gendlin (1962, 1982) is
also useful to consider here. Experiencing was originally coined by Carl Rogers
(1951) to describe the patient's sense of exploring their perceptual field. This
idea was later described by Gendlin as the basic felt sense of inwardly focused
attention, and operationalized further with Marjorie Klein and colleagues
(Klein, Mathieu, Gendlin, & Kiesler, 1969) in an observer-based measure, the
Experiencing Scale. The Experiencing Scale measures emotional involvement
and the progression of differentiating and signifying (through language) emotional experience in vivid representation as it immediately emerges in the
here and now and is deeply felt by the individual. The progression toward
higher experiencing is a movement toward greater granularity. A spate of
research over the past 30 years has demonstrated emotional experiencing as
an important change process in psychotherapy across various models (see
Auszra, Greenberg, & Herrmann, 2013; Castonguay, Goldfried, Wiser, Raue, &
Hayes, 1996; Pascual-Leone & Yeryomenko, 2017; Pos, Greenberg, Goldman,
& Korman, 2003; Whelton, 2004). Metacommunication should facilitate experiencing for both patient and therapist.

Mentalized affectivity (Fonagy, Gergely, Jurist, & Target, 2002; Jurist, 2018),
a notion derived from "mentalization" in the attachment literature (i.e., the
capacity to understand the mental states of self and others), provides another

useful lens. It is defined as "the process of making sense of emotions in light of one's autobiographical memory . . . [that] includes identifying, modulating, and expressing emotions" (Jurist, 2018, p. 83). Similar to experiencing, mentalized affectivity probably differs most significantly in its interpersonal referent (its orientation in relation to another). In psychotherapy, it is considered an important change process for the therapist to mentalize and thus stimulate mentalization in the patient. This includes mutual mentalization, when therapist and patient mentalize collaboratively, sharing their respective thinking processes in listening and reacting to each other. Here, judicious self-disclosure by the therapist is advocated (Bateman & Fonagy, 2006). Elliott Jurist (2018) described mentalizing about emotions "as the path to knowing what one feels and to action. . . . It adds fine tuning, or . . . granularity to our experience . . . [and promotes] seeing things in focus, in detail" (pp. 130–131). Research on mentalization in psychotherapy is still in its infancy (see Talia, Muzi, Lingiardi, & Taubner, 2018). Metacommunication should increase mentalized affectivity for both patient and therapist.

Metacommunication can also be understood as a technical strategy that can bring intersubjective negotiation into relief: the respective subjectivities of patient and therapist (their mentalized affectivity) and their underlying (unformulated or unspoken) desires and needs. As a result, it can make mutual recognition (mentalization of the other) more possible. As Donnel Stern (1997) suggested in his application of Gadamer's model, metacommunication can be understood as an effort to make visible "the very tailored prejudices" that two people bring to their encounter and develop between them (p. 216)—or put another way, to make explicit implicit biases. This characterization is comparable with Darlene Ehrenberg's (1992) notion of working at the "intimate edge" of the ever-shifting interface between patient and therapist— which for her refers to both the boundary between self and other and the boundary of self-awareness—"a point of expanding self-discovery, at which one can become more 'intimate' with one's own experience through the evolving relationship with the other, and then more intimate with the other as one becomes more attuned to oneself" (p. 34).

Metacommunication can reveal various selves or self states in communication between patient and therapist (Bromberg, 1998), including the power plays, accommodations, and refusals to accommodate inherent in patient–therapist interactions (J. Benjamin, 1995). As Pizer (1998) suggested, patient and therapist ongoingly negotiate what to make of each other. Metacommunication can make these subjective states plain, and thus it can promote the potential for mutual recognition—or what has been described as "an I–Thou relation" (Buber, 1923/1958), "a meeting of minds" (Aron, 1996), "a moment of meeting" (Boston Change Process Study Group, 2010), and "a genuine conversation" (D. B. Stern, 1997). This strategy can also make the dialectical tensions of agency/communion and objectification/subjectification more apparent, and thus more likely resolvable (see Muran, 2007b, 2007c, 2019; Safran & Muran, 2000).

How we describe metacommunication has technical implications, but we are not promoting a technical prescription. Rather, we are suggesting a sensibility to guide and organize intervention. In this regard, we previously outlined a number of general and specific principles of metacommunication (see Safran & Muran, 2000, for a comprehensive list). Here we present some basic ones.[3]

Invite Collaboration and Establish a Climate of Shared Dilemma

Patients can often feel alone and demoralized during a rupture, with the therapist becoming one of a string of figures who are unable to join with the patient in their struggle. The therapist is yet another foe rather than an ally. To counteract this expectation, the implicit message should be an invitation for the patient to join the therapist in an attempt to understand their shared dilemma—maintain a sense of "we-ness." Therapists should establish a climate that emphasizes the subjectivity of the therapist's and patient's perceptions. No perspective should be treated as absolute. Therapists should encourage a collaborative effort to clarify the factors influencing the emergence and maintenance of a rupture. Framing the impasse as a shared experience can transform the experience from one of isolation and demoralization for the patient to one of openness and honesty, where the patient feels safe speaking directly to the therapist about his or her feelings or overall treatment experience. This framework begins the process of transforming the struggle by diffusing the patient's defensiveness against the therapist and acknowledging that the therapist and the patient are stuck together.

Focus on the Immediate Details of Experience and Behavior

The process of metacommunication is formed around the examination of the immediate experience within a session rather than on events that have taken place in the past, such as previous sessions or at different points in the same session. Remember that what happened just a moment ago can be ancient history. Focusing on the concrete and specific details of the here and now of a therapeutic interaction promotes an experiential awareness. It lays down the groundwork for exploring a patient's actions and the internal experiences associated with those actions. Often when a therapist or patient feels anxious about a particular topic, they tend to pull the focus away from the source of conflict by deviating from the present feelings or by falling back on abstract, intellectualized speculation. Even talking about the therapeutic relationship can be done in a removed fashion, disconnected from the present. Refocusing

---

[3]Many principles are adapted from "Power Plays, Negotiation, & Mutual Recognition in the Therapeutic Alliance," by J. C. Muran and C. Hungr, in *Transforming Negative Reactions to Clients: From Frustration to Compassion* (pp. 32–38), edited by A. W. Wolf, M. R. Goldfried, and J. C. Muran, 2013, Washington, DC: American Psychological Association. Copyright 2013 by the American Psychological Association.

and opening up to exploring the present moment in concrete and specific terms can prevent this defensive deviation. Explorations of the present moment can also guide patients in becoming observers of their own behavior, promoting the type of mindfulness that fosters change.

Maintaining a focus on the here and now also encourages a respect for the uniqueness of each encounter. Each interaction between the patient and therapist is an individual moment influenced by both players. As the therapist is a key player in the dynamic, drawing premature parallels between the therapeutic relationship and the patient's other relationships can isolate the therapist's contribution and be seen by the patient as blaming. Therefore, attempts at identifying how patterns in the therapeutic relationship generalize to other relationships should be kept as an open question and should generally be left to the patient to draw. In general, such observations and explorations should be made in a tentative fashion from a stance of genuine uncertainty. In addition, therapists should try to convey the message to resist the urge to just make things different or better. They should privilege awareness over change. They should also remember that the aim is to use the therapeutic relationship to facilitate *awareness in relation*, which can then be brought to other relationships. Change (any new or different experience) instead should be understood as born in awareness, or as a by-product of awareness.

Explore One's Own Subjectivity and Contribution

Therapists' formulations should be grounded in an awareness of their own emotional experience. Therapists must work toward identifying feelings and responses that the patient evokes in them. Always try to start from where you are. This involves a careful awareness of the nuanced changes experienced by the therapist. These shifts may sometimes be difficult to articulate, but the process of attempting to articulate—both to oneself or directly to the patient— can help clarify the experience. The process of acknowledging one's contributions to the patient can also play a critical role in beginning to clarify the nature of the cycle that is being enacted. For example, a therapist could say, "As I listen to myself talk, I hear a kind of stilted quality to what I'm saying, and I think I've probably been acting in a pretty formal and distant fashion with you. Does that fit with your experience?" If the patient is receptive, this type of disclosure can lead in the direction of either clarifying factors influencing the therapist's actions or exploring the patient's feelings about the therapist's actions.

Encouraging a sense of "we-ness" involves being open to exploring the therapist's own contribution to and experience of the interaction. This process requires accepting responsibility for one's own influence in the development of a rupture with the patient. We all have a hand in an interpersonal process. When therapists disclose their own experience, they invite the patient to include their therapist as an active factor in their self-exploration. A therapist's self-disclosure may include simply asking patients if they have any ideas about what may be going on within the therapist. The therapist may also suggest possibilities for what is occurring between them and check in with the patient. For instance, the therapist could state, "I have a sense of being defensive and critical. Are you sensing this from your side?" This form of self-disclosure can help patients become aware of inchoate feelings that they are not comfortable facing, such as feeling criticized by the therapist, and can validate patients' experience of their therapist. These self-disclosures should always be presented judiciously and tentatively, again with the recognition that all perceptions are subjective and nothing is objectively absolute. Such an emphasis will invite more from the patient.

Monitor Relatedness and Responsiveness

Therapists should continually track how the patient responds to what is being said within a session. In this regard, therapists should pay close attention to their emotional experience as an important source of understanding the quality of relatedness with patients in a given moment. How connected or engaged does one feel? How compassionate? How uncomfortable? A therapist's intuitive sense of the relational atmosphere can inform them whether patients are getting closer to or distancing themselves from the therapist. The therapist may examine factors such as whether a particular interaction is facilitating or hindering the strength of the relationship, whether the discussion of an experience is elaborative or foreclosing, or whether the patient is expressive of their subjective experience or simply compliant to the therapist's view.

It is important to be aware that a patient may have difficulty acknowledging feeling hurt or criticized by the therapist or feeling angry at the therapist. Admitting such feelings may be threatening to the patient's self-esteem and in their mind may risk offending or alienating the therapist. Therefore, if an intervention fails to deepen exploration or further inhibits it, or if the therapist senses something peculiar in the patient's response, an investigation of the way in which the patient experienced it is critical. Over time this type of exploration can help to articulate the nature of the enactment taking place and assist in fleshing out an interactive matrix being enacted by the therapist and patient. It can also lead to a progressive refinement in the therapist's understanding of their own contribution to the interaction by encouraging a retrospective awareness of their own actions.

Recognize That the Situation Is Constantly Changing

The process of metacommunication is just that, a *process*. We should always try to use whatever is emerging in the moment as a point of departure for further metacommunication. Bear in mind that the therapeutic situation is constantly changing. This is a return to the concept of appreciating each experience with a patient as a unique configuration of the current encounter, with each instance leading to a further configuration. The need to recognize the fluidity of experience, where what was true about the therapeutic relationship a moment ago may not be true now, is highlighted here. From this stance, all situations are workable provided that one fully acknowledges and accepts the situation. The critical idea here is the importance of the inner act of acceptance of the changing experience. This inner act facilitates a type of "letting go" and an increased attunement to the unique configuration of the moment.

Even the position of "being stuck" is workable once one ceases to fight against it and accepts it. Metacommunication emerges from the inspiration of the moment, whether or not the moment is familiar or clearly understood by the therapist. Acknowledging and accepting the situation as it is can be an emotionally freeing experience that makes room for new possibilities and interpretations for what is occurring—what Neville Symington (1983) referred to as an "act of freedom." For example, therapists who say "I feel stuck" to the patient may in the process free themselves up sufficiently to see what had eluded them before, such as an aspect of the patient's behavior or an angle of their own bias. A disclosure of this type may contribute to a shift in the interactional dynamic, reframing the situation in a way that might uncover a new jumping-off point for exploration.

Expect Initial Attempts to Lead to More Ruptures and Expect to Revisit Ruptures

The therapist should be aware that initial attempts to uncover relational patterns in a therapeutic rupture can lead to further ruptures and will likely need to be revisited. The overarching aim of the resolution process is to stimulate curiosity about the patient's internal experience: Court surprise. This process involves working toward awareness of the feelings and behaviors associated with the style of relating, rather than trying to force things to be different. Awareness of one's self-experience and self-structure is a challenging process that can take time and repetition of certain interventions. In this process, there is always a risk that in working with alliance ruptures, a moment of metacommunication with a patient can further aggravate the rupture. The paradoxical truth remains that we are always embedded *in relation* to another while we try to become mindful and thus disembed from some relational matrix. Perpetuating one versus entering another remains a challenging question.

Regardless of how skillful the therapist may be in framing their comments in a nonblaming, nonjudgmental way, metacommunication may be implicitly suggesting that patients should be saying or doing something other than what they are currently saying or doing. For example, the observation "I experience you as withdrawing right now" may carry with it the implication that it would be better not to withdraw. In light of this risk, the therapist should remember that facing one rupture is the beginning of a resolution process that may involve further ruptures. In other words, the experience of working through a single rupture may not stand alone as an ultimate intervention but should be viewed as one step in building awareness of the internal experience and consequent maladaptive relational matrix or pattern.

There is nothing magical about the process of metacommunication. It is designed to explore at a level near experience to avoid the potential negative trappings that have been shown to be more likely with cognitive challenges or transference interpretations (see Chapter 2, this volume), but there is no guarantee. Interventions aimed at metacommunication do not always follow the notion of mindfulness with nonjudgmental thinking and emotional neutrality; they can also arise defensively. Regardless of the tension from which metacommunication arises, it should be understood that it is a single moment within a string of learning experiences between the patient and therapist. One must accept the inevitability of revisiting ruptures that have not yet been fully processed or internalized while appreciating that each repetition of a parallel rupture holds a unique configuration within the ultimate process. Along similar lines, it is also important to remember that hope will wane in certain moments within the therapeutic relationship. During periods of a prolonged rupture or an impasse, the therapist can easily lose hope in the possibility of moving forward. Such periods of hopelessness and demoralization are part of the process, just as working through impasses is the work of therapy rather than an obstacle to therapy.

Beware of Overemphasizing the Explicit and Disrespecting the Private

One of our favorite principles in the assertion literature is "Being assertive all the time is nonassertive"—and actually annoying (Jakubowski & Lange, 1978). In a similar sense, the emphasis in metacommunication is on the explicit (i.e., make the implicit explicit), and this can be overemphasized and become intrusive. It remains important to respect privacy—both the patient's and the therapist's—to allow each participant the space to self-reflect, to be alone with themselves (see Ogden, 1997). The challenge is to balance the public with the private, to protect the boundary. Here, as with self-disclosure, we are recommending a measured or judicious approach, or respect for the natural flow of approach and avoidance in human encounters, especially intimate ones. There is the apropos notion of "titration of the intimacy" (E. A. Levenson, 1991; Sullivan, 1953) and the recognition that there are times when it is prudent to refrain. The aforementioned principle regarding relatedness and responsiveness is relevant to knowing when in this regard.

EMOTION: FROM PATIENT TO THERAPIST

Basic Negative Emotions

In this section, we review basic negative emotions that are common challenges for therapists (intrapersonal rupture markers) and present some vignettes based on my [JCM] clinical experiences that illustrate metacommunication as a process toward rupture repair—emotional regulation and mutual recognition. In most of these vignettes, we are introducing beginnings to conversations that involve a more complicated process. It is important to remember, as previously suggested, that emotional experience is complex and idiosyncratic. How therapists experience and negotiate any of the challenges that we describe is highly variable and dependent on a number of factors. Therefore, these are not presented as prescriptive but as possible pathways—as regulation—and recognition-in-action.

Anxiety and Panic

Anxiety is an unpleasant state of uneasiness, worry, or dread in response to a potentially negative event characterized by uncertainty about its predictability as well as one's ability to effectively respond to it. Anxiety typically triggers defensive, avoidant, or security operations. It differs from *fear* primarily in that it is in response to a threat that is more diffuse and is future oriented. The most common negative emotion, anxiety is arguably the most challenging experience for therapists to navigate. In response to states of vulnerability and confusion, and emotions of anger and sadness, therapists often experience anxiety, which can sometimes lead to panic. The experience of anxiety can be unwitting and insidious in its effect on therapists, their attention, and experience of other emotions that may be primary (as exemplified previously).

On being personal: "Tell me something personal." "Tell me something about yourself, something personal," Tom asked me not too long into our work together. He was an imposing figure in his early 60s, considerably older than I at the time. He was a union employee who had worked almost 30 years for an airline that had recently closed its operations, so he was forced into retirement. He was alone in the world, never married and with no significant relationships when I met him, and he was looking for a new direction. I was immediately made uncomfortable by his request, very aware of my anxiety peaking. I remember responding, "I'm not sure what you mean, but I have to confess feeling wary about doing something like that and I'm not sure why." He turned silent, and after a while a smile came across his face. When I asked about the smile, he went on to say that he was just trying to set me up. When I asked what he meant by that, he explained he was looking for something "personal" to criticize me about—to knock me down from my "pedestal" in a sense. It was a startling revelation. I was impressed that he disclosed this so readily, that he was so candid. We then went on to explore why that was important to him, his regard to authority figures, especially to "false" figures. A year later, we were discussing something in session, and he asked me something rather personal. This time I didn't hesitate to reveal and responded directly, but shortly thereafter I was struck by the difference in our exchange. I brought this to his attention, and we were able to discuss the difference and how far we had come.

On being ignorant: "Why didn't you know?! Why didn't you tell me?"[4] Richard's accusatory words struck me hard. He expressed these upon discovering that his partner was cheating on him. His expression alternated between heart-wrenching sorrow and rage at me for not having known in advance. I was very aware of his pain: I could see his tears pour effusively; I could hear his chest heave palpably. And at the same time I felt anxious about approaching him. At first, I felt jerked back and forth, pulled in and then pushed away. After a while, it became harder to approach him even when he cried. When I finally found the courage to describe this experience—"I want to help you right now. I'm feeling pulled to but also pushed back, so I'm finding it hard to approach you"—it gave him pause. Eventually, he began to muse about what he was making of me. He moved from "You don't understand!" to "You can't understand!" which then led to an exploration of his fears and expectations regarding me, as well as my own regarding him. It brought into greater relief his struggles with independence and dependence that we had touched on before. Richard was a middle-aged, biracial gay man who came to me because he was struggling in his relationship with a partner of 1 year. He had two unfortunate experiences with gay therapists, so on one hand he was relieved I was straight. On the other, he was wary about whether I could fully understand his situation. He had a history of relationships in which he was ultimately betrayed by a lover. He was also physically and verbally abused as a child by his mother. As a result, he felt doomed to be forever untrusting and hypervigilant. He was also convinced that fidelity was an anomaly in the gay community. This latter conviction was something he believed I could not appreciate. Our accusatory encounter allowed us to explore his wish to trust me and his fear that he could not because of his history and the way he was objectifying me as a straight White male. This allowed me to become more than that for him.

On being careless: "You revealed your true colors!"[5] Bea started our session with this pronouncement of disappointment in me. Our previous ended with her conveying dismay over Martha Stewart's recent conviction. She had asked my opinion, and I responded rather casually, saying something about Greek tragedy and the downfall of another larger-than-life figure. She declared her dismay by my assessment of Martha, and I was taken aback, as I had not given much thought to a comment I made in passing. When I asked what she meant, she said that she found my judgment harsh and that it revealed a

---

[4]Adapted from a vignette previously presented in "A Relational Turn on Thick Description," by J. C. Muran, in *Dialogues on Difference: Studies of Diversity in the Therapeutic Relationship* (pp. 270–271), edited by J. C. Muran, 2007, Washington, DC: American Psychological Association. Copyright 2007 by the American Psychological Association.

[5]Adapted from a vignette previously presented in "A Relational Turn on Thick Description," by J. C. Muran, in *Dialogues on Difference: Studies of Diversity in the Therapeutic Relationship* (pp. 267–268), edited by J. C. Muran, 2007, Washington, DC: American Psychological Association. Copyright 2007 by the American Psychological Association.

surprising lack of compassion, "especially given my profession." At first, I was defensive, explaining that I wasn't really following Martha's situation: Admittedly, Martha Stewart was more of a cartoon figure to me. Bea was quick to cut me off—"No," and repeated, "Your colors are revealed!" Seconds of silence passed, and then I anxiously ventured, "I'm afraid to say anything right now." She appeared to soften a bit in response; her eyes turned downward, and her hands trembled. I took the opportunity here to ask what was going on for her. After some pause, she replied, "It makes me wonder what you must think of me." When I gently asked for more, she reflected on all her confessions to me, all her transgressions over the course of her life: all the lies and manipulations she described. She was 30 years older than I was at the time, a 72-year-old woman who at the age of 17 took over running her family business when her father tragically died. She developed quite an armor over the years, wary of all humanity—and especially a male therapist considerably younger. She went on to defend Martha, her strength and independence, her industriousness and fearlessness. With each word, she became increasingly emotional and was moved to tears. Eventually, she looked to me. "Why am I crying?" I suggested that maybe she was defending not only Martha but also herself. She paused and then replied, "You know, when I was running the family business, I always thought, 'I made it in a man's world!'" This moment made Bea less of a cartoon character, more of a person of greater complexity to me, and allowed her to consider that I might be able to understand despite all our differences and my inevitable misunderstandings.

On being too nice: "We're so f'kin' polite to each other!" At the start of a session, Valerie plopped herself down in her chair and blurted out this observation with a laugh: "We're kinda like Heckle and Jeckle." She went on to mimic a routine of the talking magpies. "No, after you . . ." "No, no, after you," as the birds would so pleasantly say to each other with a slight bow. When patients colorfully make you think twice about your relationship and what you might unwittingly be doing or feeling, it should be appreciated. With my request for meaning, she went on to describe how she saw us both painstakingly treating each other with "kid gloves." She appreciated my gentle manner: It often suggested care and consideration, but sometimes it felt to her as if I were treating her like a "china doll"—"fragile and maybe even cracked"—as if I were afraid of her. This revelation brought to my attention my anxieties when I was with her, which in turn allowed her to put words to her own and allowed us to address various disowned impulses. For her, she was better able to experience and express her frustrations and desperations with me as a result (see the upcoming and more elaborate illustration with Valerie on hopelessness). For me, it brought to light the subtle ways I avoided and aggressed against her at times.

Anger and Hate

Anger is a powerful and intense emotional state experienced in response to an attack or intrusion, some form of violation or abuse. It typically triggers adaptive actions with regard to assertion and control. Important distinctions have been made with anger (see Harmon-Jones & Harmon-Jones, 2016): There is *passive* anger—that is, anger kept in, including suppression and passive aggression, or anger turned toward self, such as self-blame; there is *aggressive* anger—that is, anger turned toward or against another, attacking behavior; and there is *assertive* anger—that is, standing up for or protecting oneself. *Hate* has been defined as an extremely intense version of anger or as extreme dislike or disgust regarding the other. Some have distinguished it as a rooted belief rather than a passing emotion like anger, but extreme or sustained anger and frustration can lead to hate; here we address it as an emotional state. For therapists, the challenge is to not disown their anger or aggressive impulses by acting on them without awareness. Awareness is key in this regard, and anxiety about anger, especially its expression, is a major obstacle. As has been long noted (e.g., Spielberger, Krasner, & Solomon, 1988), there is a difference between the experience and expression of anger. In the face of patients' sometimes ruthless attacks or intrusions, it is understandable to experience anger and counterhostility. As some theorists have noted, the therapeutic aim in this regard is to survive these aggressions, and in many instances this includes more than just tolerance. The aim can also include therapists making controlled expressions of anger that demonstrate strength and resilience (L. Epstein, 1984; Slochower, 1996): Defending oneself with firm limits and playful repartee are examples. It is also not unusual for therapists to move from not liking a patient at first (hate is probably too strong here) to a position of compassion and love as the patient reveals other, more vulnerable aspects of themselves.

On being nonassertive: "It's a little too late to be angry!" These were the final words I heard from my patient Rachel before she fired me. They still cut to the quick to this day. I was a newly minted PhD who was still trying to figure out my boundaries and limitations. Rachel presented with panic disorder as her chief complaint when we started to work together. I provided her with the current cognitive-behavioral technology at my disposal, relying heavily on Barlow's (1988) empirically supported contributions (e.g., psychoeducation, breathing retraining, cognitive reappraisal). In addition to our once-weekly sessions, I made myself available for phone consults when she was in a panic or at risk for panic. I even made myself available to be present at a dental appointment that was extremely anxiety provoking. I worked very hard at teaching her how to manage her breathing and thinking in the face of her fears. At first my efforts appeared to be appreciated by Rachel, but soon they were not enough. Our sessions became filled with complaints about the limitations of these techniques and my availability plus ability to help. My experience in our sessions became fraught with my own anxiety. I remember even saying a little prayer and pointing to the sky as I waited for her to come in and start a session—much like a baseball player before stepping into the batter's box. At some point, I became aware of feeling anger: This awareness first came to me between sessions when my anxieties receded. I took what felt like a big risk of disclosing it in our next session. "You know, after our last session, I became aware of feeling angry toward you." I was not sure how she would respond, but to my relief she was curious. She became open to exploring her fears in what felt like a more in-depth way: She talked about her experience of isolation and vulnerability in the world. She seemed to appreciate the impact of her anxieties and consequential criticisms on me (and maybe others). This exploration, in turn, brought another dimension to our work on her anxieties and really helped me to reapproach her in a more compassionate way. This process brought new fuel to our collaboration, or put more precisely, to my commitment to her. For a while this seemed to work. In time, though, the demands on my availability took its toll. Calls came at all hours, and I became very anxious when checking my voice mail and at seeing my phone flashing. Then came the criticisms of my ability again. At last, on our final call, I anxiously tried to talk about being angry again, to which she responded, "It's a little too late to be angry!" and hung up. To be fair, I was more anxious than angry. In retrospect, I realized I did not mind my anger sooner: I did not respect my limitations and recognize when I was being exploited and abused earlier in our work. How she would have responded remains an open question, but this was the lesson learned.

On being repulsed: "To know me is to hate me!" Bea came to me to address her interpersonal difficulties, her conflicts, and her isolation. In our first meeting, which was explicitly set up as a consultation to explore the possibility of working together, she began by informing me of a problem with my voice mail system. This issue would be a forerunner of her knack for finding wrinkles in my practice. She then asked about my phone policy, to which I asked what she meant. "Do you return calls?" I responded, "Yes." "How about after hours?" Again, I asked what she meant. She referred to calls late at night and during the weekend. I told her about my general policy of returning calls within a reasonable time frame, but I added that much is dictated by the nature of the specific case. She was not impressed. It seemed to her I had set up a practice primarily for my own convenience. During the course of the session, she expressed skepticism about therapy and her ability to change. She had a long history of being in therapy with some bad experiences. She also expressed some concern with my age and ethnicity, wondering aloud whether I could truly understand her. When she finally asked if I would be willing to work with her, I confessed I was not sure. I said I was intrigued by her situation. But I didn't say that I was drawn in by her apparent difficultness. I thought, "If you really want to study negative process, this is the patient for you!" I also told her that, given her expressed concerns about me, I was wary that I might never, in a sense, be good enough. But I didn't say that she reminded me of Rachel. So I was wary and very measured.

Bea was taken aback by my disclosure. She seemed to soften her position when she realized that our working together was not just up to her. She went on to say she wanted to work with me. She thought I was sharp and liked my ability to smile. When I asked how she felt about my disclosure, she said she didn't like dealing with the "person" behind the "professional"—her words. She went on to describe all her difficulties dealing with and relating to others. With our time up, I suggested that we meet again, and as she walked out of my office, she stopped with a smile and said to me, "You know, I've always thought, 'To know me is to hate me!'" It was a startling declaration and introduction.

As we worked together after this, Bea would occasionally poke a criticism at my various policies, attack me about something I said that she considered insensitive, and test the limits of my frustration and anger. To some extent, being upfront and mostly nondefensive about what I could and could not do for her and knowing and accepting my limitations helped me to tolerate her movements against me and to recognize my resulting anger in an immediate sense. We were able to have a number of candid conversations about our mutual frustrations, which allowed us to come to a greater appreciation of our respective personhoods. To some extent, I learned a lot from my experience failing Rachel.

Sadness and Despair

Sadness is an emotional experience of pain that emerges in response to a misfortune, separation, or loss. It initially results in a turning into oneself to mourn; it can be experienced as a deeply painful emotion, but it can ultimately mobilize the individual to recover or replace what was lost. Sadness can also result in a reevaluation of life goals and in aid and comfort from others. Thus, the sad person is at once pained and hopeful. In contrast, depression involves sadness about everything (in a global sense) and is often characterized by blunted or restricted emotional expression and by the experience of self-preoccupation or rumination and disconnection or isolation from others; it is founded on hopelessness or despair, such that the depressed person has given up (A. T. Beck, 1967). Therapists typically experience compassion in the face of a patient's sadness and are drawn toward the patient. In the face of a patient's depression, therapists can feel disconnection and, especially with regard to despair, futility, which mirrors the patient's experience. Typically, therapists champion hope and resist and avoid the patient's despair.

On being hopeful: "I'm just confused all the time!"[6] Valerie entered treatment in a severe depression that had debilitated her both mentally (she had great difficulty concentrating) and physically (she had great difficulty maintaining a working schedule). In the early stages of therapy, she described herself as in a perpetual state of confusion. She would often begin sessions in a half-humorous and half-poignant manner, which would confuse me and which became a marker that something was amiss. For example, she once

---

[6]Adapted from "Meditations on Both/And," by J. C. Muran, in *Self-Relations in the Psychotherapy Process* (pp. 357–360), edited by J. C. Muran, 2001, Washington, DC: American Psychological Association. Copyright 2001 by the American Psychological Association.

settled herself in her chair, turned to me with a smile on her face, and laughingly said, "Oh, sure, just look at me. I don't get it. I'm just confused all the time. I don't get it." I responded, "Well, let's start with the 'Oh sure, just look at me.' What's that all about?" Valerie responded, "Like you're all focused to start, and I don't even know what planet I'm on." When I asked her to elaborate, she went on to describe how she gets confused by some of her reactions and to wonder why (specifically) she had an "outburst" at the end of the last session ("It was probably one of those things that went over your head, but in my mind it was a big outburst"). I had not remembered any outburst and so asked for more detail. Valerie then went on to describe the end of the previous session, which I had punctuated with "To be continued." The expression sent her into a panic, as she experienced it as "Here, now take your problems and go away, go work on them on your own." She had jokingly blurted out halfway out the door, "Yeah, right, like you really want to." This was her so-called outburst.

Prior to this encounter, Valerie had been discussing the experience of feeling ignored by one of her brothers. She had also had a dream in which I was portrayed as impatiently waiting for her to leave me alone. When I had previously asked her if she experienced me as ignoring her or as impatient with her, she could not link the experience to anything particular that I had done. In this instance, when I raised it again and wondered aloud about what I did specifically to provoke this experience, she responded, "Well, it's based on something, but you didn't do anything terrible. . . ." I chose to focus Valerie on the "something" that she was picking up rather than focus on her characteristic tendency to dismiss, forgive, and attribute the blame to herself, which we had explored before in some detail.

In the ensuing exploration, I invited Valerie to explore my subjectivity, to speculate on what might have been going on for me when I ended the previous session ("So what do you imagine was going on for me?"). In response, Valerie elaborated on her sense that I was feeling a bit overwhelmed by her dependency and experiencing her as "too much" to handle and tolerate. She then disclosed her fear of being too dependent on me and her fundamental fear of being abandoned by me. As a result of these fears, she was exquisitely sensitive to my movements toward and away from her. She revealed that sometimes she experienced my "careful" approach to her as gentle and caring and other times as cautious and fearful of her. This revelation stirred me to explore my experience further and to begin to identify my subtle reactions to and anxieties about Valerie and what she needed from me. It helped me become more aware of how much she scared me at times, how much I felt wary of her dependency needs.

Subsequently I disclosed moments in sessions with her in which I felt anxious and guarded toward her as junctures to begin to explore what was going on between us and to discern our respective subjectivities. These disclosures helped orient our focus to the concrete and specific of the here and now and ground our awareness of our actions and self states, facilitating the experience of mindfulness in a sense for both of us. Earlier in treatment, Valerie responded to my transgressions with extended periods (sometimes days) of confusion and despair. These disclosures helped her to become more aware and vocal about her discontents with me, quicker and clearer in recognizing what she did not want from me and ultimately what she did. Of course, this process included my being mindful of my own desires with respect to her needs.

For example, when she would enter one of her self states of confusion and despair, she would frequently contact me by telephone (sometimes at the most inopportune times) but then would not be able to articulate what she wanted. The challenge I faced in these instances was to somehow try to create an optimal space for exploration and expression in an abbreviated time and without visual cues. In this regard, as I learned by my mistakes, it was important for me (and for her) to attend to what extent I resented the intrusion and to what extent I could hear her in the given moment. Sometimes this led to my asking her to call at another, appointed time or to wait until our next session. Simple, but not easy. Valerie appreciated knowing where I stood. It helped her recognize and express her own needs. It helped her move from a diffuse state of confusion and upset marked by occasional "outbursts" to a more differentiated state in which she could more readily discern her desires in contrast to mine. So it became an important, never-ending task to try to figure out where I stood. It was impossible to always or absolutely know, but it was a process—an ongoing negotiation between us.

Typically, Valerie would slip from a hypervigilant state, in which she paid exquisite attention to my position vis-à-vis her, into a dissociative self state of confusion and futility when I would be neglectful by an act of either commission (e.g., asking the "wrong" question) or omission (e.g., being nonresponsive). When faced with her futility, I often found myself feeling ineffectual and hopeless. In response, sometimes I would anxiously or angrily move away from this state and would commit another neglectful act (e.g., by imposing a sense of hope, sometimes a disingenuous assurance). When I was able to become mindful of this hopeless state, I was more able to meet her where she was. As she described, in my efforts to face and stay with my despair, she felt there was room for her to hope and to begin to talk about her specific fears and expectations.

On being stuck: "They'd be better off without me!"   Jen had said something to this effect before, but this time she sat in front of me with a look of despondency I hadn't ever seen. She was in an especially dark place—devoid of any reason. We had discussed her suicidal impulses before, but the thought of leaving her two young daughters behind was always unthinkable. She was caught in a horrible, long-drawn-out divorce proceeding, and her husband by more than one account was a bastard (her medicating psychiatrist who also saw the husband said as much). Jen was involved in a long-standing extramarital affair with a colleague at a management consulting firm: He was also married with no intention of leaving his wife. On this day, Jen could not assure me she would not take her life. She had a plan and now was convinced that her daughters would be better off with their father. To hospitalize her would probably increase the likelihood she would lose her children in the custody battle and provided no guarantee she would not try to kill herself after her release—especially if she were to lose custody. In a word, I was stuck—perhaps as she felt—and in stare down. All I could think of was I couldn't let her leave, and I told her so. Fortunately, I didn't have an appointment in the next hour, but I did call and cancel my subsequent appointment. I cleared some space (3 hours) for us to just talk, to articulate her feelings of despair—not to try to talk her out of it but rather to be there with it. (Certainly, my experience with Valerie helped here.) By doing so, Jen began to feel less isolated and alone. This required me to be aware of and tolerate my own anxieties regarding despair and provided her with the experience of being cared for and connected to another in her pain. Thus, I became a conduit for her to return from exile to being a member of the human community, a loving mother and a "doing" person.

Self-Conscious Emotions

Here we introduce so-called self-conscious emotions (see Lewis, 2016; Tangney, 1999) that develop with the emergence of consciousness and involve complex cognitive processes, including standards, rules, or goals shaped by family and culture.

Embarrassment and Shame

Embarrassment (or *shame* as a more intense version) is an anxious state that is based on the fear of another's negative evaluation and characterized by the phenomenological experience of wishing to hide or disappear and an action tendency toward inward withdrawal (Gilbert, 1998; Lewis, 2016; Tangney & Dearing, 2003). For therapists, this state is typically experienced in the face of explicit attacks by the patient on their professionalism or personhood. The challenge is not to succumb to the wish to withdraw.

On being wrong: "How could you?!"   A silly joke on my part drew this sharp rebuke from Mathew. "That's not very professional," he went on to say. Mathew was a peer in many respects but always called me "Dr. Muran" even though I would often return his calls with "Hi, Mathew, this is Chris," thus indirectly inviting him to address me informally. When I asked him about his apparent resistance to take up my invitation, he first said I needed to be more direct, but then talked about the importance of formality to him. More to the point, he needed to see me just as a professional, not as a person. He declared this even though he would occasionally relate to me in more familiar terms: For example, he would ask how I handled disciplining my son (his was always a challenge for him) or how I dealt with my aging parents (his relationship to his own was fraught with anger and guilt in addition to love). So the pull for mutuality was strong at times for me, but as we explored, he acknowledged being wary of seeing me as a flawed person. The pull to be authoritative was equally strong. Making a silly joke was an unwitting attempt by me to relate to him on mutual grounds: It undermined my authority in his eyes. It scared him and led to his rebuke—and a moment of embarrassment for me. I was not only unprofessional but also misread him badly. It was important here not to shrink away or to simply apologize: Here was an opportunity to explore his anxieties while they were palpable. Apologizing was beside the point and could have undermined the opportunity to explore his anxieties by defusing them. Here was an opportunity for Mathew to see me as both professional and person.

On having to succeed: "Too much on the line!"   Early in my career, I was asked to see an elderly gentleman who was a major benefactor to the medical center where I worked. The directive came from upper administration. Needless to say, I was in a difficult situation with no easy answer (one ripe for embarrassment among other emotional challenges). One senior colleague advised without hesitation, "You can't take this case." At the time, I was in supervision in the New York University postdoctoral program, and I brought my dilemma to my then supervisor, a very senior analyst who had built a practice (maybe better put, a career) as "the analyst's analyst," which invariably involved negotiating complicated relationships. He replied, also without hesitation, "Well, do you want to learn how to do this now . . . or later?" I was curious and so proceeded to work with the gentleman. He presented with a severe case of covert compulsions that seemed to serve to redirect his attention away from his experience of anger or sadness. He was some 80 years old when we started our work. He had survived a betrayal by his wife, who had an affair with a friend, and the suicide of his son, who overdosed as a young adult. Maybe better put, he was trying to survive these experiences. In most respects, this case was as challenging as any other. In time, the pressure to perform seemed to recede as I believe he appreciated my earnest efforts. I also believe he became very fond of me and a father–son dynamic emerged: In some respect, I filled the void left by the death of his son. We never talked about our relationship in this way. The relationship was more uncomfortable and challenging for me when he discussed the money he bequeathed to the medical center, which he did without designating how it should be used. One time, he told me how a development officer had called him and asked if he wanted to assign his bequest to the psychiatry department. His response was that he could never associate his family name with psychiatry. Apart from a few clarifying questions, I didn't say much, though much was going on in my mind: I knew what other departments (including oncology, surgery, and urology) could and did do to solicit funding, and I knew it was different for our discipline, right or wrong. We never talked about how this impacted our relationship. To this day, I wonder about my silence on our parental dynamic, including its relation to his bequest. I think in the end I did not trust how the conflict of interest within me would play out if we engaged in a conversation about it. I feared that such an explicit communication would be an implicit form of coercion on my part. So I kept my silence on this matter and my focus on his experiential avoidance of painful feelings.

How this focus intersected with what we did not address and whether it would have been worth addressing remain intriguing questions for me—and are posed here for your consideration.

Guilt and Self-Doubt

Guilt is an anxious state based on negative self-evaluation or self-criticism and motivates an action tendency toward correction or reparation, toward atonement for wrongdoing (Baumeister, Stillwell, & Heatherton, 1994; Lewis, 2016; Tangney & Dearing, 2003). If no remedial action is available, guilt can result in paralysis and turn to shame (and depression). For therapists, self-doubt (especially as self-reflection) can serve to make critical changes or adjustments in their actions, but in the extreme, hyperreflexivity and self-castigation can lead to rigidity and isolation—difficulty in being responsive to the other.

On being inexperienced: "You just don't have the experience!" I was a predoctoral extern when I heard these words from Campbell. He was a middle-aged basic science researcher who was "all but dissertation." My first thought when I heard that was an angry, "Well, I bet I get my PhD before you!" Of course, this thought was founded on my own insecurity: I was new to practice and only in my mid-20s. He accentuated his point by raising his pinky finger and indicating that the extent of my experience was equal to this finger. I don't remember much of that session, except for this exchange and that it was our last session together. It would forever remain a formative experience—an important memory of a missed opportunity. Years after this experience, I supervised a predoctoral intern who was facing a similar challenge. A patient who was a recovering alcoholic entered an early session and proclaimed, "I don't think this is going to work!" This was no surprise, as in previous sessions the patient had communicated her doubts in several less direct ways and supervision had focused on the intern's own self-doubts that were especially stirred by the patient's. We spent significant time putting words to my student's feelings in this regard. "I don't think you have the experience to help me with my addiction." My student responded, "Can you say more about what you're concerned about?" The patient accepted this invitation and began articulating her concerns, elaborating on her fears, and my student just listened and invited more expression. It was not so much what she said in response but that she remained open and nondefensive. She did not let her own doubts, which remained present, loom so large that they interfered with her ability to approach and explore the patient's feelings. The result was that the patient continued to work with her.

On being rejecting: "You got married!" Doris stood at the threshold of my office door and immediately broke into tears. She could see my wedding band from 10 feet away. I did not tell her in advance and had been away for 2 weeks for my honeymoon. It all hit her at once. I knew she had a bit of a crush on me. It was something we had talked about before, something we had explored to some extent, and something that always made me feel uncomfortable in our relationship. But in this tearful recognition, the depth and complexity of her feelings came crashing down upon me. Doris lived a reclusive life, alone and on disability, with her sister who also had long-standing psychiatric issues as her only close relationship. On the rare occasions Doris left her apartment, she would carry at least three bags full of stuff: She was a hoarder and remained one on the go. Her presenting concerns and goals were to redress her hoarding and to find part-time work—the latter to help also her re-engage with the world. Her tears made her wish to re-engage more profound. Her therapeutic relationship with me had become an important attachment, but one ripe with fantasy that precluded her from more realistic pursuits. I became a love object that she could count and settle on. When I saw her cry, I was first overcome with guilt: Should I have told her? Had I betrayed her? What had I become for her? And what had I missed? "Come in, Doris, and let's talk," I had the wherewithal to invite her to express and resist the trappings of guilt. With this watershed moment, we addressed these questions and then some. We reached a new depth of understanding of our relationship, including what she made of me and what I could be and do for her—namely, I couldn't care for her as a husband, but I could as her therapist.

Pride and Hubris

Pride involves personal satisfaction based on a positive evaluation of a successful action and associated with achievement motivation and constructs such as efficacy and mastery: Pride that turns to arrogance is *hubris* (Lewis, 2016; Tracy & Robins, 2014). For therapists, helping another, relieving suffering, seeing change in behavior can result in a tremendous amount of personal satisfaction. The challenge is to not get carried away with oneself and one's evaluation of self-efficacy. Slipping from pride to hubris on occasion is not as unusual as we would like to admit. "You're my last resort!" Patients make such expressions in many different ways. Sometimes explicitly: "You're the only one who really understands me!" Sometimes implicitly: "That's really helpful." These are expressions that can seduce us into feeling masterful. But as Dirty Harry pronounced on the death of the villain in *Magnum Force*, "Man's got to know his limitations" (yes, this would include women too; Daley & Post, 1973). Humility is essential: As the performance science literature cautions (Kahneman, 2011; Redelmeier, Ferris, Tu, Hux, & Schull, 2001), we should mind the trappings of overconfidence.

On being competitive: "Pride of the Yankees!" Oliver was about my age, highly educated, extremely smart, and very successful in the financial industry. He liked to show off—sometimes with regard to his financial success, but more often with regard to his intelligence. Often he liked to test mine and would reference something he read in the *Science Times*. There was a competitive edginess to our interactions. Sometimes there were repartees, some playful teasing. Touché, he liked that I could keep up with him. When we would explore this dynamic, he would acknowledge that he appreciated that he saw me as a worthy adversary. Oliver was also a rabid Boston Red Sox fan. And he noted I was a devoted (alright, rabid) New York Yankees fan (a mood-dependent fanatic since I first saw Mickey Mantle in pinstripes): I did drink my coffee from a Yankees mug depicting all the championships and with the caption "Hard to be Humble!" Admittedly, I didn't feel any competition in this regard . . . at least at the time.

We started working together in the summer of 2004. Oliver presented with frustrations in finding meaningful relationships: He had many male friends but no one with whom he could share his fears and insecurities, and he seemed to move from one short-lived romantic relationship to another. He was aware I was married by my band and once asked how long I was married. When we explored why he wanted to know, he expressed he was curious about my personal experience with sustained intimate relationships. So apparently I had credibility—or some kind of status. Then came October 2004, the American League Championship series, and another showdown between *my* New York Yankees and *his* Boston Red Sox. It didn't take long for my boys to take a 3–0 series lead and for me to have my World Series tickets in hand and clipped in my daily planner calendar book. Yes, it was hard to be humble as a Yankees fan!

Then came the unthinkable: The hated Sawx, the self-proclaimed "idiots," started to come back. At first, no big deal, I couldn't take this rally seriously. I survived my Boston-based uncle's merciless teasing back in the 1978 when the Sawx led my boys by 14½ games, only to see the Yankees stage a historical comeback and beloved Bucky "F'kin'" Dent punctuate it with an improbable home run. And of course there was the most recent 2003 championship series when the Yankees were at the brink and staged another comeback, capped by Aaron "F'kin'" Boone's home run. So there was nothing to worry about as I sat down to watch the deciding seventh game on October 20, 2004. Well, I was wrong, and I stared in disbelief at the television as the final out was recorded. The Red Sox won! My first thought was to turn off the television: I couldn't bear to watch this celebration. My second thought was, "F . . ., I have a session with Oliver first thing tomorrow morning!" I went on, "This is going to be the hardest session!" It is hard to be humbled. I didn't really know what to expect from Oliver, but he was incredibly gracious . . . and very curious about my experience—and not in an intrusive or "conquering" way. Even though I wanted more time to lick my wound, to process *my* loss, it was time to get to work, and I remember recognizing that this would be a challenge for my competitive impulses. I remember reminding myself to "mind and mine" those feelings, and it really mattered how Oliver approached me. The result was an in-depth and intimate conversation—about competition, winning and losing, camaraderie and loneliness—about self-definition and relatedness.

On not being as good: "My old therapist would have assured me." Grant pointed this out, and not for the first time. He had described how he had just gone on a mental journey of illness and death on the heels of stomach cramps. His previous therapist would automatically and emphatically assure him whenever he would go "hypochondriacal—'That's not gonna happen!'" Then she would explore. I was less generous with the assurances, I suppose because there were times such symptoms led to some kind of illness for Grant and I was trained to try to avoid arguments of probability with very anxious patients.

"So tell me more about your experience that I didn't respond as assuredly here." I focused on my most recent failing, trying to stay grounded on the immediate details (and not to drift to a more abstract discussion of patterns, which could obscure meaningful differences and emotional definition). It can be difficult for therapists to invite negativity or criticism—and I did *not* explore the first time Grant made such an expression, letting my anxieties move me to avoid—but ultimately I did. I have always been encouraged in this regard by the Chinese proverb "Go to the heart of danger, for there you'll find safety" (of course, this might strike some as counterphobic, and so one should strive as much as possible to do so in awareness). In response, Grant was able to explore in depth his sadness regarding the loss of a very important maternal figure in his life: His previous therapist died after a prolonged illness and, as he described, filled a very important void in his life, as he always found his mother lacking. In this context he was able to express his need for support and nurturance from me—his wish for assurance that I was there and that I cared.

Other Challenging Emotional States

In this section, we present other emotional states commonly experienced by therapists that can pose challenges.

Boredom and Neglect

Boredom is an unpleasant emotional state characterized by problems in engagement of attention, "a pervasive lack of *interest* and difficulty concentrating on the current activity" (Fisher, 1993, p. 396). Lack of stimulation and bouts of disinterest are not unusual experiences. Often we are not so aware of drifts to inattention. Whenever we are a bit bored, our minds naturally begin to wander. Much has been written about mind wandering: Research indicates we wander 47% of our waking hours (see Killingsworth & Gilbert, 2010). Also, increasing demands on our attention have resulted in large measure from excessive social stimulation and ever-expanding communication technologies that dominate our professional and personal lives (see Gergen, 1991, for an early discussion of this experience). Therapists are not above this. When sitting with a patient, a therapist can commonly find their mind wandering or trafficking in thoughts that concern matters apparently apart from the patient. Some authors have written in depth about this in the clinical setting (e.g., Ogden, 1997). When these wanderings become more pervasive, they are often meaningful markers of what's going on in the therapeutic relationship. Here are some illustrations of how such experiences can be negotiated in therapy.

On mind wandering: "Sorry, I was multitasking." In modern-day terms, mind wandering can take the form of "multitasking" whereby one can find oneself working on other tasks in addition to or sometimes instead of the therapy task at hand with a particular patient. I suspect this is as common in psychotherapy as it is in everyday life. The questions are whether it is more than usual, whether it interferes with the psychotherapy process, and whether it bears some significance about the intersubjective negotiation between patient and therapist.

After several weeks of working with Peter, who presented with concerns about social anxiety and relating to others in an intimate way, I began to recognize my attention often wandering. I could and would return to engaging with his concerns. At first I just shrugged this experience off. Then I started noticing it happening again and again, and it seemed too often to not be meaningful. I tried to tie my wanderings to an interpersonal marker and thought it might have something to do with how he spoke about his worries, his various machinations in negotiating social situations. At some point I shared, "Peter, I find myself getting lost in all your worries and wondering what that means. Does that make any sense to you?" Peter initially smiled in response, but that quickly disappeared. He then confessed he felt at times that I wasn't present. When I asked about his experience of my absence, we were able to move to a place where we could explore his sense of isolation in the world and his profound sense of sadness regarding feeling disconnected. Here I could more meaningfully recognize and connect with him.

On being neglectful: "I rarely worry about you."   One day before the start of a session with Emily, it occurred to me that she didn't occupy much of my attention between sessions. I began to wonder to what extent I took her too lightly. Emily was a high-achieving professional who came to see me after ending a 5-year relationship when she discovered that her boyfriend had no desire to marry and start a family. Our work together seemed to proceed smoothly—probably too smoothly. She seemed willing and able to grapple with her perfectionism and overdeveloped work ethic and to examine her recently failed relationship and why it took so long for her to discover that her boyfriend had different aspirations. My realization and growing unease regarding my apparent neglect led me to take a risk.

I decided to explore this feeling in session, first by grounding it in the specifics of how we interacted and then by metacommunicating: "You know, it recently dawned on me that I rarely worry about you between sessions. And I became concerned that I might be taking you for granted. Does that make any sense to you?" This stirred a tearful reaction in Emily, as she acknowledged feeling neglected by me. In the exploration that ensued, she associated to always feeling compelled to be self-reliant and began to identify the ways in which she tended to smooth things and communicate that all was fine when it wasn't. She described this as a profoundly lonely experience. It was important for me to acknowledge my participation or collusion in this process. In time, she was able to explore the way in which her fear of being too demanding and of driving the other person away led her to disown her own desires.

Love and Seduction

Love is a positive feeling of strong attraction and emotional commitment that Robert Sternberg (1986) described in terms of three components: *intimacy* (shared confidences and personal details), *commitment* (expectation of a meaningful relationship), and *passion* (infatuation and sexual attraction). Love has also been defined as involving an intricate balance between recognizing the subjectivity of the other and objectifying the other (see J. Benjamin, 1988). Objectification can be what excites or tantalizes one about the other, but it can also lead to depersonalization, degradation, or dehumanization of the other (see Kant, 1797/1996). Martha Nussbaum (1995) and Rae Langton (2009) identified several features involved in objectification: treatment of the other as a tool, as a possession, as interchangeable with other objects, as lacking autonomy and agency, as lacking boundary-integrity, as without subjectivity, as silent, and as reduced to appearance and body. For therapists, the challenge is to resist becoming fully engaged in objectification as both perpetrator and sufferer.

On being seduced: "How about a hug?"   These were James's words as he got up to leave our session. It was our first session in a number of years: We had worked together for a brief spell before he moved away from the New York area. James was gay, and though we were close in age, he was quite childlike. In fact, he did not work but was rather kept by his partner of many years. I had forgotten how flirtatious and provocative he could be. In the moment, I was caught off guard and let him hug me. It was brief and probably awkward, though I tried to appear cool with it. I reciprocated with a simple pat on his back.

In subsequent sessions, James would occasionally make an off-color remark that would make me feel uncomfortable. Increasingly I felt sexualized and objectified. At some point, I "screwed" up my courage to share my discomfort after another sexual comment. "At the risk of sounding prudish, I have to say that I do feel uncomfortable about what you just said." James went silent. It appeared I hurt him. When I asked him what was going on for him, he confirmed the hurt. I acknowledged that my disclosure was also a form of pushing back. James appeared to appreciate my candor and was able to articulate his fear that I would reject him. This in turn allowed us to explore our respective subjectivities and differences in a much richer way, including his feelings of alienation, his needs for nurturance—and more constructive ways to address these.

On being starstruck: "Look at me!"   Paulo was an artist who created in various media, from painting to photography. He was well travelled, though his renown was based solely in South America, which was always a source of great disappointment to him. He was just 50 when came to see me. His presenting complaint was long-standing depression. Our sessions typically concerned his latest creations and frustrations with finding a New York gallery to exhibit them. He often brought in a sample of his work—a form of show-and-tell. And I was enthralled not only by what I saw but also by what I heard of his creative process. I became starstruck as our sessions became exhibitions, which he seemed to really enjoy. He was so animated that I could hardly tell he was depressed.

At some point, though, I was also struck by the unusual nature of our encounters, so I explored. "I'm so impressed by this photo of yours. Can I ask what it means to you that I am?" Paulo acknowledged how much he appreciated my appreciation but also his wanting for more recognition. This allowed us to explore his ambitions and failings in more depth. This also allowed us to better understand his desires and frustrations regarding others. He was able to give definition to how he was approaching me, how hard he was working to impress me, and how much he feared further rejection.

Misempathy and Overidentification

Empathy is the ability to understand another individual's emotional experience or internal state, to feel from within another's frame of reference, to make less distinct the differences between the self and the other, having the separateness of defining oneself and another blur (Zaki & Ochsner, 2016)—to put oneself in another's skin and walk around in it, to paraphrase Atticus Finch in *To Kill a Mockingbird* (H. Lee, 1960). *Compassion* and *sympathy* are other terms associated with empathy but are oriented more toward feelings of concern for another in need. Empathy has been operationally defined as comprising multiple abilities or tendencies, including (a) *experience sharing*, or to take on an emotional state of another; (b) *mentalizing*, or to explicitly theorize about the internal states of another; and (c) *prosocial motivation*, or to want to help another as a result (Zaki & Ochsner, 2016). Empathy has long been considered essential in psychotherapy (see Bohart & Greenberg, 1997; Elliott, Bohart, Watson, & Murphy, 2018). For therapists, the challenge is to recognize misempathy (the belief that one knows exactly how another person feels when in fact one doesn't) and overidentification (when one excessively identifies oneself with another to the detriment of individuality), both of which involve missing the difference between self and other.

On being overidentified: "Why do you care?"[7] Over the first few months in our work, Michael would often start our sessions by describing a problem—whether it had to do with moving to a new apartment, approaching a woman he was interested in, or resolving a conflict at work—and my efforts to try to clarify the situation or even provide advice were met with quick dismissals. When I would explore his reaction to my efforts, he would criticize them as

---

[7]Adapted from vignette previously presented in "A Relational Turn on Thick Description," by J. C. Muran, in *Dialogues on Difference: Studies of Diversity in the Therapeutic Relationship* (pp. 268–269), edited by J. C. Muran, 2007, Washington, DC: American Psychological Association. Copyright 2007 by the American Psychological Association.

"idealistic and ill-conceived." After some time, I became increasingly wary when confronted with this scenario. In one session when I finally revealed my wariness, he was able to acknowledge that he realized he was setting me up and testing me in a sense. He recognized that he wanted me to succeed *and* that he wanted me to fail: The former was his hope, the latter his expectation. Although this seemed an important exploration and revelation, it still seemed as if we continued to repeat this enactment of my trying to solve his problems and trying to save him.

In another effort to talk about what was going on between us, he stopped and asked, "Why do you care?"—a simple-enough question, but one that gave me great pause. Was it because I liked him? I knew I experienced him as a pain in the ass when he was being particularly enigmatic and impossible to help, and yet I did like him; and I was aware of a strong investment in him. I shared these thoughts with him, which led him to ask another significant question: "What is it that you want *for* me?" As I reached for an answer to this, it occurred to me that maybe I had designs for him that had more to do with my own aspirations than his, that maybe I saw him as a younger version of me. I was blind to a prejudice of mine and to a critical difference between us. When I considered this aloud, I realized how neglectful I had been of him. This seemed to open up some space for us to begin to define with greater resolution what he wanted for himself, what he needed from me, and his fears in both regards.

On being different: "Are we much more simply human than otherwise?"
This question is based on a famous acknowledgment by Harry Stack Sullivan (1953) that was meant "in most general terms" (p. 35). The interpersonal tradition has also promoted the notion that each of us is highly idiosyncratic—"totally unique and singular as our fingerprints" (E. A. Levenson, 1991, p. 83). Both these truths stand in dialectical relation to each other. A. R. was an African American man in his mid-70s, some 30 years older than I, when he came to see me to discuss his adjustment to life in retirement. An academic, he was politically active throughout his life. Our differences (or at least some of them) were obvious, but over time I felt our mutual humanity prevailed. He was a man in existential crisis, trying to sort out what to do in the next chapter of his life. We had engaging conversations about his life in academia and his accomplishments and regrets, and I felt that we shared a lot in this regard. He also captivated me with an occasional anecdote about the civil rights movement back in the day, and he gave me great insights on a history I studied as a youth. In time, I grew in my empathy and affection for him. Then came Election Day, November 2008: We met for our regularly appointed session the day after. A. R. walked into my office and broke into tears. These were tears of joy and then some for the election of the first Black president of the United States. The depth of feeling woke me from my illusion of understanding the man. "I didn't really understand," I confessed, which allowed us to converse in an entirely different way. I learned another lesson on difference and its scale.

CODA

Ruptures as Emotional Challenges

Alliance ruptures represent opportunities to explore core relational themes for both participants in the therapeutic relationship. For therapists, they invariably involve emotional challenges marked by various basic and complex emotions, but these can provide guidance: Therapist internal experience can serve as an internal compass to what is going on *within* the patient and *between* the patient and therapist.

Rupture Repair as a Change Event

Therapist emotions can be used to build bridges to dissociated states, to repair misattunements, to resist interpersonal pulls, to disembed from relational matrices or unhook from vicious circles, and to bring an intersubjective negotiation between patient and therapist beliefs and identities into relief. Their definition can provide regulation for the therapist and coregulation within the therapeutic relationship.

Metacommunication as a Technical Principle

Metacommunication, or communication about the communication process, is a technical principle founded on collaborative inquiry that can facilitate rupture resolution, promote emotional regulation for both patient and therapist, and increase the likelihood of mutual recognition by patient and therapist of their respective subjectivities—a moment of I–Thou meeting or meeting of the minds.

5

A Way to Therapist Training

Don't practice until you get it right. Practice until you get it wrong.

—UNKNOWN

Across therapeutic approaches and disciplines, there is widespread agreement that therapist training and supervision are important. However, as Hill and Knox (2013) observed in their review of the research literature on therapist training, "we were struck by how little we actually know about the effects of training and supervision" (p. 801). Given the complexity of the interlocking patient and therapist variables that contribute to therapy outcome, it can be challenging to identify and isolate how therapist training and supervision actually impact patient care. For example, an analysis of 5 years of outcome data from a community counseling center found that supervisors accounted for only .04% of the variance in patient outcome (Rousmaniere, Swift, Babins-Wagner, Whipple, & Berzins, 2016). Gaining more insight into how supervision can be enhanced to improve clinical care will require creative approaches to both training and the research methods used to study its effects. In this chapter, we first briefly review recent efforts to improve our knowledge of what constitutes effective training and supervision, with a particular focus on helping trainees enhance their abilities to cope with challenging moments in therapy. We then present our supervisory approach of alliance-focused training (AFT; Eubanks-Carter, Muran, & Safran, 2015; Muran, Safran, & Eubanks-Carter, 2010), which focuses on helping therapists negotiate alliance ruptures

http://dx.doi.org/10.1037/0000182-006
Therapist Performance Under Pressure: Negotiating Emotion, Difference, and Rupture,
by J. C. Muran and C. F. Eubanks

with patients. We present the theoretical and empirical support for AFT, review its underlying principles, describe strategies for implementing it, and conclude with an illustration of an AFT session.

OTHER SUPERVISION AND TRAINING MODELS

In recent years, the growing emphasis on evidence-based approaches to therapy has also begun to influence models of supervision. This has led to an increase in supervisory approaches that focus on identifying specific skills that therapists need to possess, targeting those skills in training, and using structured assessments to measure trainees' progress toward reaching competency and to document the efficacy of training programs.

One prominent example is the helping skills training program developed by Hill and colleagues (Hill, 2020). This training aims to teach therapeutic skills related to exploring, facilitating awareness and insight, and helping patients take action toward their goals. The training includes attention to specific interventions, such as reflecting the patient's feelings or asking open questions. Helping skills training is geared toward trainees at the undergraduate or early graduate level who have not yet begun seeing patients, with the hope that the training will give them a good foundation of basic counseling skills before they learn a particular therapy approach. Studies of helping skills training have found that it leads to improvements in the specific skills targeted in the approach (Hill & Kellems, 2002; Hill et al., 2008).

Competency-based supervision (Falender & Shafranske, 2017) focuses on identifying the knowledge, skills, attitudes, and values that are needed to achieve competency in specific clinical tasks such as diagnosis and crisis intervention. In this approach, the supervisor and the trainee collaborate to identify the competencies that will be targeted and employ behaviorally anchored assessments and benchmarks to track the trainee's progress during training. This approach emphasizes the importance of clear communication about goals and expectations. Both supervisor and supervisee need to develop *metacompetence*, or the ability to know what they know and what they do not know so that they can identify which skills they need to improve. In addition, this approach emphasizes the importance of a strong *supervisory alliance*. Given the power differential between trainees and supervisors, it is incumbent upon the supervisor to be particularly alert to signs of strain in the alliance with the trainee.

The critical events in supervision model (Ladany, Friedlander, & Nelson, 2016) is an empirically informed approach to supervision that conceptualizes supervision as a series of tasks to be accomplished or resolved. The approach focuses on identifying critical events or dilemmas that can hinder trainee growth. Once the critical event has been identified, the supervisor focuses on specific tasks that will work toward resolution of the critical event. These tasks commonly include remediating trainee skill deficits; increasing multicultural awareness; negotiating role conflicts; working through countertransference;

managing sexual attraction; repairing gender-related misunderstandings; and addressing problematic thoughts, feelings, or behaviors. The approach aims to help trainees develop greater knowledge, skills, self-awareness, and a stronger alliance with the supervisor. This approach emphasizes the importance of attending to the supervisory process, as supervisors can become so focused on addressing the needs of the trainee's patient that they overlook the needs of the trainee.

SUPERVISORS AS RESPONSIVE MODELS AND SECURE BASES

Regardless of which supervision approach one espouses, it is critical to recognize how the supervisor serves as a role model for the trainee. To be maximally effective, a supervisor must be able not only to teach the trainee relevant skills but also to display those skills in their interactions with the trainee.

One of the most important therapeutic skills for a supervisor to possess is *responsiveness*, or behavior that is influenced by emerging context (Stiles, Honos-Webb, & Surko, 1998). As Friedlander (2015) observed, just as a therapist's ability to responsively adjust their behavior to meet the needs of a specific patient is at the heart of good therapy, supervisor responsiveness is essential to good supervision. Supervisors need to be sensitive to their trainees' developmental level, providing feedback and guidance that is appropriate to a trainee's skills and understanding (Bernard & Goodyear, 2019). In addition, they need to be sensitive to the trainee's anxiety level, respecting what Sullivan (1953) described as the "gradient of anxiety" and the optimal level for communication. Bernard and Goodyear (2019) drew on the Yerkes and Dodson (1908) inverted U-hypothesis as a way of conceptualizing the optimal range of anxiety—not too little, not too much—within which a supervisee will best perform. Responsive supervision can also be characterized as working within the trainee's zone of proximal development (ZPD; Vygotsky, 1930/1980), the distance between the trainee's current developmental level and the more advanced level the trainee could reach with the guidance and collaboration of the supervisor. Responsive supervisors balance an appreciation for where the trainee currently is with the ability to challenge trainees to stretch themselves.

Supervisors' responsiveness needs to be grounded in humility. Supervisors need to recognize their own limitations and mistakes. As Watkins, Hook, Mosher, and Callahan (2019) observed, supervisor humility "is eminently fundamental, foundational, and transformational in enhancing supervision processes, the supervisory relationship, and buffering against harmful supervision" (p. 2). They noted that supervisor humility can enhance trainees' comfort in and receptiveness to supervision, and strengthens the alliance between the supervisor and trainee.

Supervisor responsiveness may be most important when helping trainees navigate alliance ruptures (Friedlander, 2015). The supervisor has to help trainees negotiate a challenging clinical situation and also help them manage their own reactions to what has happened. In a study of therapist trainees who had a rupture with a patient (Kline et al., 2019), trainees reported experiencing difficult emotions during the rupture, such as tension, anger, and decreased self-efficacy. If a supervisor is not responsive, particularly in these challenging moments, trainees are less likely to disclose difficulties that they are encountering in therapy. In one study (Ladany, Hill, Corbett, & Nutt, 1996), 97.2% of surveyed supervisees reported that they withheld information, including clinical mistakes, from their supervisors and they were more likely to withhold important information from supervisors regarded as unsupportive or unresponsive.

Supervisor responsiveness facilitates a strong supervisory alliance, which not only will improve the process of supervision but could positively impact the process of therapy with the trainee's patient. For example, one study found an association between the supervisory alliance and patient ratings of the therapeutic alliance (DePue, Lambie, Liu, & Gonzalez, 2016). One possible way that the supervisory alliance may impact how therapists build and maintain alliances in treatment is by providing the trainee with a secure base. Scholars have suggested that Bowlby's attachment theory can provide a useful lens for thinking about the supervisory relationship (see Watkins & Riggs, 2012, for a review). Bowlby (1988) noted that in psychotherapy, the therapist should provide a "secure base" for the patient, which allows patients to safely explore both their own internal experience and the world around them. Similarly, supervisors can provide a secure base for trainees, which should help trainees develop and maintain the courage needed to engage with difficult moments in therapy rather than avoiding them. Mehr, Ladany, and Caskie (2015) found that supervisee ratings of the supervisory alliance were related to less trainee anxiety and greater willingness to disclose in supervision. Likewise, a strong supervisory alliance should help a trainee to feel secure enough to take the risk of expressing and exploring in therapy their encounter of a rupture with a patient.

ALLIANCE-FOCUSED TRAINING: HELPING THERAPISTS REGULATE EMOTIONS AND NEGOTIATE RUPTURES

The Evidence for Alliance-Focused Training

As we noted in our discussion of the Vanderbilt studies in Chapter 2 in this volume, training therapists to navigate moments of rupture can be quite challenging. Strupp and colleagues found that their efforts to train therapists to respond effectively to negative patient reactions were not successful: After training, therapists displayed an increase in negative behaviors toward patients (Henry, Strupp, Butler, Schacht, & Binder, 1993), and analyses of outcome found that training did not result in better patient outcome and that a majority of the therapists did not achieve competence in the alliance-focused approach (Bein et al., 2000).

Several research groups have developed and tested forms of therapist training that focus on improving trainees' abilities to build and maintain strong alliances with their patients (see Eubanks, Muran, & Safran, 2019). For example, Bambling, King, Raue, Schweitzer, and Lambert (2006) developed two alliance-focused forms of supervision—one that attended closely to increasing therapist awareness of interpersonal processes that impact the alliance, and another that focused on helping therapists apply specific skills likely to improve the alliance. In a study of patients receiving an eight-session problem-solving treatment for depression, they compared therapists receiving each of these forms of supervision to unsupervised therapists. They found no significant differences between the two alliance-focused forms of training with respect to ratings of alliance or outcome. They did find that patients in the alliance-focused supervision conditions reported higher alliance and achieved better outcomes and greater retention in treatment than patients working with unsupervised therapists.

Crits-Christoph et al. (2006) developed an alliance-fostering therapy for depression that combined interpersonal-psychodynamic interventions with techniques designed to strengthen the alliance by maximizing agreement on goals and tasks and enhancing the bond. In a pilot study of five therapists, the authors found that most therapists forged stronger alliances with patients they saw after the training compared with those they saw prior to training, but these improvements were not statistically significant. The alliance-fostering training was also associated with small improvements in patients' depressive symptoms and larger improvements in ratings of quality of life, particularly for therapists who used more alliance-fostering techniques. One interesting finding was that one of the five therapists actually obtained weaker alliance scores after training. The researchers observed that this therapist missed more supervision sessions than the other therapists, and they speculated that this therapist had a weaker alliance with her supervisor. This observation points to the importance of the supervisor's ability to recognize and address ruptures with trainees.

Helping therapists learn to recognize and negotiate challenging moments in therapy, which we conceptualize as alliance ruptures, has been the focus of our research program for more than 30 years. This work is grounded in the rupture resolution stage-process model discussed in Chapter 2 of this volume. The model developed by Safran and Muran (1996) in a series of task analyses informed a clinical approach to addressing alliance ruptures that has been studied in two ways: as an approach to training and supervision, referred to as AFT, and as a time-limited manualized treatment referred to as brief relational therapy (BRT). A randomized controlled trial comparing BRT to cognitive behavior therapy (CBT) and a short-term dynamic psychotherapy (STDP) in a sample of patients with diagnoses of Cluster C personality disorders or personality disorder not otherwise specified found that BRT was as effective as the other treatments on standard measures of change and was more successful than the other two treatments with respect to premature dropout (Muran et al., 2005).

A small study of patients with personality disorder diagnoses provides further evidence supporting BRT's success at keeping challenging patients engaged in treatment. In Safran, Muran, Samstag, and Winston (2005), patients were randomly assigned to STDP or CBT, and their progress was monitored. Potential treatment failures were identified on the basis of a number of empirically defined criteria. These identified patients were offered the opportunity to change treatments. The 10 patients who agreed to the change were randomly assigned either to BRT or to another treatment (STDP or CBT). Results showed that all five patients reassigned to CBT or dynamic therapy and seven of the eight patients who declined reassignment terminated treatment prematurely. By contrast, only one of the five patients reassigned to BRT dropped out of treatment (and that patient relocated to another country because of a job opportunity).

Further support for Safran and Muran's approach to alliance ruptures is provided by studies that integrated this approach into cognitive-behavioral treatments. Castonguay (1996) developed integrative cognitive therapy for depression (ICT), which integrates Safran and Muran's rupture resolution strategies (Safran & Muran, 2000; Safran & Segal, 1990), as well as strategies developed by Burns (1989), into cognitive therapy. When ruptures are identified, the therapist breaks from the cognitive therapy protocol and addresses the rupture by inviting the patient to explore the rupture, empathizing with the patient's emotional reaction, and reducing the patient's dissatisfaction by validating negative feelings and taking at least partial responsibility for the rupture. In a pilot study, Castonguay et al. (2004) found that patient symptom improvement was greater in ICT than a wait-list condition. In a randomized trial comparing ICT to cognitive therapy, Constantino et al. (2008) found that patients in ICT demonstrated greater improvement on depression and global symptoms and more clinically significant change than patients in cognitive therapy. ICT also yielded better patient-rated alliance quality and therapist empathy, and there was a trend toward better patient retention in ICT than in cognitive therapy.

Newman and colleagues (2011) drew on Safran and Muran's approach to develop a treatment component that targeted interpersonal problems and emotional processing. Participants with generalized anxiety disorder were randomly assigned either to CBT augmented with the interpersonal/emotional processing treatment component or to CBT augmented with supportive listening. Participants in both conditions showed significant improvements, and there were no significant differences between the treatment conditions, suggesting no advantage for the interpersonal/emotional processing component. However, a secondary analysis of this data set (Newman, Castonguay, Jacobson, & Moore, 2015) found that the CBT condition augmented with the interpersonal/emotional processing component yielded greater improvements in generalized anxiety disorder symptoms for patients with self-reported dismissing attachment styles. An intensive qualitative analysis of one of the cases from this study (Castonguay et al., 2012) illustrates how the interpersonal/emotional processing component may have helped dismissing patients. In this case, the therapist's use of alliance-focused strategies such as metacommunication, exploration, and experiential interventions (e.g., two-chair exercises) helped the patient explore difficult emotions related to his relationship with the therapist and to recognize how similar patterns emerged in his other interpersonal relationships. In addition, the therapeutic relationship appeared to have an impact on the patient. The therapist, through encouragement and modeling, helped this usually avoidant patient to express his feelings more openly. The patient found that his disclosures were met with acceptance and validation rather than the criticism and anger he anticipated. In this way, the therapeutic relationship provided a corrective experience that helped to change how the patient approached other relationships.

In a recent study (Muran, Safran, Eubanks, & Gorman, 2018), our group examined the impact of introducing rupture resolution supervision, or AFT, to trainees implementing CBT for patients with diagnoses of Cluster C or personality disorder not otherwise specified. In this study, trainee therapists began conducting a therapy case in CBT with CBT group supervision. Therapists were randomly assigned to switch from CBT group supervision to AFT, also conducted in small groups, after either eight or 16 sessions. This study design aimed to control for individual and dyadic differences by having therapists continue to work with the same patients before and after changing to AFT. Further, by having therapists switch to AFT at different time points (multiple baseline design), we aimed to pinpoint changes in interpersonal process (measured by the Structural Analysis of Social Behavior; L. S. Benjamin, 1974) that could be attributed to the switch to AFT, as opposed to the passage of time. We found that AFT facilitated decreases in therapists' controlling and blaming behaviors and patients' dependent behaviors. In addition, we found that AFT facilitated increases in patient and therapist expressiveness and therapist affirmation, and several of these changes were linked to positive treatment outcome. These findings suggest a movement away from negative interactional cycles of therapist blaming or controlling and patient submitting and toward more positive cycles of therapist affirmation and patient and therapist mutual expression of their inner experience. This study provides support for the idea that AFT can help therapist trainees to become more skilled at navigating challenging moments in therapy in a way that helps both patient and therapist regulate and communicate their emotions. As we discuss further in the next section, facilitating this emotion coregulation is a central aim of the AFT approach.

Principles of Alliance-Focused Training

The main goal of alliance-focused training is to improve therapists' abilities to navigate alliance ruptures by strengthening their emotion regulation skills—including their ability to facilitate bidirectional emotion regulation (or coregulation) between patient and therapist. As we discussed in Chapter 3, regulating emotions in an interpersonal context like therapy involves recognizing, accepting, and being capable of exploring both one's own emotions and the emotions of the other, even when those emotions are painful or aversive. In this process, the therapist is not only regulating his or her own emotions, and thereby modeling emotion regulation to the patient, but also interacting with the patient in a way that facilitates emotion regulation for both members of the dyad. Here we are suggesting self and interpersonal (or co-) regulation. In other words, through my interaction with my patient, I become more aware of both my patient's emotions and my own emotions. This awareness helps me to better understand my patient's reactions and my own. With this understanding, I am better able to explore our reactions in an open, collaborative, attuned manner rather than pushing against or pulling away from my patient in frustration or anxiety. This, in turn, invites the patient to participate in a parallel process.

To teach therapists-in-training these skills, AFT is grounded in several key principles. The first three of these principles center on focusing trainees' attention. Research comparing novices and experts in various fields has found that novices have more difficulty recognizing patterns and processes (see Caspar, 2017). For example, a study of inexperienced behavior therapists found that they neglected to pay attention to nonverbal patient behaviors because they were so focused on what they were going to say next (Caspar, 1995). In AFT, we want to help trainees shift their focus in three specific ways: to recognize the relational context, to emphasize self-exploration, and to focus on their experience in the here and now.

The first principle is to *recognize the relational context*. Trainees are often very focused on their patients, almost as a problem or puzzle to be solved as the trainee tries to pin down a diagnosis and a treatment plan. We want to shift their view from just trying to solve the problem of the patient toward attending to and being curious about the space between the patient and therapist. The patient and therapist are constantly moving toward, against, and away from each other—two subjects with needs, wishes, and fears. If the patient is not cooperating with the therapist's suggestions, and the therapist is responding by either doubling down on their approach in a confrontational way or anxiously generating many other suggestions in an effort to win the patient over, we can encourage the therapist to pause and take a step out of this entanglement and recognize what is happening. We can shift the trainee's focus away from the specific content that the trainee and patient are disagreeing about and toward observing the nature of the interpersonal struggle that is taking place.

The second principle is to *emphasize self-exploration*: to expand the trainee's awareness of his or her own experience of what is happening. We want to help trainees recognize and appreciate how their own feelings of anxiety or frustration or boredom—or for that matter, affection and fondness—are impacting how they respond to and interact with the patient. When trainees focus on a patient as a problem, they often miss their own contributions to what is happening. For example, a therapist notes that a patient is defensive and fails to recognize how this defensiveness is in response to the therapist being critical. Or a trainee recognizes that he or she is being critical but then becomes mired in his or her own self-criticism about this criticalness in a way that prevents the trainee from being attentive and attuned to the patient—a process that has been referred to as hindering self-awareness (Williams, Hayes, & Fauth, 2008). Perhaps a trainee believes that they have "broken a rule" by failing to follow part of a treatment protocol or making an ill-timed interpretation, and in response becomes overly and rigidly adherent to the treatment approach in a manner that the patient experiences as unresponsive or robotic. In AFT, we want to encourage trainees to look inward with curiosity and openness, as exploring what is happening for the trainee will shed light on what is happening with the patient. Feeling frustrated by a patient does not mean the patient is bad or the therapist is bad; it means something is going on that is causing the therapist to feel thwarted. Nurturing curiosity about this experience (What is happening between the patient and the therapist? What might this tell us about the therapist's goals and the patient's goals?) will be infinitely more useful than trying to ignore, deny, or disparage the therapist's experience.

The third principle is to *establish an experiential focus* on the here and now. There is always the risk that in looking at the space between the patient and therapist and what is happening inside the therapist, the therapist will intellectualize. Trainees are often very comfortable getting in their heads in their efforts to understand their patients and themselves. We want them to connect more with their bodily felt sense (Gendlin, 1982). We want them to take advantage of the fact that their bodies may be able to tell them what is going on in a more immediate and powerful way than their conscious cognitions. This orientation toward the experiential will not only give trainees access to more useful data, as it were, but also help them in session, when the ability to tune in quickly to what is transpiring will help them respond to an alliance rupture with a nimble sensitivity.

The remaining three principles concern the supervisor's focus—principles that the AFT supervisor needs to keep at the forefront of their mind. First in this set is the idea to *practice in simulated conditions and under pressure*. Trainees will be best equipped to handle the pressure of a moment of rupture if they have practiced how to handle tense, stressful moments "under pressure." As we noted in Chapter 1, practicing under pressure can help prevent choking in an athletic or academic performance (e.g., Beilock, 2010; Oudejans, 2008). As we describe next, we draw on several strategies in AFT that can be anxiety-provoking for trainees. Although anxiety that is too high is not conducive to learning, some anxiety is important, as it will better prepare trainees for the strong feelings that can arise in a therapy session. When thinking about how much to challenge trainees, it is important that supervisors—and peers in a group supervision—work within the trainee's ZPD (Vygotsky, 1930/1980) and provide sufficient scaffolding. If the trainee is not challenged at all, he or she will not learn and grow; but if the trainee is pushed too far too quickly, with an intervention that is aimed beyond the trainee's ZPD, then the training experience will be overwhelming for the trainee and most likely ineffective.

The principle of practicing under pressure is important to explain to trainees so that they have some understanding of the rationale for AFT tasks, which ask a great deal of trainees. This principle is also important for AFT supervisors to hold on to, particularly because we usually conduct AFT in groups; asking trainees to explore difficult moments in therapy in the presence of their peers can be very challenging for both trainees and supervisors. We may be tempted to let them off the hook, and we need to remember the value of practicing under pressure so that we can tolerate it ourselves.

The next principle is to *be responsive*. Similar to the supervision literature referenced earlier in this chapter, in AFT we recognize the necessity of being responsive to trainees' developmental level and anxiety. Each trainee presents with their own developmental trajectory and own personal and cultural history. As supervisors, we need to pay attention to how a trainee is doing so that we can adjust as needed. In a qualitative study of 36 former AFT trainees, the importance of supervisors providing support, validation, and a safe space to explore negative feelings (Eubanks, Muran, Dreher, et al., 2019) emerged as a theme. Although the majority of trainees who participated in the study reported experiencing these factors in AFT, some expressed the desire for greater support and a stronger sense of safety. Insufficient support could take different forms. One trainee described experiencing "benign neglect" from supervisors who were overextended. Another trainee observed that supervisors were not as open and vulnerable as they had asked trainees to be, which, the trainee noted, is "kind of weird when you want to create a very safe and creative space" (Eubanks, Muran, Dreher, et al., 2019, p. 128). The most concerning form of insufficient support is when the supervisor is experienced as invalidating or critical. Trainees who felt that they were not a good fit for AFT appeared to be most likely to report feeling misunderstood or invalidated by the supervisor, suggesting that supervisors should be especially attentive and responsive to trainees who are struggling to acclimate to the supervisor's approach.

It is imperative that, as supervisors, we create a secure base before we ask our trainees to take risks in supervision. We need to develop a culture of openness and willingness to be vulnerable by encouraging trainees to share their honest, personal reactions in supervision and by discouraging efforts to "show off" their knowledge or insight. We also can model openness and receptivity by showing our own videos at the outset of supervision and giving trainees the opportunity to give us feedback. Supervisors can engage in this useful exercise periodically, both to contribute to creating a supportive and open culture with trainees and to remain empathically connected to the anxiety that showing one's videos can engender.

The final principle is of AFT is to *practice what you preach* (so-called walk the talk) by attending as closely to the supervisory alliance as you do to the therapeutic alliance. As previously highlighted, we need to pay attention to the relational context between ourselves and our supervisees; be aware of our own wishes, needs, and concerns in supervision; and make sure that we do not get so caught up in helping our trainees with their cases that we neglect what we and the trainees are experiencing in the supervisory alliance in the here and now. We need to attend to possible ruptures in the supervisory alliance and address them in a manner that is sensitive to our trainees' developmental levels.

More research on supervisory ruptures is needed, but we can make some observations based on our clinical experience and the qualitative study of AFT trainees' experiences (Eubanks, Muran, Dreher, et al., 2019). Supervisors and trainees may experience confrontation ruptures in which the trainee pushes back against the supervisor's suggestions (similar to the 3RS code of *reject intervention*) or challenges the supervisor's authority (similar to *complaint about the therapist*), and the supervisor may feel pulled to respond with criticism or defensiveness. Trainees who are struggling with a case may put pressure on the supervisor (*control/pressure*) to quickly help them solve the problems they are experiencing with their patient. The supervisor may conclude that this is a form of parallel process, particularly when a supervisee's demands mirror the demands that their patient is making on them. However, in the AFT model, just as we caution therapists against moving too quickly to the resolution strategy of *linking the rupture to larger interpersonal patterns in the patient's other relationships,* we advise supervisors not to jump too quickly to an interpretation of parallel process, especially if making that link is a way for the supervisor to manage their own anxiety about exploring a supervisory rupture—a form of supervisor withdrawal. The supervisor should start by collaboratively exploring what is happening in the here and now of supervision and be open to exploring what is unique and particular about the interaction unfolding between supervisor and supervisee rather than rushing to contain it with a label.

Confrontation ruptures in supervision can be very challenging and uncomfortable, but we suspect that the most common types of rupture in supervision are withdrawal ruptures. Well-meaning supervisors may be so reluctant to say something that might be perceived as critical, especially with an anxious trainee, that they might sit back and allow a trainee to consume large parts of the supervision with extended descriptions of the patient and events in his or her life (similar to *avoidant storytelling*) or overly intellectualized applications of theory to the case (similar to *abstract communication*). A supervisor might be so pleased that a trainee is paying attention and following the supervisor's direction that the supervisor fails to recognize that the supervisee is just trying to appease the supervisor and does not really understand or agree with the supervisor's approach to the case (similar to *deferential and appeasing*). Or a supportive supervisor may be reluctant to acknowledge—even to themselves—concerns or criticisms that they experience regarding a trainee, and these concerns may then "leak" in ways that negatively impact the supervision. As one trainee described in reference to a supervisor who was not forthcoming with personal views, "The feeling I got was that the criticism was too harsh to be delivered directly, so that it was only implied" (Eubanks, Muran, Dreher, et al., 2019, p. 127).

Consistent with AFT's emphasis on viewing ruptures as dyadic phenomena to which therapists also contribute, AFT supervisors need to attend to the role they play in creating or exacerbating supervisory ruptures and be willing to discuss this with their trainees (the resolution strategy of *acknowledging one's contribution to a rupture*). Supervisors have to be comfortable enough in their role that they can tolerate not having all the answers and sometimes being wrong but still communicate a sense of fundamental self-assuredness that meets trainees' developmentally appropriate need for a secure base. The nonjudgmental, accepting, mindful awareness that we recommend for therapists is also helpful for supervisors, as it encourages a stance of recognizing and owning one's limitations with compassion rather than judgment.

It is also important that once supervisors acknowledge and discuss a supervisory rupture, they take responsibility for actually responding to the trainees' concerns. Awareness of a rupture should lead to changes in behavior. As one trainee lamented, "Good conversations occurred but there was very little change" (Eubanks, Muran, Dreher, et al., 2019, p. 128).

Attending to supervisor ruptures can be particularly challenging in group supervision, as we have to balance drawing trainees' attention to how they are contributing to a rupture with making sure we do not shame or embarrass trainees in front of their peers. If a supervisor is struggling with how to broach a supervisory rupture with a specific trainee in a group context, one option is to schedule an individual meeting with that trainee to begin exploring the rupture. However, the supervisor still needs to be mindful that any rupture taking place in a group setting impacts the other members of the group. If all resolution efforts happen outside the group meetings, the supervisor might be failing to address the needs of other group members, as well as inadvertently communicating an avoidant response to ruptures.

The process of emotional coregulation that we are trying to encourage between trainee and patient should also play out between trainee and supervisor and can develop among trainees in a group supervision as trainees work together to become more aware of and curious about their differing experiences of a particular case. In recent years, our growing awareness of the importance of supervisors attending to the supervisory alliance has pointed us toward the need for supervision for supervisors, so they too have a safe space to explore supervisory ruptures (Eubanks, Muran, Dreher, et al., 2019).

Strategies of Alliance-Focused Training

AFT uses two types of strategies to fulfill the six principles just described. The first is *didactic training* (which can facilitate emotion regulation and mental representation). Specifically, this training includes orienting trainees to the concepts of the alliance and alliance ruptures. Training can also include discussion of various theoretical lenses, such as resistance, defense, countertransference, interpersonal transformations, vicious circles, reinforcement patterns, relational matrices, dissociative selves, experiential avoidance, and projective identification, to highlight a few examples. These lenses can provide some understanding of negative interpersonal process and, as some have argued (Aron, 1999), an emotion regulation effect on therapists' emotions by providing a means of organizing their experience, which helps trainees to better manage their anxiety. Another organizing lens is the evidence-based stage-process model described in Chapter 2 of this volume, which suggests various pathways for how a rupture can be addressed and helps trainees develop effective mental representations of rupture resolution.

Training in various assessment tools can help trainees better understand and identify negative process and ways to better facilitate positive process. These tools include coding measures such as the Structural Analysis of Social Behavior (L. S. Benjamin, 1974), the Experiencing Scale (M. H. Klein, Mathieu-Coughlan, & Kiesler, 1986), Vocal Quality (Rice & Kerr, 1986), and our 3RS. Trainees have often told us that learning these coding systems informs their therapeutic work by increasing their sensitivity to subtle shifts in the therapeutic process. Not all supervisors will be part of a research program in which coders are regularly trained to reliable standards on coding measures, but supervisors can draw on these measures for useful language and examples. Learning to attend closely to what is unfolding can be a powerful training experience: I (CFE) can distinctly remember the "aha" moment when I first grasped the idea of paying attention to the process, and not just the content, of a session. Giving trainees concrete descriptions and labels for common rupture markers such as those provided in the 3RS can help trainees more quickly recognize when a rupture is occurring.

Once trainees start seeing therapy cases, supervision can shift from didactic to *experiential training* (which facilitates awareness through practice). We typically begin our AFT sessions with a mindfulness exercise, such as attending to the breath, in order to help orient everyone—both trainees and supervisors—to the type of nonjudgmental, present-focused awareness that is central to our approach. We also encourage trainees to identify ways to practice mindfulness outside of supervision, such as before therapy sessions, to further support their skills of acceptance and awareness.

After grounding ourselves with a mindfulness exercise, we usually move to videotape analysis of a trainee's therapy session. Trainees are encouraged to bring moments of rupture for analysis—their most vulnerable moments, rather than their greatest successes—which is one reason why it is so important for the supervisor to create an environment that feels safe for trainees. As we watch the tape together, we all try to be attuned to what we are experiencing. The trainee can benefit from becoming more aware of what he or she was experiencing in the room with the patient and starting to put words to that experience, which facilitates mental representation and emotion regulation. Sharing reactions with other trainees is also valuable. A trainee may receive important validation that they are not alone in having a negative reaction to a patient. A trainee may become more aware of feelings that they have avoided when a peer is able to acknowledge the feelings. For example, trainees who are afraid to admit, even to themselves, that they feel angry with a patient may be able to recognize this feeling when a peer voices it. Or trainees might realize that something more is going on than they realized when the patient whom they find frustrating arouses sympathy or affection from other members of the group. Different reactions from different group members also shed light on how complex an interaction can be—how multiple processes can be at play at one time—and this can lead to a better understanding of the richness and diversity of conflicting thoughts and feelings a patient may be experiencing and the variety of reactions the patient may elicit from others in the patient's life. The variety of reactions can highlight the idiosyncratic nature of an individual response—that everyone is different and each has a unique interpersonal and emotional history. This concept is important to recognize and to take into account.

The video analysis will often lead to identification of a moment that is more difficult or challenging, a place where the therapist feels stuck. This can provide an opportunity for awareness-oriented exercises, which draw on techniques similar to gestalt empty-chair and two-chair exercises. Trainees might be asked to play their patient while another group member plays the therapist. This gives trainees the opportunity to gain a new appreciation of and greater insight into their patient's experiences while seeing different ways of responding to the patient that they may not have considered. I (CFE) recall role-playing one of my patients in a group supervision during my training. As other trainees took turns sitting in the therapist's chair, I channeled my patient's critical, skeptical stance and realized how removed I felt from the therapists, and how almost pitiful their attempts to reach me seemed; I could see them coming from a mile away. This experience surprised me and gave me a completely different sense of my patient—a quiet, subdued young woman who also, I was realizing, was determined not to be controlled or intruded upon by others.

Alternatively, trainees might be asked to play themselves in an exercise while another group member plays the patient, giving the trainee the opportunity to engage in deliberate and reflective practice by experimenting with metacommunication that feels risky. We can encourage the trainee to say whatever comes to their mind without filtering. This experience frequently yields greater insights, as trainees make better contact with feelings they had been trying to keep at bay, such as frustration with a patient or self-criticism or anxiety. We often find that trainees have been censoring themselves excessively out of fear of making a mistake or harming a patient, and when encouraged to express the thoughts or feelings they have been holding back, trainees bring forward expressions of their experience that are completely appropriate to share with the patient and hold great promise for moving the treatment forward.

The most challenging form of role-play is the trainee playing both patient and therapist roles by moving from one chair to the other. This technique can be very powerful, potentially revealing implicit expectations and fears held, but because it requires so much of the trainee, potentially evoking too much anxiety regarding performance and disclosure, we usually reserve it for trainees who have had some experience with less demanding role-plays and seem ready for this challenge.

The overarching goal of the role-play exercises for trainees is to become more aware of what they and their patient are experiencing in a moment of rupture. That greater awareness will facilitate emotional coregulation, which will help the trainee to become unstuck and better able to move, explore, and navigate their way through an alliance rupture. With awareness-oriented role-plays, the word *play* is important: we want trainees to feel free to experiment, to take creative risks, to *play* with different approaches in a way that they might be afraid to with a real patient. Out of this greater freedom may come greater recognition of new options and avenues, such that trainees are no longer trapped in a vicious cycle of a rupture. As one trainee noted, awareness-oriented role-plays facilitate "speed learning" (Eubanks, Muran, Dreher, et al., 2019).

The Structure of Alliance-Focused Training

Our supervisory sessions run 75 minutes and follow a specific structure, beginning with a mindfulness exercise and then a check-in with the trainees about how their cases are progressing. From there, one case is identified as the focus of the supervision session. Typically, we focus on a case that is posing a particular problem and for which the most recent video-recorded session that illustrates this problem is available. The video provides the basis for defining the rupture event for an awareness exercise. Sometimes a trainee will describe a problem with such clarity that a supervisor might forego asking to see the video and move directly to inviting an exercise. When it comes to playing video segments, we often invite trainees to provide narration of what they remember experiencing during the session to the best of their ability as they watch it in the group setting. For the other trainees, we often direct their attention to their emotional awareness rather than exhibiting their conceptual skills, as conceptualizing too often results in competition in the group and defensiveness in the presenter. We recognize that in the final analysis, the resolution of rupture is both "personal" (depending on the trainee's own history and experience) and "interpersonal" (requiring the participation of the patient). We conclude each session by debriefing the group, gathering any final impressions, and checking in with the trainee who presented to see where they are experientially with regard to the group and the case presented.

Illustration: Alliance-Focused Training in Action

In this section, we illustrate many of the principles and strategies of AFT by drawing on an actual supervision session that JCM led with four trainees in our research program. We present work with a trainee, identified here as James, who was struggling in the termination phase of a time-limited treatment. The focus of the transcript that follows is on the work around an awareness exercise.

JAMES: I've been thinking a lot about termination, for example, and noticing that I wasn't bringing it up. And so my patient came in last week and basically started off by saying like, "Are you aware that your entire profession in a sham?" and "What you're going into is like a bunch of lies?" So then it became sort of like he was trying to kill everything that we'd done to this point, like right before we finish basically. We spent the latter half of the session talking about control, I guess, and his need for control. I tried to make him aware of the fact that him coming and saying that my profession is a pack of lies is a way of controlling the experience to a certain extent. So I think I feel like there was something there, but I don't know. I'm feeling like a little bit de-skilled by him or something like that. I'm not sure kind of what it is.

TRAINEE 1: Like his power in some sense?

JAMES: Yeah. And I guess like my fantasy or my fear about termination is that he's just going to continue in this very rigid way. What he said directly was this kind of therapy, whatever you're doing here, may be effective for some people, but for people like me it's not effective. He doesn't give up easily. He likes to prove himself to be right.

SUPERVISOR: So how did the session end?

JAMES: It's funny, I'm having a hard time recalling specifically. I mean, I think it ended with like an acknowledgment that, you know, on my part I was trying to push some awareness of his like, his need to control things. And he, I guess he is a little bit more willing to see things from my perspective than he was when we started. So he's able to leave that kind of a question. I don't remember really where we ended.

James is clearly dealing with a challenging patient. This patient is contributing to a confrontation rupture as he disparages James's chosen profession. At the same time, by criticizing the entire field of psychology, the patient is also avoiding being completely direct with the therapist about his complicated feelings about their work together, consistent with a withdrawal rupture. This mixture of hostile confrontation and intellectualized withdrawal can be confusing and disorienting for the therapist. It is leaving James feeling "de-skilled," and his struggle to remember the end of the session points to his difficulties regulating his own emotions with this patient. The supervisor sees this as an important opportunity to use an awareness-oriented role-play to help James become more aware of what is happening between him and the patient. As James has experience doing role-plays, the supervisor determines that his developmental level warrants moving directly into the most challenging form of role-play, in which the trainee plays both the patient and the therapist roles.

SUPERVISOR:	So, okay, so let's try this. [Supervisor moves an empty chair in front of James.] Try to imagine he's there in front of you. And try to articulate this experience of feeling disempowered. And I always think it's important to try to link it. So this is a tricky thing because you don't want to get caught into a blame game, but you do want your metacommunications to be really grounded in specific behaviors so that it's something really tangible.
JAMES:	And this is, as an aside, this is what—the problem with metacommunicating with him is that it gets so intellectualized because things that are happening are sort of like kind of paranoid and intellectualized themselves. And I start presenting the evidence while it's happening, and five minutes later I'm thinking, what am I talking about? That's part of the feeling of being de-skilled.
SUPERVISOR:	Okay, which is I think important because I think that having that awareness down the road will be important to help ground yourself again. So let's just begin and play it out. Take a moment to gather yourself and imagine him sitting across from you.

James is somewhat anxious about engaging in the role-play and notes how he has difficulty maintaining his awareness in the moment in the session. The supervisor addresses the trainee's concerns in way that is responsive to his anxiety and to his skill level by balancing support—validation that even a delayed awareness of an intellectualization process is useful and grounding—with encouragement to move forward with practicing under pressure.

JAMES ROLE-PLAYING HIMSELF AS THERAPIST:	"So, um, you know, I'm noticing that a lot of what we've been talking about today is sort of whether or not therapy in general or this therapy in particular is useful to you. And what I hear you saying is that this therapy that we're doing here is not effective, and that therapy in general is only effective for people who are sheep, as you say. Um, I guess I'm noticing that really leaves me completely out of

the picture. So, like, it doesn't matter what I do here, um . . . there's nothing I can do." [James moves to sit in the other chair.]

JAMES ROLE-PLAYING HIS PATIENT: "Um, I don't know what you mean. What, how, how's that important?" [James moves back to the therapist chair.]

JAMES AS THERAPIST: "Um, I guess it's important because I'm trying to make sense of the work that we're engaged in here. You're sitting here telling me that it's pointless, and I guess I'm trying to keep it together." [James turns to the supervisor.] I don't know if I would really say that.

SUPERVISOR: Okay, so what's going on for you right now?

JAMES: I guess I'm aware of not wanting to make myself overly vulnerable with him because I think it's like so easy for him to reject vulnerability because he kind of detests it so much himself, but also it's very hard to put myself in a position of weakness with him.

By taking a risk in the role-play and metacommunicating to the patient about how hard it is to "keep it together" in the face of the patient's critical attack, James becomes more aware of his fear of being vulnerable with this patient. This is an important advance in self-awareness, and the supervisor encourages James to explore it further:

SUPERVISOR: So how might you do that? What would be weak? When you say make yourself vulnerable, how so?

JAMES: Um, I guess by articulating to him the way in which he sort of like actively seeks to undermine any power that I have in the relationship. So acknowledging with him that is actually happening seems to me to sort of hand over the reins. But even as I'm saying that, it doesn't seem a weak move.

As James further explores his own fears of expressing vulnerability to his patient, he becomes aware of another feeling—a sense that sharing his reaction to his patient is not necessarily a display of weakness. The supervisor responds by validating James's recognition that there is a strength in owning his reactions but then encourages James to continue to explore his apprehension about metacommunicating with his patient.

SUPERVISOR: Yeah, I mean, I have two thoughts. One is that we talk about acts of freedom: in some sense I feel it's like an act of power in a way to be able to own feeling useless or rendered useless. So I don't necessarily see that as a vulnerable position. So that's one thing. The other thing: There's something else that you were saying that I think is important. I'm trying to remember exactly how you put it, but you're really reticent to do that because of your fear of him just being rejecting.

JAMES: Yeah, and he rejects that in himself so readily.

SUPERVISOR: And I think like that's like an important aspect of the meta-communication too. Not necessarily the interpretive part that you do that to yourself, but the part that, you know, I'm also wary of making this disclosure for fear of you just being very rejecting and dismissive of what I'm saying and of me, as a person and a professional.

For trainees, it can be very helpful to learn that when they have complex or mixed feelings, such as both wanting to share something with a patient and fearing what will happen when they do, they do not have to force those feelings to neatly align. A metacommunication that acknowledges how one feels simultaneously pushed and pulled can be illuminating for the patient and liberating for the therapist. The challenge is to try to put words to a full spectrum of feelings—however mixed or conflicting.

JAMES: Okay. So then it could be something along the lines of: [James as therapist]: "I'm aware of, as we talk about this that like I'm sort of hesitant to agree with the way you're characterizing the profession and this therapy, because I have some sense that you're very rejecting of any weakness or any vulnerability."

SUPERVISOR: So what's going on for you now?

JAMES: I'm not sure that's um . . .

TRAINEE 2: . . . clear enough?

JAMES: Yeah, yeah.

James is still struggling to metacommunicate in the role-play, which suggests that he is still having difficulty regulating his emotions.

SUPERVISOR: See I think you use—back to what we were talking about before about your own anxiety and how that kind of muddies up the water: It makes it hard to be clear and succinct about things. So say a little bit more about what you're afraid of—what the anxiety is about.

JAMES: He like—the anxiety is really about like how, how nitpicky he is about words. I mean he picks apart the things that I say all the time—especially when it gets to be higher stakes moments in the session. Uh, so there's that, but the fact is that I'm used to that.

TRAINEE 3: He does that all the time!

Validation from other group members is very helpful and extremely important if trainees are going to feel safe making themselves vulnerable in front of
the group.

JAMES: Yeah, and there are many moments where I notice that I'm
                not really making much sense.

SUPERVISOR: Well, it's one thing being accustomed, but it still creates
                defensiveness—puts you on guard. I think that's important
                as well. And you do feel on guard and it makes it sort of dif-
                ficult to be useful, in so many ways, even in terms of being
                clear about what you're saying.

JAMES: Uh huh, so then maybe metacommunicating more about
                the defensiveness is more useful.

The supervisor is helping James recognize his own defensiveness in his
interactions with his patient. This could easily be experienced by a trainee as
a criticism, so it is imperative that the supervisor proceed thoughtfully and in
a way that the trainee experiences as supportive and validating. In addition to
being aware of words, tone of voice, and body language, the supervisor can
enlist the group's help. Feedback from group members can feel less threatening than feedback from the supervisor, and it helps to keep group members
engaged when they are not the focus of the discussion. Of course, the supervisor should do this only if they have already cultivated a supportive atmosphere in the group so that group members do not use this as an opportunity
to try to one-up each other.

SUPERVISOR: It's interesting. What did you all experience when James
                started the role-play?

TRAINEE 3:   I really felt for you. I think this patient is impossible, and
                the way you are still hanging in there with him—I couldn't
                do that.

TRAINEE 1:   I felt something sort of similar. I felt protective of you.

TRAINEE 2:   I noticed—it seemed like, when you played him and then
                went back to playing yourself, you went right to like trying
                to justify why you were doing what you were doing. You
                kind of moved away from metacommunication and to a more
                defensive position.

JAMES: Huh, yeah.

SUPERVISOR: I think the defensiveness is insidious here.

JAMES: Yeah, totally!

SUPERVISOR: It's subtle: Before you know it, you're cloaked in it again.

The supervisor, building off the observations of the trainees, points to James's
defensiveness. But he proceeds gently: by referring to "the defensiveness" as
a process that James can be cloaked in, the supervisor avoids equating James

with his defensive reaction and helps James stand outside his defensive reaction to look at it. This distancing makes it easier for James to be less defensive about being defensive. It also helps create space for James to explore how the defensiveness serves multiple functions, both protecting him and enabling him to tolerate staying in the room with the patient but also contributing to a barrier that makes it harder for him to be fully present in the session.

JAMES: And I think that explains the distance I'm feeling sort of. It's weird because I guess in my mind I imagine that more work with him would make me sort of less defensive about how attacking he is.

SUPERVISOR: Well, I think they're both true in a way. I mean, I think you've developed a thicker skin, but a thicker skin means [chuckling] a better defensive skin. Um, they're both true, actually. You've developed a hardiness to him, but that doesn't mean that you should become oblivious to the attacks that are continuing.

JAMES: Right.

SUPERVISOR: It sucks! This is really hard.

The supervisor, aware of the relational context of supervision, tries to make sure James feels safe and supported by validating James's experience of how challenging it is to regulate and communicate about his feelings with this patient.

JAMES: Yeah, yeah, to communicate in a simple way is hard.

SUPERVISOR: Yeah.

JAMES: So okay, he's says that like the field of psychology is corrupt and the therapy is useless. Then I'm just not as surprised that he's saying that, which in a way is a bit defensive, right?

James is now more aware of his defensive reaction but is still feeling stuck and unsure how to proceed, as he keeps feeling pulled to join the patient's intellectualized way of communicating at an abstract level by talking about psychology or psychotherapy in general. Next, the supervisor encourages James to use metacommunication to shift the therapeutic focus to the immediate relational context—to talk about what is happening between the patient and him right now.

SUPERVISOR: Yeah. But you can ask, "Why are you bringing this up now?" And "What does this mean about our work?" Or, "What's going on?" [laughter] "What's up with this?" You know? Make it personal.

JAMES: Okay.

SUPERVISOR: I do think it's always a challenge to make it personal. We don't want to be overly narcissistic, but it is personal.

Trainees can be uncomfortable metacommunicating about their own internal experience of the therapeutic relationship. They often worry about shifting the focus too much onto themselves. The supervisor anticipates that concern here and offers some reassurance that James has good reason to try to shift the focus to how the patient's words are impacting him.

JAMES:	So something along the lines of like saying: "I notice we're getting to the end of the session, and most of the session today has been discussion about the uselessness of therapy, um, or the, how useless therapy can be. And I'm also noticing that we're having this discussion at the end of the therapy itself, like we're getting closer to the end." [Pause]
SUPERVISOR:	Yeah.
JAMES AS THERAPIST:	I'm not sure I have a sense of what you're trying to convey. That I can't help you? Is that what you mean? [Pause. James turns to the supervisor.] It doesn't touch the defensiveness though. Not at all.
SUPERVISOR:	I think the bottom line is you feel kind of shut down.
JAMES:	Yes.
SUPERVISOR:	Human relations are a tricky business. And this is who he is; this is why he's here to be—to be able to relate better to others, and this is what he does to put people on guard, shut the other person down and out. And now you feel shut out.
JAMES:	Yeah.
SUPERVISOR:	But when you make a statement like that, then check how does he process it? Don't defend it. Find out—"Okay, so I just told you that you rendered me useless. How did you experience that?"

The supervisor has noted a link between the way the patient is with James and how the patient behaves in his other relationships. This insight can be a helpful framework for the therapist, but the supervisor does not encourage the therapist to share this with the patient yet. He encourages James to explore the patient's experience in the here and now—to regulate his own defensive reaction by being curious about how the patient is experiencing what James is saying in this moment.

JAMES AS THERAPIST:	"What is your experience of my saying that?"
SUPERVISOR:	Right. Stay with the details of the interactions. Keep working it. And when you find yourself getting defensive say, "Oh, I'm becoming aware of myself getting really defensive."

JAMES:	Okay. He would become very defensive in that. Like he would definitely move to saying like um, "Well, you know, I think I've been very open here. You know, I've definitely shared a lot of my problems and my difficulties."
SUPERVISOR:	Well, so then, "It seems like you're feeling criticized by what I just said. Um, so it feels like I pushed you back, and maybe I did. You know, maybe I did." I mean, there is reality to that. You are calling him on it. So you are giving a little bit of a pushback. So if he does that, okay. So now we've explained this part. "Yeah, you're right, okay, I just pushed you back. You're being defensive because I just pushed you back. Now what do you think?" [laughter]
JAMES:	It's funny because there's oscillations, um, because there are moments when I like, really, you know, like reach out empathically to him because when he gets kind of defensive like that, I want to acknowledge that he actually has, you know, he has gone through a lot. There have been moments when he's been crying, you know, like that's a very hard position for him to take.
SUPERVISOR:	Yeah. And you could say, "This is difficult for me because I feel this impulse to try to defend, and show the importance of some of the work we've done, and I've seen you make yourself vulnerable. I've seen you do these things. But look at me trying to like to defend that right now. Obviously I'm feeling kind of under attack." So you're laying it all bare.
JAMES:	Yeah. Hmm.
SUPERVISOR:	And it seems all so simple, but it's not easy.
TRAINEE 3:	No, this is so hard.
SUPERVISOR:	Right, because of the damn anxiety. [laughter] But, you know, that's okay, so that's the human condition, right? That's what you're working with, so you find yourself going off task and you're like, oh shit, I don't know, okay, I'm feeling really anxious right now. I feel myself moving away. So you can just do that internally, or you can do that externally. But all to get back to the moment.
JAMES:	Hmm, you know, what's interesting is that I hadn't, like I hadn't really been aware of how the defensiveness is really just like a representation of the anxiety. Um, and I hadn't been so aware that I was being more defensive with him, in these kind of more subtle ways.
SUPERVISOR:	Now, I also think that we affect change on so many different levels. I also don't want to take away how—I think

you've also been really important to him and effective because you've been resilient and caring at the same time.

TRAINEE 2:   Yeah, you have really hung in there with him.

TRAINEE 1:   I think that's really powerful. He hasn't had that before. He's so used to being rejected or ignored. I think all this hostility is his way of trying to deal with losing you.

Next, the supervisor agrees that the trainee's interpretation of the patient's behavior could be right but does not want that to become the focus in a way that forecloses more exploration of the patient and therapist's immediate experience. He emphasizes the importance of continuing to unpack the many layers of experience and gently encourages James to have realistic expectations of what can be done in the few sessions he and his patient have left.

SUPERVISOR: I think that that's all true too. It's layered. So it works on one level, and there's still another level which you got to still work to unpack things. And you may run out of time because it's 30 sessions, and you just have so much space to work with. Okay?

JAMES: Yeah, okay. There's definitely more for me to be aware of at this point. . . .

As can be seen from this illustration, the AFT supervisor strives to provide support and to promote expression—all at once. The supervisor provides support by validating the trainee's experience and helping the trainee to conceptualize what is unfolding between the trainee and the patient. The supervisor challenges the trainee by encouraging the trainee to keep exploring both the trainee's and his patient's experience of the process by practicing under pressure. In a group supervision setting, the AFT supervisor also balances focusing on one trainee with engaging the other trainees in the group, minding group cohesion. This transcript illustrates the notion of *scaffolding*—the use of "support points" by the supervisor to permit work in the ZPD. It also illustrates *responsiveness* by the supervisor to the trainee's current level of anxiety and their supervisory alliance.

CODA

What We Have Learned From Other Training Models

There is growing recognition in the field that supervision needs to focus on identifying, targeting, and measuring trainees' progress toward competency in specific therapeutic skills. There is also increasing attention to the skills that supervisors need to possess, such as responsiveness and humility, which help the supervisor build a strong supervisory alliance that provides trainees with a secure base.

What the Research Says About AFT

Research on AFT has demonstrated that therapists who receive AFT can achieve patient outcomes comparable with therapists receiving supervision in other approaches and that AFT may be more successful at retaining patients in therapy, that integrating AFT principles into CBT may improve outcomes for some patients, and that providing AFT as an adjunct to CBT supervision leads to positive changes in patient and therapist interpersonal process.

What Are the Organizing Principles of AFT?

AFT is grounded in principles that center on drawing the trainee's attention to the relational context, emphasizing self-exploration, and establishing an experiential focus. AFT also emphasizes the importance of practicing under pressure, of supervisor responsiveness, and of supervisors "practicing what they preach" by attending to the supervisory alliance and ruptures that emerge in supervision.

What Are the Essential Strategies of AFT?

The essential strategies of AFT include didactic training to facilitate emotion regulation and mental representation, and experiential training, which facilitates awareness through practice. Experiential training in AFT takes the form of mindfulness exercises, video analysis of rupture moments, and awareness-oriented role-plays.

6

A Way to Therapist Self-Care

Be sure to adjust your own oxygen mask before helping others.
—EVERY FLIGHT ATTENDANT EVERYWHERE

Throughout this book we have emphasized the importance of therapists paying close, mindful attention to both the patient's behavior and their own internal experience. This nonjudgmental awareness facilitates attunement with the patient and the ability to identify and not only repair an alliance rupture but also use a rupture as an entry point to a deeper understanding of the patient's underlying relational schemas or fundamental needs. Athletes and performers must take care of their bodies and minds to perform optimally; so must therapists. Therapy can be demanding work. Professional psychologists report high levels of work-related stress and burnout (Barnett, Baker, Elman, & Schoener, 2007; Smith & Moss, 2009). As Norcross and VandenBos (2018) observed, the emotional arousal that characterizes clinical interactions can be "simultaneously a curative agent for the client and a damaging one for the therapist" (p. 52). It is a very tall order to be attuned to both our patients and our own internal experience if we are drained, depleted, or demoralized.

SOME BASIC ATTITUDES

We have presented several ways in which pressure can impair our clinical performance: Our clinical judgment and decision making can become more

http://dx.doi.org/10.1037/0000182-007
Therapist Performance Under Pressure: Negotiating Emotion, Difference, and Rupture,
by J. C. Muran and C. F. Eubanks

narrow and rigid; we can rely excessively on biases and heuristics, and our emotions can color our beliefs and opinions; and we may remain unaware of how these factors are impacting us because of a lack of consistent and reliable feedback. As we noted in Chapter 1 of this volume, research on resilience (e.g., Bonanno, 2004) suggests that our ability to navigate stressful events depends largely on how we perceive or appraise them. Consistent with this idea, in this chapter we focus on how therapists view their patients and themselves in moments of rupture—on the attitudes we believe that therapists need to embrace to be in the best position to navigate challenging moments in therapy: maintaining humility, cultivating compassion, courting curiosity, being patient, and balancing our tendency toward the negative with positivity. Therapists who approach a rupture from a humble, compassionate, curious, patient, and balanced stance will be more aware of how pressure impacts them, better positioned to effectively regulate their emotions, and less vulnerable to the errors that can arise from anxiety or overconfidence.

Maintaining Humility

We conceptualize alliance ruptures as dyadic phenomena, coconstructed by patients and therapists. To identify and address ruptures in a productive and nondefensive way, it is essential that therapists acknowledge and take responsibility for their contributions to ruptures. This requires humility on the part of the therapist. By *humility*, we mean the recognition that we do not know everything and we never achieve a perfect understanding of the patient, the therapeutic process, or ourselves—we are always learning and working toward greater understanding. Furthermore, we are flawed, and we make mistakes. When there is a problem in the alliance, we recognize that we have played some part in it—we are always growing and working toward greater skillfulness as therapists.

As we noted in Chapter 1, Redelmeier, Ferris, Tu, Hux, and Schull (2001) suggested that maintaining greater humility was important to guard against factors such as overconfidence, unquestioning self-approval, and unawareness of the limits of one's judgment, which can increase the likelihood of clinical errors. The need for humility can be a straightforward one, in the form of excessive confidence in one's abilities. For example, in a survey of 129 therapists in private practice, when asked to compare their clinical skills to other mental health professionals, everyone in the sample rated themselves as above average, and more than 90% of the sample rated their clinical skills to be at or above the 75th percentile (Walfish, McAlister, O'Donnell, & Lambert, 2012).

Although therapists are certainly not immune to narcissism, clinical overconfidence can also be due to the way psychotherapy is typically practiced and assessed. Tracey, Wampold, Lichtenberg, and Goodyear (2014) observed that therapists often lack consistent, reliable feedback about the long-term effectiveness of their interventions with patients. Given that patients may defer to therapists and may be reluctant to fully voice their concerns with therapy (see

Rennie, 1994), therapists may not be aware of patient dissatisfaction. Other research indicates that therapists can be quite oblivious to their patients' dissatisfaction (Regan & Hill, 1992) and that this lack of awareness is associated with patients quitting therapy (Rhodes, Hill, Thompson, & Elliott, 1994). Alternatively, lack of reliable feedback for therapists may mean that even when a patient is fully satisfied with treatment, the therapist will never have the opportunity to learn that the patient's improvement could have been greater or faster had the therapist approached the case differently.

Therapists may also fall prey to excessive confidence, not because they place too much faith in their own clinical skills but because they trust too much in the effectiveness of the type of therapy they practice. According to social identity theory—a metatheory in social psychology—the self is defined largely in terms of membership in a group or groups (Mackie & Smith, 2015). Per a related concept—uncertainty-identity theory—social categorization is related to the desire to reduce uncertainty (Abrams, 2015). Identifying with a clearly defined group can provide group members with greater certainty about the appropriate way to behave. The challenges of doing therapy—the unpredictable ways patients can behave, the numerous paths therapists can take in response—may make therapy a fertile ground for practitioners to seek out group identities such as theoretical orientations that provide not only community but also affirmation that a particular approach to therapy is optimal. The fact that empirical investigations of bona fide therapies have failed to identify one therapeutic approach as consistently more efficacious than others (e.g., Wampold & Imel, 2015) suggests that a degree of humility about the type of therapy we practice is also in order.

According to research on therapist burnout, an important predictor is overinvolvement with patients, as measured by therapist self-report items such as "I feel that at times I'm working harder for change than the client" (J. Lee, Lim, Yang, & Lee, 2011, p. 254). Burnout is often conceptualized as comprising higher levels of emotional exhaustion and depersonalization and lower levels of personal accomplishment (Maslach & Jackson, 1981). Of interest, overinvolvement has been associated with greater emotional exhaustion and depersonalization but higher levels of personal accomplishment (J. Lee et al., 2011). In other words, working too hard for the patient is both draining and rewarding for therapists. This points to another form that therapist overconfidence or narcissism can take: an inflated sense of how much our patients need us. We may feel that we are so needed by our patients that we cannot take time for ourselves and practice appropriate self-care. What seem on the surface like selfless devotion to our patients may actually be more about serving our own need to be needed, and neglecting the fact that we have an ethical responsibility to practice self-care so that we are in optimal shape to work effectively with our patients (Barnett & Cooper, 2009; Maranzan et al., 2018). Ironically, for some therapists, embracing greater humility may take the form of engaging in more activities that seem self-indulgent, such as taking more time off work and getting together with friends.

Cultivating Compassion

Another attitude that is important for navigating pressured moments in therapy is compassion. As Rogers (1957) observed, for therapy to be effective, therapists need to work toward possessing and communicating positive regard for their patients and empathic understanding of their patients' experience. The importance of taking a warm, empathic, and compassionate stance toward one's patient is crucial in moments of rupture. Metacommunication about a rupture involves making a tension or difficulty in the therapeutic relationship explicit. If a therapist metacommunicates from a place of only anger and frustration, the patient is likely to feel criticized or attacked. Therapists can and inevitably will feel angry and frustrated at times, but these emotions need to exist in the context of a sense of compassion for the patient: a nonjudgmental openness to the patient's suffering and a desire to relieve that suffering (Gilbert, 2005). Therapists can cultivate compassion through emotion regulation strategies, such as self-awareness and reattribution of motive, or reframing the patient's behavior with the understanding that he or she may not be intentionally trying to be difficult (Wolf, Goldfried, & Muran, 2017). Even when a patient seems to be actively resisting the therapist's efforts—such as a patient who was mandated to treatment and does not want to cooperate—the therapist can draw on theory and case conceptualization to provide a larger framework for understanding the patient's behavior. For example, is a patient who refuses to cooperate trying to defend their autonomy and self-respect in the only way they know how? A thoughtful analysis of the links between the patient's wishes, fears, past experiences, and current behaviors can help the therapist to see the patient as complex and three-dimensional, and not just "difficult."

In addition to fostering compassion for their patients, therapists need to nurture compassion for themselves. Adequate self-care requires self-compassion (Maranzan et al., 2018). Maintaining humility and acknowledging one's contributions to ruptures require a particularly compassionate stance toward oneself: to be able to admit one's mistakes and shortcomings without surrendering to shame, and to be able to forgive oneself for mistakes so that anxious self-criticism does not get in the way of being present for the patient. Self-criticism can be deafening. Self-compassion facilitates compassion for the other by making space for the therapist to continue to hear and see the patient, even when the therapist realizes that he or she has made a poor choice. Self-compassion also provides an important form of modeling for the patient. For the patient who is afraid of making themselves vulnerable, seeing a therapist nondefensively acknowledge their contribution to a rupture and invite an exploration of what happened could provide a powerful corrective experience that challenges the patient's prior understanding of relationships (Christian, Safran, & Muran, 2012). The patient could experience firsthand how vulnerability does not have to lead to the destruction of the self or the relationship but, rather, can foster greater intimacy. Winnicott (1971) argued that children do not need perfect parents, that they actually benefit from "good enough" parenting that prepares them to deal with the frustrations of life. Similarly, we should not strive for the impossible goal of being perfect therapists. By being "good enough" therapists who inevitably fall short at times but are able to acknowledge and explore our missteps, we create opportunities for connection and growth for our patients and ourselves.

Courting Curiosity

As we discussed in Chapter 1, research on cognition and decision making has found that our thinking tends to become more rigid and narrow when we are under stress. It is important that we strive to counteract this tendency by continuously courting a curious stance toward our patients, as well as ourselves. Curiosity can help us guard against snap judgments and biases. Curiosity can also be a tool for maintaining engagement with a patient when we are struggling to feel compassion for them: If your empathy is running low, can you still be curious about your patient? Can you acknowledge that you find a patient irritating or boring and then be curious about that experience? What about this patient, and you, and the interaction between both of you in this moment, is giving rise to this experience? This orientation "to the details" of experience or behavior is consistent with perspectives presented by phenomenologists (Gendlin, 1982; Rogers, 1951), interpersonalists (E. A. Levenson, 1991; Sullivan, 1953), and behaviorists (S. C. Hayes, 2015). Darlene Ehrenberg (1992) and Donnel Stern (1997) encouraged a dialogic version of this orientation by suggesting that only in an "intimate" or "genuine" conversation with patients can therapists come to define their own prejudices, beliefs, or aspects of themselves.

The sense of curiosity we are referring to also draws on the notions of "beginner's mind" (S. Suzuki, 1970) and "mindfulness" (Kabat-Zinn, 1991/2013). This is not a curiosity that leads the therapist to pull away from the patient into abstract intellectualizations (markers of therapist withdrawal) but a movement toward greater engagement with the patient. In fact, curiosity can be a way not only to stay engaged when empathy is lacking but also a way toward developing greater empathy. There is a small but growing research literature on the concept of therapeutic presence (e.g., Geller, 2019). Therapeutic presence can be defined as "a state of being aware of and centered in oneself while maintaining attunement to and engagement with another person" (J. A. Hayes & Vinca, 2017, p. 86). Research suggests that therapeutic presence is positively associated with a better alliance and good treatment outcome (Geller, Greenberg, & Watson, 2010). Therapeutic presence is also associated with empathy (Geller et al., 2010), and it has been argued that, in fact, it is a prerequisite for empathy (J. A. Hayes & Vinca, 2017). Another way of thinking about therapeutic presence is as a form of intense curiosity: close attention to the patient's moment-to-moment experience in the therapy room. Such close attention will facilitate greater attunement to the patient, which is fertile ground for empathy. If "familiarity breeds contempt," curiosity breeds compassion.

Being Patient

Just as it is important to pay attention with mindful curiosity to what is unfolding moment by moment in the therapy room, particularly in moments of tension or strain, it is also important to hold on to the ability to take the long view. We can become so engaged in a moment of conflict that we fail to recognize that we have become stuck—in an enactment, a vicious cycle, or a self-defeating pattern. We have to be able to recognize this and disembed and see what is happening in a larger context. This requires patience: the ability to take a step back instead of immediately reacting. In a moment of conflict, we may feel the need to try to fix things, the urge to rush to soothe an angry patient and smooth over tension, or the impulse to defend ourselves when we feel we have been wronged. In a moment of stagnation, we may feel compelled to *do* something, anything, to assuage our sense of helplessness and uselessness in the face of a patient who is not getting better. In these moments, we would benefit from an attitude of patience that gives us space to pause, take a breath, and reflect on what we and the patient are experiencing.

One way to nurture an attitude of patience is to pay attention to the process and not just the content: to see not only what we and the patient are talking about but also *how* we are talking about it. The process is often more important than the content. A therapist may encourage an unassertive patient to assert themselves and fail to recognize that the therapist is telling the patient what to do in an overly didactic manner, the patient is doing their best to comply, and therefore even the patient's "successful" completion of an assertiveness homework assignment is actually another example of the patient deferring to and appeasing an authority figure. Or a therapist might become tangled up in a disagreement over fees or session meeting times and become so focused on maintaining rules and regulations that the therapist fails to see how the therapist and the patient have become ensnared in a power struggle that warrants an invitation to mutual exploration, not a punitive and self-righteous retreat behind "the frame."

Balancing With Positivity

In addition to being able to step back and see the process that is unfolding, we also have to be aware of our tendency to focus on and even exaggerate the negative. As we discussed in Chapter 1, negative emotions can have a greater impact on our behavior than positive ones: "Bad is stronger than good" (Baumeister, Bratslavsky, Finkenauer, & Vohs, 2001, p. 323). We also discussed how research on resilience in the face of trauma has pointed to the importance of our cognitive appraisal of negative events (Bonanno, 2004). These literatures suggest that we have a tendency to concentrate or dwell on the negative, but if we can balance this tendency with attention to the positive as well by attending to our perceptions and resisting the inclination to just focus on the negative, we have the capacity to be more resilient in the face of challenges. This is where our conceptualization of alliance ruptures can prove very useful.

If we think of ruptures as not just obstacles to treatment but also potential opportunities to increase the patient's—and our own—awareness of relational schemas and needs, and to provide the patient with a corrective relational experience, then we can reframe our perception of difficult moments in therapy. We can be more curious about a difficult moment, open to its possibilities. We can be more patient to let it unfold rather than rushing to end it before we even understand what is happening. Recognizing ruptures are inevitable, we can optimize our ability to observe and tolerate the ways our patients move against and away from us. We can be more curious and patient with ourselves, and the ways we contribute to ruptures. We can put less pressure on ourselves to avoid ruptures or fix them immediately, which creates more room for us to be curious about them and explore them, mining them for greater insight and understanding. We can even try to be grateful for ruptures: as much as they can be uncomfortable and stressful, they are always teaching us something. As we often tell our trainees, every difficult moment is more "grist for the mill." After all, some research suggests that experiencing a rupture and repairing it is associated with better outcome than not having a rupture at all (Eubanks, Muran, & Safran, 2018). If we can also maintain this perspective—patiently seeing a moment of rupture as part of a larger, and potentially profoundly therapeutic, process—then we can become more resilient and responsive therapists. Of course, we caution against overconfidence and minimizing or dismissing the negative; we are just advocating for "balance."

SOME USEFUL STRATEGIES

We started this chapter by discussing attitudes that we think are important for therapists to develop and nurture in order to perform well under pressure. We now propose some useful strategies for therapists to refine their rupture resolution skills and to continue their professional development beyond their formal training: mindfulness exercises, emotion journals, video review, critical inquiry, practice under pressure, and the development of a competence constellation. We intentionally discussed the attitudes first because they are paramount; a strategy that is implemented without the right attitude will likely be less useful, and potentially counterproductive. As you read about these strategies, please keep in mind that they need to be practiced in the context of humility, compassion, curiosity, patience, and balanced positivity.

Before the Session: Mindfulness Exercises

There is a small but growing literature on the value of mindfulness practices for therapists. Randomized controlled trials of mindfulness training for therapists have found evidence that mindfulness can lead to reductions in symptoms and stress and improvements in self-compassion (Eriksson et al., 2018; Grepmair et al., 2007). Consistent with our emphasis on the value of bringing a mindful curiosity and nonjudgmental awareness to the therapy session, we encourage therapists to develop mindfulness practices, but we appreciate that this idea may seem unappealing or impractical for busy clinicians. We think a promising possibility is to consider practicing brief mindfulness exercises right before a session.

A few researchers have investigated the impact of presession mindfulness exercises. Dunn, Callahan, Swift, and Ivanovic (2013) provided therapist trainees with a 5-week mindfulness training program. They then randomly assigned therapists to different tasks before each therapy session: either a 5-minute mindfulness centering exercise or a control activity such as checking e-mail. They found that therapists who engaged in the mindfulness activity reported being more present in the session, and their patients rated the sessions at a higher quality level, compared with the control condition. Stone, Friedlander, and Moeyaert (2018) followed a modified version of the Dunn et al. protocol and closely examined the impact of presession mindfulness exercises (specifically engaging in a 3-minute guided exercise of attending to the breath) on therapy process in two dyads. Across both dyads, they found positive effects of therapist mindfulness exercises on patient ratings: in one dyad, mindfulness practice before the session was associated with higher patient ratings of therapist empathy, and in the other dyad, it was associated with higher patient ratings of the personal quality of the therapeutic relationship.

More research is needed, but these initial efforts suggest that engaging in brief mindfulness exercises right before a session may help therapists to be more attuned and empathic in the session. In addition to exercises focused on centering or attending to the breath, therapists could consider exercises for cultivating therapeutic presence (see Geller, 2017). Just taking a moment to take a deep breath and gently note how one is feeling could be a valuable way to prepare oneself for a session. Such exercises might be particularly useful when one anticipates a difficult session with a challenging patient.

After the Session: Emotion Journal

The influential work of Pennebaker and colleagues (Pennebaker, 1997; Pennebaker & Smyth, 2016) has established the benefits of expressive writing for improving physical and emotional well-being. In this experimental paradigm, participants are asked to write about their "deepest thoughts and feelings" about a negative life experience for up to 20 minutes a day for 3 to 4 days. In a meta-analysis of the expressive writing literature, Frattaroli (2006) found a small but significant effect for the benefits of expressive writing for psychological health, physical health, and overall functioning.

Why is writing about one's deepest thoughts and feelings beneficial? Pennebaker and colleagues acknowledged that the mechanisms by which writing confers benefits are not well understood (Sayer et al., 2015). Frattaroli (2006) examined potential moderators associated with different theories and found the greatest support for exposure theory: the idea that repeatedly describing thoughts and feelings about a negative experience leads to a reduction in those thoughts and feelings. Frattaroli also found mixed support for self-regulation theory, which posits that expressive writing allows participants to observe themselves expressing and controlling their emotions, which increases their self-efficacy for emotion regulation, which in turn reduces negative affect. Some preliminary support was also found for social integration theory, which states that disclosure via expressive writing impacts how people interact with their social world—for example, by ceasing to hold a grudge, or by seeking out more social support—which leads to improvements in health and well-being.

For therapists, writing about difficult moments in therapy could facilitate exposure, improve emotion regulation, or provide an outlet for negative feelings that helps the therapist engage more positively with a patient, or even increases the therapist's awareness of their need for social support or supervision and consultation. Here it is important to recognize the research that demonstrates the performance-enhancing and emotion-regulating impact of writing down one's feelings, however negative (e.g., Barrett, 2017; Beilock, 2010; see Chapter 1, this volume). Writing about one's emotional reactions to patients could also promote greater acceptance of or insight into one's experience. This is consonant with what many writers have noted; as Flannery O'Connor was reputed to have observed, "I write because I don't know what I think until I read what I say."

We recommend that therapists keep an emotion journal, where they make note of their emotional reactions to their patients. This useful practice can be incorporated into the therapist's routine—after writing the official session note, the therapist can make their own notes in an emotion journal. This gives the therapist a safe space to express thoughts and feelings that the therapist may not be able to freely express elsewhere because of the need to preserve confidentiality, and therefore this may be particularly useful for therapists who are not engaging in regular supervision. Reading over the journal entry before the next session with that patient may help the therapist to make connections and identify patterns, such as recognizing that encounters with a certain patient always leave the therapist feeling anxious or annoyed or bored. Or a therapist may recognize associations between emotional reactions and specific clinical situations and thereby gain greater insight into what pushes the therapist's buttons.

Between Sessions: Video Review

In the field of psychotherapy, there is often an assumption that therapists will become more skilled with more practice—hence the many requirements around acquiring certain numbers of hours of clinical experience for licensure and various certifications. However, research suggests that practice does not make perfect. For example, a study that followed 170 therapists treating 6,500 patients over several years (S. B. Goldberg et al., 2016) found that whereas some therapists improved over time, on average, therapists did not improve with more experience; rather, they became slightly *less* effective over time.

Research on the development of expertise in a number of fields—including music, chess, sports, and medicine—has identified that to improve one's skills, one must not only practice but also engage in *deliberate practice*, defined as "individualized training activities especially designed . . . to improve specific aspects of an individual's performance through repetition and successive refinement" (Ericsson & Lehmann, 1996, pp. 278–279). There exists a growing awareness of theoretical and empirical arguments for incorporating deliberate practice into training and professional development (see Bennett-Levy, 2019). Chow et al. (2015) conducted a study of 69 therapists in the United Kingdom who worked with more than 4,500 patients. The authors surveyed the therapists about the extent to which they engaged in specific forms of deliberate practice and then examined the relations between this engagement and patient outcome. The authors found that time spent engaging in deliberate practice activities, such as reviewing difficult cases, writing down reflections of prior sessions, and reflecting on what to do in future sessions, was significantly related to patient outcome. As no one specific activity reliably led to better outcome, the authors concluded that there is value in deliberate practice but that the form it takes depends on the unique needs and preferences of the individual therapist. However, the authors did note that when they looked not at the amount of time therapists spent in various activities but rather at the amount of cognitive effort they expended in various activities, ratings of one activity were significantly correlated with patient outcomes: reviewing recordings of therapy sessions.

Building on these findings, Rousmaniere and colleagues (Rousmaniere, 2017; Rousmaniere, Goodyear, Miller, & Wampold, 2017) have called for greater attention to therapist deliberate practice and therapists' need for feedback on their performance from supervisors and/or routine outcome monitoring systems, which can help them identify and address areas where they need to strengthen their skills. Rousmaniere (2019) developed a manual guiding therapists through deliberate practice exercises that include use of videos of one's therapy sessions with patients. Rousmaniere described how close attention to session videos, in particular moments that the therapist found challenging, can provide the opportunity to identify stimuli in the session that elicit strong reactions from the therapist, such as shame or embarrassment, which can interfere with the therapist's ability to remain empathically attuned to the patient. By watching these moments many times and attending to their reactions, therapists can practice recognizing and regulating their emotional responses to their patients.

As we discussed in Chapter 5 of this volume, video analysis of difficult moments is a key component of our alliance-focused approach to training and supervision. Although watching and exploring such moments with a supervisor and/or peer group is particularly beneficial, we have also observed that watching one's own videos alone can be useful. Therapists can identify difficult moments in a session and pay close attention to their reactions—both recalling the emotions they experienced in session and noting their reactions while watching the video. If therapists bring a nonjudgmental curiosity to observing their experience, and closely observing the patient's reaction to their interventions, they can gain greater awareness of ruptures that may be occurring and how they are contributing to them. It is much easier to dis-embed and observe a rupture when you are literally observing it unfold in a video. If the prospect of watching oneself on video sounds daunting, it may be helpful to keep in mind that reviewing videos does not always entail identifying and dwelling on one's mistakes: Therapists may also find that the moment they felt most uncomfortable, the part they feel they "messed up," was actually a moment they handled well. This may lead to useful reflection about the therapist's own self-criticism and the possible ways this may be hindering the therapist by negatively impacting the therapist's confidence or willingness to try something new. It is essential that the attitudes we bring to our work with patients—maintaining humility, cultivating compassion, courting curiosity, being patient, and balancing the negative with positivity—are also present when we are analyzing our work.

We appreciate that not all clinicians work in settings where video (or audio) recording of sessions is possible, but for those who can video at least some of their work, we strongly recommend it. With greater awareness of what may be happening for you, the therapist, and what may be happening for your patient, and how the two of you are moving against or away from each other, you will be in a much better position to respond with empathic engagement the next time a similar moment arises. In our experience, the moments we find most challenging always come back again; it may not be in exactly the same form, and it may not even be with the same patient, but we can rest assured that another opportunity to practice will arise.

Between Sessions: Critical Inquiry

As we discussed in Chapter 1 of this volume, Schön (1983) observed that professional development requires the ability to view one's actions through a critical lens. Taking a critical view of our own work is a way to counter the errors of judgment to which we are all subject (see Kahneman, 2011). Several writers have drawn on the work of Kahneman and other researchers to iden-tity cognitive biases to which therapists may be prone (e.g., Garb & Boyle, 2015; Lilienfeld, Ritschel, Lynn, Cautin, & Latzman, 2014; Norcross & VandenBos, 2018; Pope, Sonne, & Greene, 2006; Tracey et al., 2014). For example, naïve realism, or the assumption that the world is exactly as we see it (similar to Kahneman's, 2011, idea of "what you see is all there is"), can lead therapists to believe that they can rely on their intuitive judgments, which may lead them to assume that improvement—or deterioration—following an intervention is due to that intervention and neglect the potential impact of other variables (Lilienfeld et al., 2014). Confirmation bias may lead therapists to attend, knowingly or unknowingly, to patient information that confirms their case formulations and disregard information that runs counter to their hypotheses (Garb & Boyle, 2015). Hindsight bias can lead therapists to construct explanations after the fact, and these explanations do not help therapists learn anything new, because they are never questioned and examined (Tracey et al., 2014). For example, a patient quits treatment, and the therapist concludes that the patient had been showing signs of not being ready to change. The therapist will never learn whether this post hoc explanation is correct unless the therapist tests the hypothesis on a new patient: Does another patient who displays similar behaviors also quit? If the new patient does not quit, this evidence suggests that the therapist's post hoc assessment of the prior patient may be inaccurate or incomplete.

One useful strategy for recognizing and addressing our cognitive biases is to familiarize ourselves with the relevant literature. We can read the work of scholars like Kahneman and Tversky and actively reflect on how we enact these biases in our clinical practice. Per Redelmeier et al.'s (2001) suggestion, we can also read about probability theory and clinical judgment (e.g., Meehl, 1954, 1960) to gain a better understanding of the role randomness can play in our patients' progress or lack thereof.

We can also counter our confirmation biases by trying to adopt a disconfirmatory approach whereby we seek out information that would disconfirm our predictions (Tracey et al., 2014). In a related vein, it is useful to consider whether there is clinical information that would fit a competing hypothesis or theory about our patient. Exposure to other clinical approaches—such as other theoretical orientations—can be helpful in this regard. We can read about other approaches as a way of testing and refining our ideas about how therapy works. Many therapists choose to read about and even integrate other approaches, and although we see great value in integration (see Castonguay, Eubanks, Goldfried, Muran, & Lutz, 2015), we argue that therapists do not have to actually integrate other approaches to benefit from exposure to them. Reading about different ways to approach clinical work helps us identify our biases, challenge our assumptions, and deepen our understanding of our own models of therapy.

Another useful strategy is to explicitly identify our hypotheses about our patients and test them (see Tracey et al., 2014). We can predict what we think the results of our interventions will be and see if that is what actually happens. In this area, it is helpful to draw on multiple sources of data, because we will inevitably be tempted to focus on data that confirm our predictions. We recommend that therapists use brief, standardized measures to provide an additional source of information about how their patients are doing. Routine monitoring of patient outcome using standardized instruments that can alert the therapist to patient deterioration can positively impact treatment outcomes (e.g., Brattland et al., 2018; Shimokawa, Lambert, & Smart, 2010).

Between Sessions: Practice Under Pressure

As we discussed in Chapter 5, alliance-focused training uses awareness-oriented role-plays to provide trainees with the opportunity to practice under pressure, which is a critical component of improving performance (e.g., Beilock, 2010). Therapists who are part of supervision groups can use role-plays to explore challenging moments with patients. Therapists who are in solo practice and do not have a supervision group can also experiment with a role-play. Recall a difficult moment from a session and play out that moment. If possible, practice in your office and physically move to sit in the patient's chair while role-playing the patient, then sit in your own chair to role-play yourself. See what feelings arise for you in both roles. You may be surprised by the vantage point you gain on your patient's experience.

When you sit in the therapist's chair—your chair—take the opportunity to experiment with something new. Risk saying whatever comes to your mind first, without filtering it. Risk saying something you wanted to say but were reluctant to say to your patient. Actually say it out loud in the room. Notice what feelings come up for you. The aim here is not to practice impulsively blurting out whatever crosses your mind but to become more aware of what you are feeling, what you are holding back, and why. You may discover that you are holding something back that you do need to express to your patient, and that will benefit the treatment. Or you may discover you are holding something back that you need to process with a colleague or supervisor. Identifying and addressing what you are holding back will help you be more effective with your patients because it will free you to direct your energy and attention to your interaction with your patient rather than being consumed by the exhausting effort required to suppress powerful thoughts and feelings.

Between Sessions: Competence Constellation

One of the challenges of being a therapist, a challenge that can leave us vulnerable to burnout, is the potential for isolation when a therapist is in solo practice. In this chapter, we have described important attitudes a clinician needs to have to navigate challenging moments with a patient, and we have suggested several strategies that can help therapists to nurture and support these attitudes. We have noted the value of paying attention to one's internal experience and reflecting on one's work. The idea of self-analysis has a long history in our field (e.g., Freud, 1937). However, as one experienced therapist pointed out in a study of self-analysis, it is "too easy to fool yourself" (C. Goldberg, 1992, p. 160). Redelmeier et al. (2001) recommended the use of supervision and peer review to guard against errors of judgment. It is not a coincidence that dialectical behavior therapy, which was developed to treat some of the most challenging patients, regards a team approach to treatment as essential (Linehan, 1993b).

We also believe that therapists will perform best when they have a network of colleagues who can provide support and different perspectives. W. B. Johnson, Barnett, Elman, Forrest, and Kaslow (2012) observed that our field tends to view the development and maintenance of professional competence as an individual responsibility. They called for a reconceptualization of competence from a communitarian perspective. Clinicians need a *competence constellation*: "a network or consortium of individual colleagues, consultation groups, supervisors, and professional association involvements that is deliberately constructed to ensure ongoing multisource enhancement and assessment of competence" (W. B. Johnson et al., 2012, p. 566).

We believe that the most powerful and impactful way to address an alliance rupture is for the patient and therapist to explore it together. Greater insight and potential for change comes from a mutual engagement: two heads are better than one. Similarly, when therapists seek to identify and understand and, if necessary, change their reactions to a clinical experience, they need to engage with other people. They need supervisors, coaches, and/or peers who can give feedback, help practice role-plays, provide support, and challenge assumptions. Creating and nurturing a competence constellation is not a luxury; it is a necessity.

CODA

What We Know About the Need for Self-Care

Therapy can be challenging and demanding work. There is a great deal of pressure to perform, to relieve suffering, and to save lives. There are emotional costs and burnout risks, and much can be attributed to tensions and conflicts in the therapeutic relationship. To maintain empathic attunement and negotiate alliance ruptures, therapists should proactively pursue and practice self-care.

Some Basic Attitudes for Self-Care

We can best position ourselves to be attuned and responsive to our patients by maintaining humility about our abilities, our approach, and how much our patients need us; by cultivating compassion for our patients and ourselves; by courting curiosity about our patients and our experience of them; by practicing patience when we encounter moments of strain or stagnation in treatment; and by balancing our tendency to focus on the negative with an appreciation of the positive potential for growth that resides in each rupture.

Some Useful Strategies for Self-Care

We can adopt strategies that support our self-care and professional development. These strategies include practicing mindfulness before sessions, keeping an emotion journal to track our emotional reactions to patients, nurturing a stance of critical inquiry by engaging with the literature on cognitive biases and adopting disconfirmatory and hypothesis-testing approaches to our work, practicing under pressure by engaging in role-plays, and developing a competence constellation of supervisors and/or colleagues who can both provide support and challenge our assumptions, as we will never reach our fullest potential as therapists if we are always working alone.

Conclusion

In the Pressure Cooker

Pressure is a privilege

—BILLIE JEAN KING

Tennis great Billie Jean King was no stranger to pressure, and there was no challenge more pressure-filled than when she agreed to play Bobby Riggs in the much publicized and culturally historic "Battle of the Sexes" in 1973. For Billie Jean, this was not just a tennis match for more than 90 million viewers on prime-time network television; the women's movement and equality in sports were on the line and on her shoulders. In her 2008 book *Pressure Is a Privilege*, she reflected on her approach to pressure and a favorite saying of hers. She described the recognition that with success comes pressure—that the opportunity to reach a moment to perform under pressure is a privilege. She used this recognition to embrace such moments, to feel fortunate to be there. Such a perspective can be considered a form of cognitive reappraisal, an effective emotional regulation strategy that allowed her "to slow down and focus" (King, 2008, p. 110), which was critical to her performing at her best. She went on to describe a number of performance-maximizing strategies that have been supported by cognitive science (see Chapter 1, this volume), including experiencing the value of purposeful (deliberate) practicing, choosing positivity to offset negativity, breaking down tasks into smaller steps (taking a process orientation), preparing for negative

http://dx.doi.org/10.1037/0000182-008
Therapist Performance Under Pressure: Negotiating Emotion, Difference, and Rupture,
by J. C. Muran and C. F. Eubanks

events to promote resilience, and asking for help from others, which invariably involves humility.

For the therapist, it is a privilege to be invited to share in the anguish and anxiety of another—to be part of such an intimate relationship, to be part of *many* such relationships. Hans Sachs, an early psychoanalyst, was once asked, "Isn't what you analysts do exactly what a good friend does?" He replied simply, "Ah, perhaps so, but where could you find such a friend?" (Karasu, 2001, p. 165). It is a privilege to be such a friend. Of course, with such an invitation comes great responsibility—the pressure to perform, to provide comfort, and to effect change for the other. In and of itself, pressure can stir emotions—often fear and confusion, sometimes anger and despair—that can adversely affect performance (see Chapter 1). What is more, the emotional experience of the patient in psychotherapy can further confound the emotions of the therapist—and of course this goes both ways, cycling back and forth (see Chapters 2 and 3). The interaction of patient and therapist emotions can foster greater connection and intimacy but also disconnection and isolation. The former can result in mutual empathy. The latter can result in empathic failure, or what we have termed *rupture*.

We have described the experience of emotion as expressions of self—cultural identities, including their intersectionality, and fundamental motivations, including the needs for agency and communion. In this book, we have attended to therapists' emotions; their impact on their performance, both cognitive and behavioral; and the importance of emotion regulation in relation to their patients. More specifically, we have discussed various therapist emotional challenges or hazards and their relationship to ruptures (see Chapters 2–4). We have defined these events as fraught with power plays (from identity differences) and dialectical tensions (from basic needs) and as opportunities for self-discovery and mutual recognition. We have presented and illustrated metacommunication as a technical principle that can promote emotion regulation and realize these opportunities.

At the heart of our perspective is the continuous struggle for the therapist to know and develop oneself—and this struggle is always in relation to another, including the patient. This is consistent with Hegel's (1807/1969) existentialism—but also with the interpersonal psychoanalytic principle, according to which change invariably must include the therapist, as each therapeutic relationship involves (and demands definition of) a unique interaction between two complex selves (see Ehrenberg, 1992; J. L. Singer, 1966). Thus we have presented an empirically tested training protocol for therapists (Muran, Safran, Eubanks, & Gorman, 2018; see Chapter 5, this volume) that focuses on experiential exercises and deliberate practice to develop emotion regulation skills in therapists, and we have extrapolated from this research, as well as findings from cognitive and emotion science, to recommend strategies that can be implemented by the private practitioner (see Chapter 6).

Donald Rumsfeld, former U.S. secretary of defense, once infamously said, "There are known knowns; there are things we know we know. We also know there are known unknowns; that is to say, we know there are some things we do not know. But there are also unknown unknowns" (U.S. Department of Defense, 2002). Politics aside, we have always found some wisdom in these words, and we organize our concluding thoughts about therapist performance under pressure and in the cooker of alliance rupture accordingly.

WHAT WE KNOW WE KNOW ABOUT CLINICAL JUDGMENT, ALLIANCE, AND TRAINING

- Clinical judgment and decision making are shaped by heuristics and biases, especially in the face of ambiguity and pressure (Redelmeier, Ferris, Tu, Hux, & Schull, 2001).

  - Certain heuristics can lead to cognitive error (see Chapter 1): Perhaps the most pernicious is overconfidence—the tendency to overestimate our knowledge and control and to underestimate complexity and chance (Kahneman, 2011).

  - Implicit biases (prejudicial judgments regarding cultural groupings such as gender, race, and ethnicity) can have deleterious effects on our choices and result in microaggressions (Banaji & Greenwald, 2013; Sue, 2010).

- Clinical judgment and decision making are also significantly shaped by emotion, including feelings of liking or disliking (see Grecucci & Sanfey, 2014).

  - Negative emotions have more powerful effects on our choices than good ones, as demonstrated by better memory or recall for bad events and by more influence on subsequent emotional states (Baumeister, Bratslavsky, Finkenauer, & Vohs, 2001).

  - Emotions can also affect or elicit other emotional states experienced by an individual and by another individual in a dyadic interaction (see Rimé, 2009; Scarantino, 2015).

  - Emotion regulation—the trajectory of our emotions—has been identified as an important variable in mental health, resilience, and performance under pressure (see Gross, 2014a).

- The patient–therapist (or therapeutic) relationship (or alliance) in psycho-therapy has been shown to be an important change variable; the quality and nature of the alliance is consistently predictive of outcome (see Flückiger, Del Re, Wampold, & Horvath, 2019).

  - Certain therapist behaviors (e.g., collaboration, empathy, affirmation) have been shown to be "demonstrably" important elements, and others (e.g., genuineness, emotional experience and expression) with suffi-cient evidence have been considered "probably" important (see Norcross & Lambert, 2019b).

- Some therapists are better and more effective than others in achieving good alliances with patients (see Castonguay & Hill, 2017; Wampold & Imel, 2015).

- Rupture and repair have been shown to be prevalent events and predictive of treatment outcomes (see Eubanks, Muran, & Safran, 2019; Muran, 2019).

- Rupture recognition by the therapist is important (whether acknowledged explicitly or not), and there is evidence of at least two possible pathways toward repair: (a) changing the focus of the work and (b) exploring the rupture experience (see Eubanks, Muran, & Safran, 2019; Muran, 2019).

- Deliberate practice (i.e., well-defined regimens based on effective techniques and with expert monitoring and self-monitoring, which require full cognitive commitment, training out of one's comfort zone, and producing effective mental representations) and reflective practice (i.e., the cyclical process of reflecting while doing) have been shown to be key in developing mastery (see Ericsson & Pool, 2016; Schön, 1983).

  - Training therapists to improve their alliances with their patients has yielded modest results (see Eubanks, Muran, & Safran, 2019; Muran, 2019).

  - Our training protocol—designed to improve therapists' emotion regulation and rupture repair abilities and based on experiential principles consistent with deliberate and reflective practice—has demonstrated changes in therapist behavior, specifically decreasing therapist criticism and control and increasing affirmation and expressiveness (Muran et al., 2018).

WHAT WE KNOW WE DON'T KNOW ABOUT RUPTURE, INTERVENTION, AND TRAINING

- Are all ruptures the same or equally important?

  - Is there a difference in ruptures that occur early versus late in treatment? Is there a difference if the *same* rupture occurs early versus late?

  - Is there a difference between withdrawal and confrontation ruptures? Is one more of a risk factor?

  - Does the impact of ruptures depend on other patient and therapist and treatment variables? Which ones?

  - Is there a difference between a withdrawal rupture and what some might describe as "a titration of the intimacy," which is expected as natural in the ebb and flow of human relations (Fletcher, Simpson, Campbell, & Overall, 2013)?

- Is there a difference between ruptures that are apparently marked or effected by a patient and a therapist behavior? Is there such a thing as a rupture caused (more) by one versus the other in a dyadic relationship?

- Is there a difference between ruptures and microaggressions? Can all ruptures be attributed to identity or cultural differences?

• What are the essential elements of intervention regarding ruptures?

- Is recognition of a rupture by the therapist sufficient? In other words, will repair be a natural consequence?

- Is explicit acknowledgment of a rupture necessary? There are some small-scale studies that suggest otherwise (see Eubanks, Muran, & Safran, 2019).

- Is there a difference in appropriateness or benefit between (a) changing the focus of the work and (b) exploring the rupture experience?

- When and for whom is metacommunication appropriate? When and for whom is therapist expressiveness not appropriate?

- Are there other rupture repair or resolution pathways—as dictated by treatment orientation or patient–therapist dyad?

- How do patients contribute to rupture resolution?

• What are the essential training strategies regarding ruptures and their repair?

- How do we best train regarding emotion regulation (self-awareness and other-awareness inclusive)? How do we translate the emotion science on this subject?

- How do we best apply principles from deliberate and reflective practice from the performance science literature to training in rupture repair?

- How do we responsively tailor rupture repair training to different therapists, patient populations, treatments, and settings?

- In addition to the need to replicate our findings regarding our alliance-focused training, we could dismantle and evaluate its various elements.

- How do we best train the trainers? How do we guide supervisors to balance training therapists in emotion regulation and rupture repair with maintaining and negotiating the supervisory alliance?

WHAT WE DON'T KNOW WE DON'T KNOW ABOUT EMOTION REGULATION

We have witnessed dramatic developments in the cognitive and emotion sciences over the past 50 years that can be attributed in large part to advances in neurotechnology and that have significantly advanced our understanding of human performance. One example is the development of our understanding of self-regulation with the study of emotion regulation. It is now touted as a basic transdiagnostic mechanism (Aldao, Gee, De Los Reyes, & Seager, 2016; Sloan et al., 2017) as part of a trend toward breaking down traditional—arguably arbitrary—boundaries of diagnostic categories and treatment orientations (see Barlow et al., 2017; Barlow, Bullis, Comer, & Ametaj, 2013). With our contribution, we have aimed to advance our understanding of therapist emotional experience (in the therapeutic relationship) by shifting the focus to emotion regulation in the therapist. We do so with the humble recognition that tomorrow brings advances and realizations that we cannot anticipate or imagine. We look forward to what may be beyond the horizon.

The Rupture Resolution Rating System

The Rupture Resolution Rating System (3RS) is to date the most widely used observer-based measure of alliance ruptures and attempts to repair them (Eubanks, Muran, & Safran, 2019). A validation study of the 3RS conducted by our research group (Eubanks, Lubitz, Muran, & Safran, 2019), which applied the 3RS to early sessions of cognitive behavior therapy (CBT), found high rates of interrater reliability on ratings of confrontation and withdrawal ruptures and resolution strategies, as well as ratings of the therapist's contribution to ruptures and the extent to which ruptures were resolved. Predictive validity analyses found that the frequency of confrontation markers, successful rupture resolution, and the therapist's contribution to ruptures predicted premature dropout from therapy.

Studies led by other research groups that applied the 3RS to different populations in various settings provide additional support for the predictive validity of the measure. A study of patients receiving CBT at a university clinic in Portugal found an association between an increase in 3RS-rated ruptures and premature dropout from therapy (Coutinho, Ribeiro, Sousa, & Safran, 2014). A study of patients with anxiety or depressive disorders at a university clinic in Germany found that confrontation ruptures predicted an abrupt increase in symptoms (Ehrlich & Lutz, 2015). A study of early sessions of dialectical behavior therapy for borderline personality disorder that was part of a randomized controlled trial in Canada found some support for the predictive validity of withdrawal ruptures: unrecovered patients evidenced more withdrawal ruptures than recovered patients (Boritz, Barnhart, Eubanks, & McMain, 2018). A study of Australian adolescents with borderline personality disorder found that ruptures early in treatment were associated with worse outcome, whereas greater rupture resolution later in treatment was associated with

---

The following manual is from *Rupture Resolution Rating System (3RS): Manual,* by C. F. Eubanks, J. C. Muran, and J. D. Safran, 2015, New York, NY: Mount Sinai-Beth Israel Medical Center. Copyright 2015 by C. F. Eubanks, J. C. Muran, and J. D. Safran. Reprinted with permission.

better outcome (Gersh et al., 2017). A study of patients from a Swiss university clinic found that therapist use of challenge during rupture resolution attempts was positively associated with outcome (Moeseneder, Ribeiro, Muran, & Caspar, 2019).

3RS ratings have also been linked to a neurobiological marker. A study of 22 patients receiving therapy for depression found that increases in confrontation ruptures and therapist attempts to repair ruptures during the session were associated with larger increases in patient oxytocin levels over the course of the session and with decreases in patient self-reports of the therapeutic bond (Zilcha-Mano, Porat, Dolev, & Shamay-Tsoory, 2018).

FUTURE DIRECTIONS

Although we conceptualize both ruptures and rupture repairs as dyadic phenomena that are coconstructed by patients and therapists, the 3RS does not yet sufficiently reflect this understanding (see also Eubanks et al., 2019). In its present form, the 3RS operationalizes ruptures in terms of patient behaviors and operationalizes resolution attempts in terms of therapist behaviors. As a preliminary step toward addressing this limitation, we added a single item assessing the extent to which the therapist caused or exacerbated ruptures in the session. As just noted, our validation study of the 3RS found that higher ratings on this item were significantly associated with premature dropout (Eubanks et al., 2019). This evidence supports the need for greater examination of how therapists contribute to alliance ruptures. One important future direction for the 3RS is to create and validate therapist rupture markers. In a similar vein, we will also create items that assess patients' contributions to rupture resolution. Another future aim is to explore ways to better capture behavior at the level of the dyad, not just the individuals in the dyad. As one of our priorities has always been to balance precision with practicality, adding additional elements may require us to streamline the measure in other ways so that we do not overburden coders who are trying to achieve interrater reliability.

We also expect, and indeed hope, that as the 3RS is applied to more diverse populations—different types and modalities of therapy, different settings, different patients and therapists—both for research purposes and as a training tool, that there may be the need to further adapt the 3RS in various ways, such as adding additional rupture markers and resolution strategies and attempting to rate the effectiveness of individual resolution strategies. Future work could also examine whether some rupture markers lead to "overcoding" ruptures and whether we are casting the rupture net too wide at times and including interpersonal behaviors that are not markers of a problem in the alliance. We view the 3RS as a work in progress, and we are excited by the ways in which further use, adaptation, and refinement of this measure has the potential to deepen our understanding of the process of negotiating a therapeutic alliance.

REFERENCES

Boritz, T., Barnhart, R., Eubanks, C. F., & McMain, S. (2018). Alliance rupture and resolution in dialectical behavior therapy for borderline personality disorder. *Journal of Personality Disorders, 32*, 115–128. http://dx.doi.org/10.1521/pedi.2018.32.supp.115

Coutinho, J., Ribeiro, E., Sousa, I., & Safran, J. D. (2014). Comparing two methods of identifying alliance rupture events. *Psychotherapy, 51*, 434–442. http://dx.doi.org/10.1037/a0032171

Ehrlich, T., & Lutz, W. (2015). Neue Ansätze zur Modellierung diskontinuierlicher Verläufe in der Psychotherapie: "Sudden gains" und "sudden losses." *Psychotherapeut, 60*, 205–209.

Eubanks, C. F., Lubitz, J., Muran, J. C., & Safran, J. D. (2019). Rupture Resolution Rating System (3RS): Development and validation. *Psychotherapy Research, 29*, 306–319. http://dx.doi.org/10.1080/10503307.2018.1552034

Eubanks, C. F., Muran, J. C., & Safran, J. D. (2015). *Rupture resolution rating system (3RS): Manual.* Unpublished manuscript, Mount Sinai Beth Israel, New York, NY.

Gersh, E., Hulbert, C. A., McKechnie, B., Ramadan, R., Worotniuk, T., & Chanen, A. M. (2017). Alliance rupture and repair processes and therapeutic change in youth with borderline personality disorder. *Psychology and Psychotherapy: Theory, Research and Practice, 90*, 84–104. http://dx.doi.org/10.1111/papt.12097

Moeseneder, L., Ribeiro, E., Muran, J. C., & Caspar, F. (2019). Impact of confrontations by therapists on impairment and utilization of the therapeutic alliance. *Psychotherapy Research, 29*, 293–305. http://dx.doi.org/10.1080/10503307.2018.1502897

Zilcha-Mano, S., Porat, Y., Dolev, T., & Shamay-Tsoory, S. (2018). Oxytocin as a neurobiological marker of ruptures in the working alliance. *Psychotherapy and Psychosomatics, 87*, 126–127. http://dx.doi.org/10.1159/000487190

RUPTURE RESOLUTION RATING SYSTEM (3RS): MANUAL

Catherine F. Eubanks, J. Christopher Muran, and Jeremy D. Safran

TABLE OF CONTENTS

Introduction   154
Coding Procedures   155
Withdrawal Rupture Markers   162
Confrontation Rupture Markers   169
Resolution Strategies   178
Rupture/Resolution Marker Differential Diagnosis   188

INTRODUCTION

Our view of the therapeutic alliance draws on Bordin's (1979) three-part conceptualization: the alliance is composed of (a) agreement between patient and therapist on the tasks of treatment; (b) agreement on the goals of treatment; and (c) a personal, affective bond between the patient and therapist. An alliance **rupture** is a deterioration in the alliance, manifested by a *lack of collaboration* between patient and therapist on tasks or goals, or a strain in the emotional bond.

Note that our definition of ruptures related to tasks and goals focuses on lack of *collaboration* rather than lack of *agreement*, reflecting our experience that not all disagreements between patients and therapists are ruptures. A patient can express disagreement with the therapist in an appropriate, collaborative way that does not constitute a rupture. An emphasis on collaboration over agreement is also helpful in instances when a patient has concerns about a task or goal but expresses agreement with the therapist in an effort to appease the therapist or to avoid conflict. These surface-level agreements are actually examples of withdrawal ruptures (described next).

Ruptures are inevitable and occur in all therapies and with therapists of all skill levels. Ruptures can emerge when patients and therapists unwittingly become caught in vicious circles or enactments. A rupture may remain outside of the patient's and the therapist's conscious awareness, and it may not significantly obstruct therapeutic progress. In extreme cases, however, ruptures can lead to dropout or treatment failure.

Ruptures can be organized into two main subtypes: **withdrawal** and **confrontation** ruptures (Harper, 1989a, 1989b). In differentiating between these subtypes, we draw on Horney's (1950) concept of responding to anxiety by moving away, toward, or against others. In withdrawal ruptures, the patient either moves *away* from the therapist (e.g., by avoiding the therapist's questions) or may appear to move *toward* the therapist, but in a way that denies an aspect of the patient's experience (e.g., by being overly deferential and appeasing) and is therefore a withdrawal from the actual work of therapy. In confrontation ruptures, the patient moves *against* the therapist, either by expressing anger or dissatisfaction in a noncollaborative manner (e.g., hostile complaints about the therapist or the treatment) or by trying to pressure or control the therapist (e.g., making demands of the therapist). Ruptures can also include elements of both withdrawal and confrontation.

Although ruptures are a function of both patient and therapist contributions, this coding system focuses on *patient behaviors* as indicators or markers of ruptures. In our experience, even if a therapist behavior precipitates an alliance rupture (e.g., the therapist is critical or condescending), the patient usually responds by withdrawing or confronting the therapist; thus, we are usually still able to capture the rupture with this coding system. However, if coders feel that a therapist is playing a large role in causing or exacerbating ruptures, the coders should indicate that on the final item on the scoresheet.

The process by which a rupture is repaired is referred to as a **resolution process**. A resolution process enables the patient and therapist to renew or strengthen their emotional bond and to begin or resume collaborating on the tasks and goals of therapy. The resolution process may also serve as a corrective emotional experience for the patient. Therapists may attempt to initiate resolution processes by employing **resolution strategies**, such as changing the task, or disclosing the therapist's internal experience of the rupture. The Rupture Resolution Rating System, or 3RS, tracks resolution strategies over the course of the session as *potential* markers of resolution processes. After viewing the entire session, the coder determines the extent to which the resolution strategies were successful in actually bringing about a resolution to the rupture or ruptures in the session.

REFERENCES

Bordin, E. S. (1979). The generalizability of the psychoanalytic concept of the working alliance. *Psychotherapy: Theory, Research, & Practice, 16,* 252–260. http://dx.doi.org/10.1037/h0085885

Harper, H. (1989a). *Coding Guide I: Identification of confrontation challenges in exploratory therapy.* Sheffield, England: University of Sheffield.

Harper, H. (1989b). *Coding Guide II: Identification of withdrawal challenges in exploratory therapy.* Sheffield, England: University of Sheffield.

Horney, K. (1950). *Neurosis and human growth: The struggle toward self-realization.* New York, NY: Norton.

CODING PROCEDURES

Unit of coding: This coding system can be applied to different amounts of clinical material. The following suggestions are based on our experience:

- Coding the <u>entire session</u> as one unit: We have found that it is difficult to capture the many changes that can occur in one session with just one score. Also, it is harder to reach reliability.

- Coding <u>speech turn by speech turn</u>: This kind of coding is possible but requires transcripts. Also, it is sometimes unclear within one speech turn whether a rupture is occurring—more speech turns may be needed to clarify what is transpiring.

- Coding in <u>5-minute segments</u>: We are currently using this approach. We find that 5 minutes usually gives us enough material to identify ruptures, but not so much that we cannot reach agreement on what we are seeing. However, 5 minutes is somewhat arbitrary. Other researchers may prefer longer (e.g., 10 minutes) or shorter (e.g., 1 or 2 minutes) time bins.

Using video: Transcripts can be used in addition to video, but transcripts cannot replace video, because nonverbals are important for detecting ruptures and resolution events. You can stop, rewind, and review the video whenever necessary to complete the ratings.

Good process: Ruptures occur often, but in most cases they are not occurring every minute of the session. It is important to be clear on what process looks like when there are no ruptures before trying to identify ruptures. When there are no ruptures, the process will be marked by the following characteristics:

- Patient and therapist are attuned to each other. They are on the same page.

- Patient and therapist are both actively engaged in the work of therapy.

- Patient and therapist either agree on the tasks and goals of treatment or are actively and collaboratively working to reach clarification and agreement on the tasks and goals of treatment.

- Patient and therapist trust and respect each other and are comfortable with each other, to an extent that is appropriate for the stage of therapy (i.e., there will be more trust and comfort in the 15th session than in the first).

Note that a lack of ruptures is not necessarily the same as effective therapy. A patient and therapist could be in agreement and be working together smoothly but pursuing goals and tasks that are not the best choice for the patient's situation. When coding ruptures, one should focus on the quality of the collaboration and bond between the patient and therapist, not the quality of the therapist's case conceptualization, choice of treatment approach, or adherence or competence.

Observing a rupture: A rupture is a deterioration in the alliance between patient and therapist, manifested by a lack of collaboration on tasks or goals or a strain in the emotional bond. In a rupture, the patient moves *away* from the therapist or the work of therapy (withdrawal), moves *toward* the therapist in a way that denies the patient's own experience and thereby contributes to a movement away from the work of therapy (also withdrawal), or moves *against* the therapist or the work of therapy (confrontation).

The word **rupture** may call to mind a major argument or conflict in a session. However, with this coding system, we are coding minor tensions and strains as well as major disagreements. Even good sessions with skillful therapists may contain some degree of tension or strain. That being said, you will likely find sessions that do not contain any ruptures. As beginning coders are often eager to find ruptures, and may be tempted to overcode, we suggest this rule of thumb: *When in doubt, wait and watch.* If a rupture is developing, it will likely become clear as you continue to watch the session.

Some indications of a rupture follow:

- Patient and therapist are *not* working together collaboratively and productively. They are "not on the same page."

- There is strain, tension, or awkwardness between patient and therapist.

- Patient and therapist are misaligned or misattuned.

- Patient and therapist seem distant from each other.

- Patient and therapist are working at cross-purposes.

- Patient and therapist are acting friendly, but you sense tension or disagreement beneath the surface, such that the friendliness seems to be a pseudoalliance.

- Patient and therapist seem to be caught in a vicious cycle or enactment.

- You feel very bored while watching a session. This *might* be a sign that a withdrawal rupture is occurring and the patient is avoiding talking about genuine feelings and concerns.

Descriptions of the type of rupture follow:

- **Withdrawal:** Patient is moving *away* from the therapist or the work of therapy.

- **Confrontation:** Patient is moving *against* the therapist or the work of therapy.

- Both withdrawal and confrontation: Patient is simultaneously moving away and against. For example, the patient may criticize the therapist (confrontation) while smiling and laughing nervously (withdrawal). Patients who are dissatisfied with some aspect of therapy but at the same time want to avoid conflict with the therapist are particularly likely to exhibit mixtures of confrontation and withdrawal.

Choosing category of rupture marker: Once you decide on the type of rupture (withdrawal or confrontation), then select the rupture marker within that category that best describes what is happening. (See the category definitions and examples on pp. 162–177 for descriptions of the rupture markers.)

Withdrawal rupture markers:

- Denial
- Minimal response
- Abstract communication
- Avoidant storytelling and/or shifting topic
- Deferential and appeasing
- Content/affect split
- Self-criticism and/or hopelessness

Confrontation rupture markers:

- Complaints/concerns about the therapist
- Patient rejects therapist intervention
- Complaints/concerns about the activities of therapy
- Complaints/concerns about the parameters of therapy
- Complaints/concerns about progress in therapy
- Patient defends self against therapist
- Efforts to control/pressure therapist

Coding is not limited by speech turns: a single speech turn can contain multiple rupture markers.

PATIENT: I don't like this ridiculous homework, and I don't like the way you keep nagging me to do it.

This one speech turn contains two rupture markers and should receive two confrontation codes (complaint about activities and complaint about therapist).

Rating the clarity of the rupture marker: When you see an example of a rupture marker, put a check on the scoresheet. If it is unclear whether the behavior you observed meets full criteria for a particular rupture, you can rate it with a check minus.

✓   Meets criteria for rupture marker
✓– Unclear whether it meets criteria for rupture marker

Resolution

Observing resolution: When a rupture is repaired or resolved, there is a shift in a positive direction. Whereas the patient and therapist had seemed stuck, or locked in a vicious cycle, drifting apart, or working against one another, now they begin to come together, to understand each other, and to work collaboratively.

For an event to constitute a resolution marker, *it must be in the context of a rupture*. Usually, that means a rupture occurred prior to the resolution attempt. In some cases, a therapist may refer to a rupture from a prior session or from earlier in the same session, and then commence a resolution attempt. When you are coding multiple sessions from the same dyad, you may be able to detect subtle references to prior ruptures. For example, a therapist may try to "preempt" a rupture by employing resolution strategies because they anticipate that something they are about to say or do may precipitate a rupture. If you are able to make a link between the resolution strategy and a past rupture, current rupture, or rupture that is anticipated based on past ruptures, then you can code a resolution strategy. If there is no connection to a rupture, then the behavior cannot be considered a resolution strategy, even if it otherwise is topographically similar to one of the resolution strategies. For example, a therapist may decide to change tasks for many reasons. Only if the change in tasks is related to a rupture can it be coded as a resolution strategy.

Resolutions will usually occur following a rupture, but they may not correspond one to one. In other words, there may not be a resolution for every rupture. Also, resolutions may not follow directly after ruptures; there can be a rupture at the beginning of the session, and a resolution for that rupture may come at the end of the session. Or one resolution event may address a series of ruptures. For these reasons, we have found it easier to track *attempts* to resolve ruptures as we watch the session by coding therapists' use of resolution strategies. Only after watching the entire session do we make global ratings of the extent to which the resolution attempts succeeded in resolving ruptures.

Choosing Category of Resolution Strategy
Select the resolution strategy that best describes what the therapist is doing to address the rupture. (See the category definitions and examples on pp. 178–187 for descriptions of the strategies.)

Resolution strategies:

- Therapist clarifies a misunderstanding.
- Therapist changes tasks or goals.
- Therapist illustrates tasks or provides a rationale for treatment.
- Therapist invites the patient to discuss thoughts or feelings with respect to the therapist or some aspect of therapy.
- Therapist acknowledges their contribution to a rupture.
- Therapist discloses their internal experience of the patient—therapist interaction.
- Therapist links the rupture to larger interpersonal patterns between the patient and the therapist.
- Therapist links the rupture to larger interpersonal patterns in the patient's other relationships.
- Therapist validates the patient's defensive posture.
- Therapist responds to a rupture by redirecting or refocusing the patient.

As with the rupture markers, coding is not limited by speech turn:

THERAPIST: It makes sense that you are frustrated with me right now. I think I haven't been sensitive enough to your concerns about the homework.

The therapist's response is one speech turn that contains two resolution markers (validating the patient's defensive posture and acknowledging contribution to a rupture).

Rating the clarity of the resolution marker: When you see an example of a resolution strategy, put a check on the scoresheet. If it is unclear whether the behavior you observed meets full criteria for a particular strategy, you can rate it with a check minus.

✓ Meets criteria for resolution strategy
✓– Unclear whether it meets criteria for resolution strategy

Global Ratings

These ratings are made after watching and coding the entire session in 5-minute segments. They should be based on the entire session.

<u>Significance Ratings</u>: Rate the significance of each type of rupture marker (e.g., denial, minimal response) and each resolution strategy (e.g., clarify misunderstanding, change tasks/goals). Use the following scale:

Rating	Significance	
1	No significance	No rupture markers/resolution strategies, or only very minor ones that did not appear to impact the alliance. It is possible for a session to include a few minor ruptures (e.g., patient tells a somewhat avoidant story) and resolution strategies (e.g., therapist redirects patient) that have **no visible or lasting impact** on the bond or on collaboration on tasks and goals. Such very minor ruptures and resolution strategies can be coded here.
2	Minor significance	Rupture markers/resolution strategies have **a minor impact** on the alliance.
3	Some significance	Rupture markers/resolution strategies have **some impact** on the alliance.
4	Moderate significance	Rupture markers/resolution strategies have a **moderate impact** on the alliance. Probably the easiest way to gauge "moderate" is to use this category for markers/strategies that seem greater than 3 but not significant enough to be rated a 5.
5	High significance	Rupture markers/resolution strategies have a **noteworthy impact** on the alliance.

- Please note that you are rating significance, not frequency or duration. Numerous minor ruptures may be less significant for the alliance than one large rupture.

- **Overall Withdrawal and Confrontation:** After rating each rupture marker, rate the significance of all the withdrawal markers as a group, and all the confrontation markers as a group, using the Significance scale just presented.
  - Once you have made the Overall Withdrawal and Confrontation ratings, compare them and make certain that the difference between them reflects your overall sense of the session. For example, if the session was marked more by withdrawal than confrontation in terms of significance for the alliance, then your overall Withdrawal score should be higher than your overall Confrontation score.

<u>Overall Resolution Rating</u>: This rating is your global assessment of the extent to which resolution actually occurred across all the ruptures in the session. *This may differ from your significance ratings for the individual resolution strategies.* A session may include numerous, significant attempts to resolve ruptures (many high Significance ratings), but those attempts may not be completely successful (low or moderate Overall Resolution). Sessions may include some ruptures that are resolved and some that are not; pick the rating that best captures your global sense of the session.

Start by anchoring at 3, and then move up or down based on the extent of resolution in the session. Three is "average." In this context, average is meant to convey the idea of typical, commonplace baseline. It does not indicate the statistical average (mean) in your sample. For example, your sample may include only highly skilled therapists who are all excellent at repairing ruptures. In that case, you could give them all high ratings.

Overall resolution rating	Degree to which ruptures were resolved
1	**Poor resolution**/worse alliance—Major ruptures were not resolved. Either the ruptures were not addressed, so they continued, or attempts to resolve ruptures were unsuccessful. If attempts to resolve ruptures of any kind—major or minor—made the alliance worse, then code that here.
2	**Below-average resolution**/no improvement in alliance—Minor ruptures were not resolved, or major ruptures were only slightly resolved. Resolution strategies neither improved nor harmed the alliance.
3	**OK/average resolution**/OK alliance—Ruptures were at least partly addressed and resolved. By the end of the session, patient and therapist have some bond and are generally able to collaborate on most therapy tasks and goals. Sessions with no ruptures or only very minor ruptures that have no significant impact on the work of therapy should be coded here.
4	**Good, above-average resolution**/somewhat improved alliance—Ruptures were generally resolved well. Some ruptures may have been resolved very well and others only moderately well, but overall, problems with the bond and/or collaboration on tasks and goals were addressed with some success. If very minor ruptures were resolved very well, code that here.
5	**Very good resolution**/improved alliance—Ruptures were more than minor, and they were resolved very well. The resolution process seems to have improved the alliance—strengthened the bond between patient and therapist, and/or facilitated greater collaboration between patient and therapist on the tasks and goals of therapy.

Therapist Contribution Rating: The last item on the scoresheet asks coders to rate the extent to which the therapist caused or exacerbated ruptures in the session. We regard ruptures as relational phenomena that always involve both members of the dyad, so therapists are always contributing to ruptures in some fashion. The focus of this item is the extent to which the therapist is playing a "larger than average" role by actually initiating or exacerbating the rupture. The therapist might be actively engaging in negative interpersonal behaviors such as criticism, or the therapist might be unusually passive and seem to ignore prominent rupture markers. If you feel that the therapist is exhibiting markers of withdrawal and/or confrontation that cause or exacerbate patient rupture markers in the session, use this code to capture the therapist's behavior.

WITHDRAWAL RUPTURE MARKERS

In a withdrawal, the patient is moving *away* from the therapist and/or the work of therapy. The following section lists descriptions and examples of markers of withdrawal ruptures.

Denial

The denial marker overlaps with, but is not necessarily synonymous with, denial as a defense mechanism. The patient withdraws from the therapist and/or the work of therapy by denying a feeling state that is *manifestly* evident, or denying the importance of interpersonal relationships or events that seem important and relevant to the work of therapy. The patient's denial functions to shut down or move away from the current topic or activity, thereby hindering the work of therapy.

The patient may be aware that they are denying their true feelings to avoid discussing them. Or the patient may not be aware—they may be disconnected from their own internal state. In other words, they may be withdrawn from themselves. This constitutes a withdrawal rupture because it functions to create or exacerbate withdrawal from the therapist and the work of therapy.

THERAPIST: You look upset.

PATIENT: I'll be fine. Don't worry about me.

THERAPIST: According to what it says here, it looks like you could have died too.

PATIENT: Yeah. That would have solved a lot of problems.

THERAPIST: What would it solve?

PATIENT: Nothing. I didn't mean anything by it.

THERAPIST: It's interesting that you compare this mission with the death of your mother.

PATIENT: My mother's death was the most traumatic event of my life so far. That mission was just another mission.

Check minus rating: Patient's denial is unclear. You suspect that the patient might be trying to move away from the therapist, but it is also possible that the patient is collaborating by openly, honestly, and accurately reporting how the patient feels or thinks.

THERAPIST: You look upset.

PATIENT: (Speaking calmly.) I don't think I'm actually upset right now, I think I'm just really tired.

Minimal Response

The patient withdraws from the therapist by going silent or by giving minimal responses to questions or statements that are intended to initiate or continue discussion. The patient's minimal responses function to shut down the therapist's attempts to engage the patient in the work of therapy.

Walking out: An extreme example of a minimal response is walking out of the session.

Nonverbals: When a patient's speech does not meet criteria for a withdrawal marker, but the patient's nonverbal behaviors indicate that the patient is withdrawing (e.g., patient slumps down, sinks into the chair, avoids eye contact), this code can be used.

Cell phone: The patient stopping the work of therapy to answer or check their cell phone can also constitute a minimal response. (Note that if the patient does this in a way that reveals hostility or contempt for the therapist, then it should also receive a confrontation code. If there is a compelling external reason why the patient is answering the phone in the middle of a session—e.g., a parent taking an emergency call from the nurse at a child's school—then do not code it as a rupture.)

Overly talkative therapists: When a therapist dominates the session by talking a great deal, coders may feel that the patient has no choice but to give minimal responses because the therapist does not give the patient an opportunity to speak. Pay close attention to the patient's body language. If the patient appears to be actively listening and is engaged by what the therapist is saying, then the patient is not withdrawing. However, if the patient seems bored or disengaged, then minimal response is an appropriate code even if the therapist is not pausing to let the patient speak.

THERAPIST: That sounds like it was very difficult. How did it make you feel?

PATIENT: (Shrugs.)

THERAPIST: So is it upsetting to even talk about it right now?

PATIENT: Sort of.

THERAPIST: What type of cancer is it?

PATIENT: You know what? I don't want to talk about it.

Check minus rating: Patient gives a short response or goes silent for a few moments, and it is unclear whether the patient is withdrawing from the therapist or engaging in the work of therapy by quietly processing what the therapist just said. What a patient says *after* a long pause may help to clarify whether a short reply or silence was a minimal response. A pause followed by a thoughtful answer suggests that the patient is engaged in the therapy process. A pause followed by a terse response or a change in topic suggests that the patient's silence was part of a withdrawal.

Abstract Communication

The patient avoids the work of therapy by using vague or abstract language. The patient's use of abstract language functions to keep the therapist at a distance from the patient's true feelings, concerns, or issues.

Intellectualization: The patient may intellectualize by focusing on rational concepts and complex terminology.

THERAPIST: Did it bother you when I said that?

PATIENT: I was confused, but I think it's OK for things to be confusing a little every once in a while. It makes you think about it more and you can learn from it.

Global statements: The patient may make global statements that allude to an issue that is relevant to the treatment rather than directly stating their true thoughts or feelings.

Vague and confusing: The patient may rely on abstract and/or vague language to such an extent that the therapist (and the coder) may become confused and have difficulty following what the patient is saying.

PATIENT: But I mean, you know, I was thinking that maybe what I would do is just not let that happen, and just say, well, you know, maybe I don't even have to understand why that happened, maybe if I just don't let that happen, that I would just be in a better place to work on things.

Differentiating between collaboration and collusion: Sometimes therapists join patients in the use of abstract language, and both engage in an intellectualized discussion. To determine whether this constitutes collaboration (no rupture), or collusion (a withdrawal rupture), consider the following:

* Does the intellectualization function to strengthen the bond between the patient and therapist?
* Do they agree that this intellectual discussion is an appropriate therapy task for this moment in this session?
* Do they agree that this intellectual discussion is consistent with or in support of their agreed-upon treatment goals?

If so, then this is not a withdrawal rupture.

* If the intellectual discussion is a way of avoiding the work of therapy and/or is harming their bond, then it is a form of withdrawal.

Check minus rating: Patient is using abstract language, but it is unclear whether this is contributing to a withdrawal from the therapist and/or the work of therapy.

Note: Some patients have an intellectualized style of speaking. If this is the way the patient generally speaks, and it does not seem to interfere with the work of therapy, then it is not a withdrawal rupture.

Avoidant Storytelling and/or Shifting Topic

The patient tells stories and/or shifts the topic in a manner that functions to avoid the work of therapy. It is not uncommon for the patient to do both simultaneously—to shift the topic by launching into an avoidant story.

Avoidant stories: These stories are often long and tangential or circumstantial, but they can also be brief or even entertaining and may foster the sense of a "pseudoalliance." The key is that the stories function to move away from the therapist and/or the work. They may shut the therapist out, as if the patient were not even aware that the therapist is there.

Talking about someone else's reactions in an effort to avoid talking about oneself should also be coded here; for example, a patient who has been laid off talks about his coworkers' stress and anxiety rather than his own. (If the patient were to talk about the difficulties "many people are facing in this economy," then abstract communication would be the appropriate code.)

Stories that are efforts to engage in the work with the therapist by communicating something that the patient believes is important and relevant should not be coded as withdrawal ruptures. If the patient and the therapist chat a little at the beginning or end of the session as a way of warming up or cooling down, do not code that as avoidant storytelling unless you have a *strong* sense that they are avoiding the work of therapy in an important way.

Shifting topic: A good indication that the patient is withdrawing by shifting the topic is if the patient changes the topic from a heavy subject to a light one.

If the patient shifts the topic not to avoid but rather to enhance the work of therapy, this would not be coded as a withdrawal (e.g., "I know that we were talking about my job, but I just remembered something that happened with my boyfriend that I really want to discuss with you . . .").

THERAPIST: How do you think things are going so far in our work together?

PATIENT: That sounds like a performance review question. I had a performance review at work last week, and it was so stressful. . . .

THERAPIST: Are you experiencing me as angry right now?

PATIENT: No, no. I feel, um, actually, um, very safe talking to you. And it's not that I don't worry—I don't feel—I can say to my boyfriend . . .

Collaboration versus collusion: The patient may tell an avoidant-sounding story or make a sudden topic shift, and the therapist may go along and even encourage the story or the new topic by asking questions or making encouraging comments. To determine whether this constitutes a withdrawal rupture, consider the following questions:

- Does the story/topic shift function to strengthen the bond between the patient and therapist?
- Do they agree that this story/new topic is an appropriate therapy task for this moment in this session?
- Do they agree that this story/new topic is consistent with or in support of their agreed-upon treatment goals?

If so, then this is not a withdrawal rupture.

- If the story/topic shift is a way of avoiding the work of therapy and/or is harming their bond, then it is a form of withdrawal.

Check minus rating: Patient tells a story or shifts the topic, but it is unclear whether this functions to avoid the work of therapy. The story or new topic may be somewhat relevant but still has an avoidant quality (e.g., somehow shutting out the therapist). Or the therapist goes along with the story or topic shift, and it is unclear whether the patient and therapist are colluding in a withdrawal or collaborating.

Deferential and Appeasing

The patient withdraws from the therapist and/or the work of therapy by being overly compliant and submitting to the therapist in a deferential manner. The patient's deferential behavior functions to avoid conflict with the therapist and/or makes it harder for the therapist to know how the patient really feels or what the patient really thinks. Code deferential for patients who "yes" the therapist—who seem superficially engaged and smile and say "yes" to everything the therapist says, even when they do not really agree.

THERAPIST: How was the homework?

PATIENT: Oh, it was so helpful. You give such wonderful advice.

THERAPIST: It's a process, but I think we can both agree it's nice to have that support. What I'm hearing, and you can tell me if it's different, is that there isn't so much of that right now.

PATIENT: Yeah, totally.

THERAPIST: It can be challenging and can increase the feelings of sadness.

PATIENT: Yeah.

THERAPIST: That's what it sounds like.

PATIENT: I think that's absolutely right. I totally agree. I 100% agree.

Collaboration versus deference: Not every positive comment a patient makes is deferential. Patients can genuinely feel and honestly express positive feelings about the therapist and the work of therapy. To determine whether a patient's positive comments constitute a withdrawal rupture, consider the following questions:

- Does the patient seem genuine, honest, and engaged? (Note body language as well as tone of voice.) Then do not code a withdrawal rupture.

- Does the patient seem insincere? Does it feel as if the patient is trying to smooth things over, to avoid conflict, to win over the therapist? Then do code a withdrawal rupture.

Check minus rating: Patient is agreeing with or praising the therapist or the therapy, and it is unclear whether the patient is being overly deferential or sincere.

PATIENT: Did you do it all yourself, or did you use an interior decorator? So this is all you? I'm impressed.

Content/Affect Split

The patient withdraws from the therapist and/or the work of therapy by exhibiting affect that does not match the content of their narrative. For example, the patient is describing an upsetting event, but the affect is too positive (smiling, nervous laugh) or is very matter-of-fact.

(Patient looks tearful.)

THERAPIST: It's hard for you to tell me about those sad feelings.

PATIENT: (A bright, forced smile.) Yes, it is. It's not easy to talk about.

Content/affect splits are particularly noteworthy when the patient uses positive affect to soften or withdraw from a complaint or concern about the therapist or the therapy.

THERAPIST: What just happened? You did not like that question?

PATIENT: Well, I just felt like things were moving forward (chuckling), that question took me back a couple of steps.

PATIENT: So, first, I wanted (chuckle), after the last session, I felt like, I don't know if that was the intention or not but I felt like you were trying to tell me that I need to take more responsibility. (Smiling.) That's the impression I left with. Maybe I wasn't doing my homework, so I wasn't taking it seriously, me coming here, and that I wasn't challenging myself. Like, I was just coming in here and it became like a routine. So I took that as you want me to do my homework and I need to work on things and put more effort into this because I'm not here because someone made me, I'm here because I wanted to, so to get benefit out of it, I needed to be more proactive. (Laughs.)

Content/affect split versus humor: Do not code every time a patient laughs or smiles or makes a sarcastic joke. Upsetting events can contain within them aspects that are funny or ironic, and a patient's comfort with laughing with their therapist could be a marker of a strong alliance rather than a rupture. To determine whether a content/affect split constitutes a withdrawal rupture, consider the following questions:

- Does the split between the patient's content and their affect cause or reveal weakness in the bond with the therapist? Does the patient seem uneasy or uncomfortable? Do you have the sense that the patient does not trust the therapist enough to reveal true feelings?

- Does the content/affect split hinder the work of therapy by making it harder for the therapist to know how the patient really feels or what the patient really thinks?

- Is the patient using overly positive affect in an effort to avoid conflict with the therapist by softening the blow of a complaint or concern?

If yes, then code a withdrawal rupture.

Check minus rating: When the content and affect seem discrepant, but you are not sure if the patient is withdrawing from the therapist.

Self-Criticism and/or Hopelessness

The patient withdraws from the therapist and the work of therapy by becoming absorbed in a depressive process of self-criticism and/or hopelessness that seems to shut out the therapist and to close off any possibility that the therapist or the treatment can help the patient. The patient may make self-denigrating and self-minimizing statements. The patient may engage in this process as a means of avoiding conflict with the therapist.

THERAPIST: That sounds important. Can you tell me more about that?

PATIENT: (Sighs.) What's the point? It's not going to make me feel better.

THERAPIST: It's hard for you to tell me "no."

PATIENT: Now you see why it's impossible for me to get a job.

Patient and therapist discussing patient's sense of loneliness. Patient mentions several friends and acquaintances but for each one provides a reason that the patient cannot turn to them for support.

THERAPIST: Are there other people in your life that we can get you connected with?

PATIENT: Um . . . (long pause)—it's hard because the friends I've made here, they're not people that I really want to open up to. They're not people I think would give good advice. It's more of an informal, social friendship than in my proper friends back home. I haven't found, you know, really good friends here yet.

Help-rejecting patients like this can present with a combination of self-critical/hopeless and reject intervention. The therapist keeps trying to get the patient to identify someone they can talk to, and the patient rejects the idea that such a person exists in their life—because the patient is hopeless that the situation can be improved.

Note that patients can be self-critical or hopeless about some aspects of their situation but still be engaged with the therapist and the work of therapy and can explore these feelings with the therapist in a collaborative way, as in this example:

PATIENT: I doubted my intelligence. Like, maybe I'm just stupid because I'm having all these problems. So am I really a thinking type? Maybe I'm sensing. I don't think things through. Because I always test as thinking, but then I thought, well, these tests are subjective. So maybe I don't know who I am.

Patient is not withdrawing—the patient is sharing self-critical thoughts in an open and direct way. This is not a rupture.

Check minus rating: The patient is making self-critical and/or hopeless statements, and it is unclear whether this constitutes a withdrawal from the therapist and/or the work of therapy.

CONFRONTATION RUPTURE MARKERS

In a confrontation, the patient is moving *against* the therapist and/or the work of therapy. The following section contains descriptions and examples of markers of confrontation ruptures.

Complaints/Concerns About the Therapist

The patient expresses negative feelings about the therapist. The patient might feel angry, impatient, distrustful, manipulated, hurt, judged, controlled, or rejected. The patient might believe that the therapist has failed in being supportive, encouraging, or respectful. The patient may criticize the therapist's interpersonal style or express doubts about the therapist's competence. If the patient says or implies that the therapist does not understand the patient, or is ineffective as a therapist, then code it here.

Most patients find that it is difficult to criticize a therapist directly. If you get even a hint of negative feelings for the therapist, code it.

PATIENT: I was thinking about some of the things that you said last week. I wasn't very happy about them. Not so much what you said, actually, more the way you said them. You were pushing me into a corner. I wouldn't have thought that was the way to go about helping people.

PATIENT: I feel like you are opening me up and exploring every inch of my insides. It's really, really, really uncomfortable.

THERAPIST: And the Air Force?

PATIENT: (Said testily) The *Navy*, doctor, *listen*.

PATIENT: I can see I'm not gonna get anything useful out of you.

PATIENT: This is not for me. All this "what do you feel, what do you think?" I asked you something. I came to you to consult about something very clear and specific.

PATIENT: I can't communicate with you.

PATIENT: I just kind of resented, you know, when you came at me like that. Why didn't you just stop me?

Complaint/concern about therapist with "nice" patients: Complaints/concerns about the therapist are often expressed in a hostile manner, but hostility is not necessary for this code. Complaints/concerns can also be expressed in a subtle, polite way by "nice" patients. They may appear in conjunction with a withdrawal rupture (e.g., concern expressed with a smile so that it is both complaint/concern therapist and content/affect split). These **mixed codes** (withdrawal and confrontation) should be captured by coding both confrontation and withdrawal markers in the same time segment.

PATIENT: So, first, I wanted (chuckle), after the last session, I felt like, I don't know if that was the intention or not, but I felt like you were trying to tell me that I need to take more responsibility. (Smiling.)

Content/affect split, complaint therapist—the patient is telling the therapist "You made me feel criticized."

Complaint/concern about therapist versus self-assertion: Helping patients to express concerns about the therapist and/or the work of therapy can be a step toward healthy self-assertion and part of the process of repairing an alliance rupture. When this is happening, it is important to distinguish between markers of confrontation ruptures and self-assertion. Pay attention to the degree of hostility. Thinking about how affiliation is rated on the Structural Analysis of Social Behavior (SASB; e.g., L. S. Benjamin, 1974[1]) can be helpful. On the SASB, affiliation is conceptualized as a dimension with poles of hostility/hate at one end and friendliness/love at the opposite end. At the midpoint of this dimension is a point of neutrality. When the patient's concern is expressed with hostility, it is a confrontation rupture. Generally speaking, a healthy self-assertion will be expressed in a more neutral way.

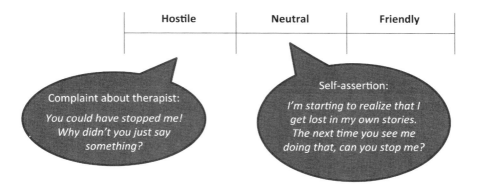

Check minus rating: It is unclear whether the patient is expressing negative feelings about the therapist.

Patient Rejects Therapist Intervention

The patient rejects or dismisses the therapist's intervention. The patient may reject the therapist's view or interpretation of the patient and/or the patient's situation, or the patient rejects or dismisses the therapist's efforts to intervene (e.g., therapist tries to offer support, and patient rebuffs therapist in a hostile manner). The patient is attacking and shutting down something that the therapist is trying to bring to the table. Rejecting a therapist's question as irrelevant or inappropriate should be coded here.

If the patient disagrees with, dismisses, or rejects a task—an activity that the therapist wishes the patient to participate in, such as completing a thought record or doing a two-chair exercise—then rate complaint/concern about activities.

---

[1]Benjamin, L. S. (1974). Structural analysis of social behavior. *Psychological Review, 81,* 392–425.

THERAPIST: It sounds like you are concerned about him.

PATIENT: (Hostile tone.) No, that is not it at all.

THERAPIST: When did your insomnia begin?

PATIENT: What difference does that make?

THERAPIST: I thought we could focus some more on your anxiety. . . . That's the thought I had. I don't know if there's anything in particular that you want to make sure we get to today?

PATIENT: (Frowning.) Yeah, I don't know if it's anxiety.

Collaboration versus confrontation: Not every disagreement is a rupture. A patient may disagree with a therapist's idea in the context of a collaborative exploration of an issue, as in the following example:

THERAPIST: You've been under a lot of pressure at work lately. Is there something at work that is contributing to how you are feeling today?

PATIENT: Work was stressing me out a lot last week, but today, no, I don't think it's work that is causing my anxiety. I think maybe it's more about what's going on with my girlfriend. . . .

Note that in the preceding example, the patient and therapist are working together to identify the source of the patient's anxiety. The patient is actively engaged, really considering the therapist's idea and taking the therapist's contribution seriously. If the patient said "no" to everything the therapist suggested, and you had the feeling that the patient was resisting the therapist's efforts, then you would code reject intervention.

To determine whether a disagreement is a confrontation rupture, consider the following questions:

• Is the patient engaging with the therapist in the work of therapy (vs. resisting the work of therapy)?
• Are the patient and the therapist on the same page? (If the therapist appears frustrated or defeated, that is a good sign that a rupture is occurring.)
• Does the patient respect the therapist's ideas and suggestions?

Check minus rating: If it is unclear whether the patient is rejecting the therapist's intervention or is thoughtfully considering it. There might be a subtle sense of pushback.

Complaints/Concerns About the Activities of Therapy

The patient expresses dissatisfaction, discomfort, or disagreement with specific tasks of therapy such as homework assignments or in-session tasks such as empty chair or imaginal exposure. Patients may directly complain about an activity, or they may express their concerns in a more subtle way by expressing some doubts about the effectiveness of a particular task.

PATIENT: I really don't understand what you're asking me to do on these thought records. I don't see the point of them at all.

PATIENT: What is this? Why are we doing this exercise? I feel really uncomfortable right now.

THERAPIST: That's the kind of pressure you're putting on yourself, the kind of stuff you wouldn't want your boss to do to you.

PATIENT: Yeah. That's true. (Pause.) Do you think this, doing this exercise is going to actually help with that? (Sounds skeptical.)

Homework: When a patient reports that they did not do the homework, code complaint/concern about activity. The patient's not doing the homework indicates a problem in the collaboration between the patient and therapist on the tasks of therapy: the patient may not agree with the homework, the patient may lack motivation to do the homework, or the homework may be problematic (e.g., too difficult) for the patient.

The only exception would be the rare instance when the patient agreed with the homework, was motivated to do the homework, and tried to do the homework but encountered obstacles that could not have been foreseen (e.g., homework was to practice assertion by speaking up in class and class was cancelled that week).

Check minus rating: It is unclear whether the patient is expressing concerns/complaints about activities of therapy.

Complaints/Concerns About the Parameters of Therapy

The patient expresses concerns or complaints about the parameters of treatment, such as the therapy schedule (e.g., appointment times, session length, number and frequency of sessions) or the research contract (e.g., completing questionnaires, being video-recorded).

PATIENT: Once a week is not enough. It's not enough time to address all my problems!

PATIENT: I don't see the point of these questionnaires I have to fill out every week. What do these questions have to do with me?

PATIENT: I can never forget that the camera is there.

Collaboration versus confrontation: When patients and therapists are trying to schedule a session, the patient may express concerns about specific dates or times. This may be part of a collaborative scheduling process in which both parties are comfortable being honest and clear about what they realistically can do. To determine whether a patient's concern about certain dates or times is part of collaborative discussion or is a complaint/concern about parameters, consider the following questions:

- Is the patient not really trying to find a time to meet?
- Is the patient putting up roadblocks to every suggestion the therapist makes?
- Is the patient inflexible?
- Does the patient seem not to want to meet with the frequency the therapist thinks is appropriate?

If yes, then code complaint/concern about parameters.

Check minus rating: It is unclear whether the patient is expressing concerns/complaints about the parameters of treatment.

Complaints/Concerns About Progress in Therapy

The patient expresses complaints, concerns, or doubts about the progress that can be made or has been made in therapy.

PATIENT: I've been coming here for four weeks now, and I really can't think of anything that has changed. Maybe this has all been a waste of time.

PATIENT: As I told you, I have the feeling we are going in circles.

PATIENT: I think I want to quit.

PATIENT: Yeah. (Sounds a little unsure.) I think I've made some progress.

In the preceding example, the patient's tone and affect revealed doubts about the patient's progress. This example should be coded as a combination of **confrontation** (complaint about progress) and **withdrawal** (deferential) because the patient is dissatisfied with the progress but reluctant to clearly state this for fear of upsetting the therapist. If the patient's tone and affect had been less clear, this could be coded as a check minus. Alternatively, if the patient said this in a straightforward way and was communicating that they really felt that they *had* made some progress and were pleased, then this would not be a rupture.

Check minus rating: It is unclear whether the patient is expressing complaints/concerns/doubts about the progress in therapy.

Patient Defends Self Against Therapist

The patient defends their thoughts, feelings, or behavior against what they **perceive** to be the **therapist's** criticism or judgment of the patient. The patient makes a case to support, validate, and defend their behavior, beliefs, feelings, decisions, and so on. Note that the therapist does not have to actually criticize the patient for the patient to anticipate or perceive criticism and become defensive. Also, what patients regard as critical can be idiosyncratic. One patient may regard being called "career focused" a compliment, and another patient becomes defensive because they regard it as criticism.

Patients who insist that they do not meet criteria for diagnoses or that they do not need treatment are usually defending themselves against a perceived criticism or judgment.

THERAPIST: That makes a lot of sense.

PATIENT: Of course it does! I'm not an idiot!

PATIENT: But I think it's normal for people to change. I'm going through a transitional period. So I have new ideas about what would help me get through this situation. It doesn't necessarily mean that I am unstable.

THERAPIST: That's the interesting thing—you always come in and you tell me that you're always listening and you always follow me.

PATIENT: And I do exactly what you suggest all the time.

THERAPIST: That's the funny thing, because you do lots of things that I never suggested.

PATIENT: My life is more complex. I did exactly what you suggested. Taking a look back, I did everything that you suggested, but it didn't help our relationship.

There are instances when a patient sounds very defensive, but it is unclear against whom the patient is defending themselves. In the following example, the patient gets extremely animated talking about her boyfriend:

PATIENT: It was like he didn't understand. . . . I had to keep up my separate household. How do you do that? How do you do that? I can't do this stuff during the day. . . .

If the coder believes that this patient is not only defending herself against her boyfriend but also trying to make her case to the therapist because she thinks the therapist might share the boyfriend's views, then use the code of patient defends self. If it seems likely that the patient is only defending herself against her boyfriend, or her own inner critic, but there is a small possibility that in some way she is trying to defend herself against the therapist, then code check minus.

The SASB coding system can be a helpful guide here as well. Patient defends self is trying to capture behaviors that are toward the hostile end of the affiliation dimension, as opposed to the neutral point of the dimension, which is more likely a healthy place of self-assertion.

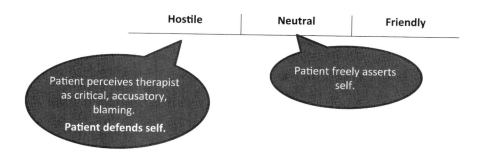

Check minus rating: It is unclear whether the patient is defending themselves against the therapist. If the patient is highly defensive, even if the defensiveness seems to be directed toward someone other than the therapist, give at least a check minus—most likely on some level, the patient's defense is partly aimed at the therapist.

Efforts to Control/Pressure the Therapist

The patient attempts to control the therapist and/or the session (e.g., patient tells the therapist what to do or what not to do), or the patient puts pressure on the therapist to fix the patient's problems quickly. Trying to push or provoke the therapist should be coded here. While watching a segment, if you can imagine feeling pressured if you were the therapist, then consider this code.

THERAPIST: And you do need to tell your parents.

PATIENT: Just stop it.

THERAPIST: Your cancer is at stage three.

PATIENT: Stop it, stop it, stop it!

PATIENT: Tell me what my problem is and what I need to do.

THERAPIST: So why have you come to see me?

PATIENT: Whoa, we'll get to that. Now, you're probably thinking . . . [Patient goes on to dominate the discussion and makes no space for the therapist to participate.]

PATIENT: I'm tired of wasting time. I want to know how this therapy works. Tell me how it's going to help me with my problems. And none of that fancy therapist talk; I want a direct answer.

A longtime patient (who is also a therapist and who often engages in power struggles with their therapist) arrives at the session and sits in the therapist's chair.

THERAPIST: That's where I sit.

PATIENT: Oh, yes, of course. (Patient gets up and moves to the other chair.)

The session of Gloria with Carl Rogers is a good example of a more subtle form of control/pressure. The following excerpt is one of the many times that Gloria asks Rogers for an answer. She is never completely direct—she hedges a little ("almost") and smiles in a forced way. There is a sense of desperation and pleading, which puts pressure on the therapist.

PATIENT: And I want—I almost want an answer from you. I want you to tell me if it would affect her wrong if I told her the truth, or what.

Control/pressure can also take the form of sexually charged, flirtatious patient behaviors that feel intrusive and demanding to the therapist. Do not automatically code all flirtatious behavior or all examples of erotic transference. The key for this code is the patient's effort to put pressure on or exert power over the therapist. For example, if a patient says the following to a female therapist:

PATIENT: That's a really pretty skirt you have on today.

This statement may feel like a friendly, well-meaning compliment from a grandmotherly patient but may feel intrusive and intimidating from a domineering male patient who often makes sexually inappropriate comments about his female employees. The latter would constitute an example of control/pressure.

Collaboration versus confrontation: Patients can directly tell therapists what they need from them in a collaborative way. To distinguish between frank collaboration and control/pressure, consider the following questions:

- Is the patient expressing their needs to the therapist in a sincere, direct way, or is the patient trying to compel (e.g., with hostile force or fawning flattery) the therapist to do what the patient wants?

- Does the patient legitimate the therapist's freedom to decline the patient's request?

- Does the patient seem so intimidating or so desperate that the therapist will have a hard time saying no?

If yes, code control/pressure.

Check minus rating: It is unclear whether the patient is pressuring or attempting to control the therapist.

RESOLUTION STRATEGIES

Resolution strategies are therapists' attempts to repair a rupture. The following section presents descriptions and examples of resolution strategies.

Therapist Clarifies a Misunderstanding

The therapist responds to a rupture by attempting to clarify a misunderstanding. Generally, the resolution effort stops here; the therapist does not go on to explore the underlying significance of the misunderstanding or try to link it to the patient's core themes.

THERAPIST: You seem a little distant right now.

PATIENT: Well, I guess I was a little bothered about what you said about how I should apologize to my sister.

THERAPIST: No, no, I said that I think your sister should apologize to you.

PATIENT: Oh. (Smiling.) I must have misheard you. . . .

PATIENT: (Said nervously.) I guess I can try reaching out to them.

THERAPIST: It's worth trying out, to see how it makes you feel to share more with them. I don't want you to misunderstand and think that I'm saying call them and just pour it out and say, this is what's going on in my life!

THERAPIST: It sounds like you clicked with CBT

PATIENT: No! I was assigned to CBT, that's totally different.

THERAPIST: What I'm saying by "you click with it" is that you seem to like it.

Check minus rating: It is unclear whether the therapist is trying to resolve a rupture by clarifying a misunderstanding. For example, the therapist may be clarifying something, but it is unclear whether this explanation is in response to a rupture.

Therapist Changes Tasks or Goals

The therapist changes the tasks or goals of therapy in response to a rupture. The therapist may change the task/goal to address the concerns of a patient who is complaining (confrontation rupture). Or the therapist may change the task/goal in an effort to engage a withdrawn patient. Changing the task can include *modifying* the task to make it more palatable for the patient.

PATIENT: We're getting off track again. I don't think this is getting us anywhere.

THERAPIST: I'm willing to follow your lead right now. What direction would you like to go in?

PATIENT: It's hard to talk about my mom. (Patient goes quiet.)

THERAPIST: So how are things at work? You were going to meet with your boss to ask about a raise, right?

THERAPIST: Today's our 15th session, so we're about the middle of our treatment. So today I was interested in reflecting back on your main concerns, the things you wanted to work on when you first came in, see how things are going so far, and also planning what we're going to do moving forward. And then I'd like to hear about how the homeworks went. Does that sound good? Do you have anything else you want to add to the agenda?

PATIENT: (Tight smile.) I have a whole list of things. So much happened since last time. I wrote it down and I wanted to talk to you about. *Content/affect split and check minus reject intervention— patient is subtly telling the therapist "no"*

THERAPIST: OK, so we can do two things. We can either assess the mid-phase today, or we can put that off until next week and work mostly on this stuff if there's a lot of stuff going on.

PATIENT: That sounds good.

THERAPIST: OK, so then next week we'll talk about where we've come.

PATIENT: I don't relate to it. It just doesn't seem the kind of thing that's useful to me, that even relates to me. *Complaint activity*

THERAPIST: So what do you feel like doesn't relate to you? *Invite thoughts/ feelings*

PATIENT: Well (looks at thought record), distressing physical sensations, I've never had that.

THERAPIST: OK, that doesn't need to apply.

PATIENT: Thoughts and images through my mind—I'm not the kind of person who thinks in images—I don't know.

THERAPIST: OK, that's also something that can be sort of removed from this. Maybe it's easier to just cross those things out.

Check minus rating: It is unclear whether the therapist is changing the task/goal in response to a rupture or if the therapist is simply doing therapy (e.g., therapist is unaware of a rupture and is moving on to the next item on the agenda).

PATIENT: It's hard to talk about my mom. (Goes quiet.)

THERAPIST: (Nods.) Well, I think we're done setting the agenda, should we review the homework?

Therapist Illustrates Tasks or Provides a Rationale for Treatment

The therapist responds to a rupture by illustrating, explaining, or providing a rationale for a therapy task or goal. The therapist may share their reasons for pursuing a particular therapy task in an effort to engage the patient or to alleviate the patient's concerns. Sometimes this may be in the form of reframing the meaning of tasks or goals in a way that is more appealing to the patient.

Do not code if the therapist is simply explaining a task as part of the regular process of treatment—for example, if the therapist is introducing a thought record for the first time and is explaining how to do it and why it would be helpful. If it is not clear whether the therapist is responding to a rupture or "just doing therapy," follow this guideline: The first time the therapist explains a task, it is most likely "just therapy." If the therapist explains the task a second time, or keeps expanding on their original explanation, that increases the likelihood that the therapist is responding to a rupture of some kind (e.g., a sense that the patient is not agreeing with the task).

THERAPIST: I'd like to spend some time trying to understand what's going on between us right now. My hope is that this type of exploration may provide us with some clues as to what may go on for you in your relationship with other people.

A patient is reluctant to complete a homework assignment that involves increasing social contact because they fear rejection. The therapist reframes the assignment as "putting yourself into the anxiety-provoking situation in order to self-monitor your cognitive processes."

THERAPIST: I'd be interested in exploring it because I learn as much as you do too. It helps me understand what's happening between us.

PATIENT: I just felt like, is that an issue? Is it?

THERAPIST: I guess I did see it as an issue that we could explore. Maybe you like to see me as older, maybe that is comforting to you? That's kind of where I was going with that.

THERAPIST: It may be frustrating to have to carry these thought records around with you, but it may be really helpful to just have them in moments when you're so overwhelmed.

THERAPIST: I do think that you are suffering from some kind of anxiety. And the only way I know to alleviate your symptoms is to figure out what's causing that anxiety. And the only way I know how to do that is to talk.

THERAPIST: You see, one thing that concerns me is, uh . . . It's no good you doing something that you haven't really chosen to do. That's why I am trying to help you find out what your own inner choices are.

Check minus rating: If it is unclear whether the therapist is illustrating a task/providing a rationale in response to a rupture or is simply doing therapy.

The Therapist Invites the Patient to Discuss Thoughts or Feelings About the Therapist or Some Aspect of Therapy

The therapist responds to a rupture by inviting the patient to express negative or vulnerable thoughts or feelings about the therapist and/or the tasks or goals of therapy. For example, the therapist may encourage a confrontational patient to expand upon their negative feelings about a therapy task, or the therapist may observe that a patient is quiet and withdrawn and may ask them to voice their concerns directly.

This code really involves two parts: the therapist recognizes that a rupture is occurring, then tries to initiate some exploration of the rupture with the patient.

Do not code every time the therapist asks the patient what the patient is thinking or feeling. Just checking in to make sure the patient is still in agreement is not acknowledging and exploring a rupture. For example, do not code if the therapist is simply following CBT protocol and asking for feedback at the end of the session. Do code if the therapist is asking for feedback in the context of a rupture (e.g., "We had a challenging session today. We didn't really agree about the thought record. How are you feeling about it now?")

PATIENT: I'm feeling a little irritated, but it's not a big deal.

THERAPIST: I understand that you're uncertain about how important your concerns are. But if you're willing to go into it, I'd be interested in hearing more.

THERAPIST: I'd like to talk about the thoughts you are having about it, specifically, this isn't going to work.

THERAPIST: So are you feeling in general frustrated with this whole thing, the thought record?

PATIENT: Yeah. (Slight smile.) *Minimal response and check minus content/affect split*

THERAPIST: So, can you say more about that? What is frustrating about it?

THERAPIST: Are you experiencing me as angry right now?

THERAPIST: So did you feel that we weren't communicating with each other?

Therapists often invite thoughts/feelings by asking questions. However, they can also invite by making observations that function to encourage the patient to elaborate about their concerns about the therapist or the therapy. For example:

THERAPIST: It almost sounds like maybe you felt like you were in trouble, maybe you weren't doing things right.

PATIENT: Yeah.

THERAPIST: Like I was disappointed.

PATIENT: Yeah. I was in trouble. That was the feeling.

Check minus rating: It is unclear whether the therapist is inviting the patient to express negative or vulnerable thoughts/feelings about the therapist and/or the therapy. The therapist may be simply acknowledging that the patient has negative thoughts or feelings, not clearly inviting and encouraging the patient to explore them. Or it may not be clear that the patient's concerns are related to the therapist and/or the therapy.

The Therapist Acknowledges Their Own Contribution to a Rupture

The therapist acknowledges their own contribution to a rupture. For example, the therapist acknowledges the ways in which they may be frustrating, confusing, or upsetting the patient and thereby harming the therapist–patient bond or hindering their work together. The therapist may acknowledge how the therapist contributed to a rupture earlier in the session or in a prior session or how the therapist is contributing to a rupture that is occurring right now. The therapist may predict, based on past ruptures, that their next response will contribute to a new rupture.

THERAPIST: I could see how this could be frustrating for you. You're asking me for a direct answer and I keep putting the ball back in your court

THERAPIST: OK, I want to stay with this for a moment because it's possible maybe I was unclear, or without realizing it, gave you certain signals or messages.

THERAPIST: I have to admit, in this moment, I feel a little accusatory. . . .

THERAPIST: I'm sure this will sound evasive to you.

THERAPIST: You know, I've been thinking about it a lot, what happened last time, I have two thoughts about it, see what you think. One is that I need to take some responsibility for not making your environment here safe, that things got farther and more emotional and more painful, um, then they needed to be and that, um, there were some mistakes that I made.

Check minus rating: It is unclear whether the therapist is acknowledging their contribution to a rupture.

The Therapist Discloses Their Internal Experience of the Patient–Therapist Interaction

In the context of a rupture, the therapist discloses their internal experience of the patient-therapist interaction.

Do not code every time a therapist shares what they think or feel. Many therapists are in the habit of prefacing statements with phrases like "I am wondering . . ." or "I feel like . . ." Only code when the therapist is sharing their thoughts or feelings about the patient–therapist interaction when the patient is confronting or withdrawing. The therapist may share their own perception of the interaction (e.g., "I feel like we are caught in a power struggle"). The therapist may share negative feelings, such as frustration or anxiety. Or the therapist may reassure an anxious patient by disclosing the therapist's positive feelings.

THERAPIST: I'm trying to answer your question, but I get the sense that nothing I say to you will be satisfying right now. I'm concerned I will antagonize you further if I continue to try.

THERAPIST: I feel like walking on ice here. . . .

THERAPIST: Yeah, so, I think just as it was difficult—You felt like I didn't understand you, I felt like, you know, every time, not every time, but sometimes when I brought certain things up and made some suggestions or maybe asked, you know like I said, presented a different point of view from the point of view that you had, oftentimes you were not really absorbing, taking in what I was saying.

THERAPIST: I have to be honest with you. I'm a little angry with you. As a therapist that's not something that's comfortable to feel.

THERAPIST: But I also had a feeling that there may have been a reason that you were saying, you know, so much and maybe keeping me away because if we picked at something, you were going to go to an emotional place.

PATIENT: Yeah. I was in trouble. That was the feeling. A lot of times with people I feel like I did something wrong.

THERAPIST: Well I'm really glad that you were able to bring that up, that's awesome, that's total assertiveness right there. The other thing is, I'm *not* disappointed. So I just want to put that out there. I don't think you're doing a bad job or being lazy. I think you're doing a great job on homework. I feel like you're really taking this seriously.

Check minus rating: It is unclear whether the therapist is disclosing their own internal experience in the context of a rupture. It may be unclear that the therapist is responding to a rupture, or the therapist may not be clearly revealing their internal experience but only hinting at it.

THERAPIST: I'm getting the sense from you that there's a lot that you're holding onto, and it sounds like there's no way to bounce it off of anyone.

Therapist is aware that the patient is holding things in and is reluctant to share. However, the therapist does not clearly disclose her own experience—she does not say, for example, "There's a lot you're holding back from me."

Therapist Links the Rupture to Larger Interpersonal Patterns Between the Patient and the Therapist

The therapist links a rupture to larger interpersonal patterns between the patient and the therapist. With this strategy, the therapist notes how the rupture that is occurring now is similar to other ruptures that have occurred in this dyad (e.g., "I think we're doing it again").

The patient has difficulty articulating what they want to focus on in the session and they criticize themselves for being confused and disorganized. The therapist draws attention to how they often blame themselves for any misunderstandings that arise.

In some cases, the patient is the first one to observe such a pattern. If the therapist then picks up on the patient's idea and agrees with it or elaborates on it, then you can still code this strategy, as in the following example:

PATIENT: I've never gotten that kind of feedback from someone. It makes me think about other situations. Is that maybe how I'm skewing some other interactions with people?

THERAPIST: You know, it's delicate, because I'm sure you're not always skewing everything and I don't want you to not trust your instincts. Lots of times our instincts are telling us useful information. But at times when you're feeling maybe not as confident, maybe a little more delicate, you may be more likely to pull for stuff like that.

Check minus rating: It is unclear whether the therapist is linking a rupture to larger interpersonal patterns between the patient and therapist.

Therapist Links the Rupture to Larger Interpersonal Patterns in the Patient's Other Relationships

The therapist links a rupture to larger interpersonal patterns in the patient's other relationships. This code will encompass many—but not all—transference interpretations in a psychodynamic therapy. This code may also be appropriate for some discussions of core beliefs in CBT. The link has to be made in the context of a rupture—the link functions to draw attention to and/or invite exploration of a rupture.

The therapist can start by acknowledging a rupture and then note a parallel with an outside relationship, or the therapist can start with an observation about an outside relationship and then draw a parallel with a rupture in therapy. The patient can be the first to make the link, as long as the therapist then agrees with or expands on what the patient said.

The patient has difficulty asking the therapist for a different session time. The therapist links this to the patient's lack of assertiveness in relationships with their family and coworkers.

THERAPIST: Well, speaking of what you were just saying about the reasons why you never developed some of these important, close friendships, around this idea of being understood, it sounds like some time in the process since we last saw each other, there was this question of how much *I* understood you.

PATIENT: And that problem came up when I was in physical therapy.

THERAPIST: Is it coming up here with cognitive therapy?

Check minus rating: It is unclear whether the therapist is linking a rupture to larger interpersonal patterns in the patient's other relationships.

Therapist Validates the Patient's Defensive Posture

Therapist responds to a rupture by validating the patient's defensive posture. The therapist allies with the resistance: instead of challenging the patient's defensive behaviors, the therapist validates the ways in which they are understandable and adaptive. This is more than just reflecting back the patient's own explanations for their behavior—this involves communicating that the patient's position is legitimate and valid. The therapist may validate a patient's complaints or concerns, or a therapist may validate a patient's withdrawal, as in the following example:

A patient cries in session and then becomes self-conscious and begins to speak in a distant, intellectualized fashion. The therapist observes that the patient now seems distant from their pain, and says, "Perhaps it's adaptive for you to have some distance from it right now."

PATIENT: (In a critical tone.) You also seemed like really stressed about being late, and you know, that was something you know like that just didn't, just wasn't an issue for me. And I don't know, I don't know why that bothered you so much.

THERAPIST: So you observing my emotion and commenting on it is exactly what we want to be doing for one thing. And you're right about everything you said.

PATIENT: You will never understand me. I cannot express myself so it's much better to quit.

THERAPIST: Actually, I appreciate your honesty, and if you want to quit of course that's your choice.

THERAPIST: And let me know if you have any other questions, too, like if it doesn't make sense. I'm glad that you came in and—some people might come in and say, "Oh yeah, I like the thought record" even though they hate it.

PATIENT: (Smiling.) Oh, OK, oh that's not my style.

THERAPIST: No, it's great! I'm very happy that, you know, you're telling me exactly how it's going and what you think because there's no point if you don't like it.

Check minus rating: It is unclear whether the therapist is validating the patient's defensive posture. For example, the therapist validates the patient, but it is unclear whether this validation is in response to a rupture.

Therapist Responds to a Rupture by Redirecting or Refocusing the Patient

When the patient moves away from the tasks of therapy (e.g., by telling avoidant stories), the therapist responds to the rupture by redirecting the patient back to the task at hand or by refocusing the patient on the present moment.

Session begins with a focus on the patient's anxiety, which was one of the patient's presenting problems. Patient begins by talking at length about going to clubs to hear music. Patient is not engaging with the therapist at all and seems to be avoiding the tasks of therapy—this is a withdrawal, avoidant storytelling.

PATIENT: It's really hard to find a club that has consistently good music without having to pay through the nose.

THERAPIST: Yeah.

PATIENT: And not having to buy a drink, which sometimes I do and sometimes I don't. It's like, if I'm going to listen to this music, I'm going to have to get a pint of beer and I'm not in the mood for a pint of beer.

THERAPIST: Right.

PATIENT: I'd rather leave my system alone.

THERAPIST: Yeah, OK, I hate—not to change pace too much, but I know that the last time we met, you had a lot of doctor's appointments, a lot of health concerns. Is that contributing to your anxiety right now? *(The therapist attempts to stop the patient's avoidant storytelling by redirecting the patient back to the task of therapy, discussion of the anxiety.)*

PATIENT: They were huge for me, it was like he didn't understand. The thing is, we lived two doors apart, and that was like a big mistake so there was an expectation both on his part so really what it was doing was that we lived together but at the same time there was I had to keep up my separate household. How can you do that? How do you do that? Laundry, letters, I can't do this stuff during the day, you know, going out, buying cards. I'm a woman. It takes me an hour to get ready and I'm not even high maintenance. I was looking like a slob. I have a living animal in my house, you know, that I have to take care of. I take the responsibility of a pet seriously! I made a commitment to her, and it isn't like I put her before him—In reality, of course, I do. Does he have to know that? No—but she still has to get walked and taken care of . . .

THERAPIST: So let's check in with how you're feeling right now. What are you feeling now?

In this vignette, the therapist is not trying to expand the discussion of the patient's feelings about a rupture (which would be an example of invite thoughts/feelings). Rather, the therapist is trying to rein the patient in and bring her focus back to the present moment.

Check minus: It is unclear whether the therapist is redirecting/refocusing the patient in response to a rupture or whether the therapist is simply doing therapy.

RUPTURE/RESOLUTION MARKER DIFFERENTIAL DIAGNOSIS

The following lists present guidelines for deciding between two or three rupture or resolution marker codes that coders sometimes have difficulty distinguishing.

Deferential versus minimal response

- If the patient is just being quiet and seems withdrawn—code **minimal response**.

- If the patient is nodding, agreeing with the therapist, and seems at least superficially engaged, trying to be a good patient—then code **deferential**.

- If the patient is giving very brief, minimal responses *and* behaving deferentially (e.g., quiet nods, smiles), then code both **deferential** and **minimal response**.

Denial versus deferential

- If the patient denies feeling upset at the therapist when the patient seems to actually be upset (e.g., "I'm not upset!"), code **denial**.

- If the same patient then goes on to say that he/she has very positive feelings toward the therapist or therapy (e.g., "I'm very happy with how therapy is going"), code **deferential**.

Avoidant storytelling versus abstract communication

- If the patient talks about the experiences of other people—specific people—in an effort to avoid talking about themselves, code **avoidant storytelling**.

- If the patient talks about the experiences of people in general—people in the abstract—in an effort to avoid talking about themselves, code **abstract communication**.

Denial versus reject intervention

- If the patient's response is best characterized as an attempt to move away from the therapist or the task of therapy—to avoid something painful, to avoid conflict—then code **denial**.

- If the patient's response is best characterized as an attempt to move against the therapist—to show the therapist that the therapist is wrong, to put the therapist in his or her place, to assert the patient's independence from or superiority over the therapist by saying that the therapist's idea is wrong—then code **reject intervention**.

- If the patient seems to be doing both—simultaneously trying to avoid *and* trying to move against the therapist—then code both **denial** and **reject intervention**.

Reject intervention versus complaint/concern therapist versus complaint activity

- If the patient's response is focused on the therapist's intervention—the interpretation is wrong, the assessment is inaccurate, the question is the wrong question to ask—then code **reject intervention**.

- If the patient's response is focused on the person of the therapist—the therapist is incompetent or misguided or confused or confusing—then code **complaint/concern therapist**.

- If the patient's response is focused on a specific activity—homework, an in-session exercise such as two-chair—then code **complaint activity**.

- Note that the patient may do all of the above in a single time segment.

Patient defends self versus reject intervention

- If the patient's response is focused on making a case for themselves— I didn't do anything wrong, it's not my fault, I did the best I could—then code **patient defends self**.

- If the patient's response is focused on criticizing or dismissing or attacking the therapist's position—your idea is wrong—then code **reject intervention**.

Reject intervention versus denial versus defends self

- You said that I have a problem with depression. That is not true. **Reject intervention**
- I am not depressed. **Denial**
- I am dealing with a lot at work, and anybody in this situation would feel stressed. **Patient defends self**

Self-critical versus reject intervention versus complaint/concern therapist

- If the patient is giving up on the therapist or the therapy because the patient feels that they cannot be helped—I'm too depressed, too lazy, too weak—then code **self-critical**.

- If the patient says the therapist cannot help the patient because the therapist's intervention is flawed, insufficient, or irrelevant—then code **reject intervention**.

- Help-rejecting patients who reject the therapist's suggestions AND convey a sense of hopelessness, of giving up on the therapy can present with a combination of both **self-critical** and **reject intervention** (mixed codes).

- If the patient says the therapist cannot help the patient because the therapist is incompetent, inexperienced, or a poor match—then code **complaint/ concern therapist**.

Mixed codes—both confrontation and withdrawal

- Ruptures can include elements of both confrontation and withdrawal, and when this occurs, both should be coded.

- As just noted, help-rejecting patients may present with both **reject formulation** and **self-critical/helpless** markers.

- Patients who are uncomfortable criticizing the therapist may present with a confrontation marker (e.g., **complaint therapist, complaint progress**) in combination with a withdrawal marker. For example, the patient may smile or laugh nervously (**content/affect split**) while voicing a complaint, or the patient may try to soften the complaint by expressing it in an indirect or veiled way in an effort to avoid conflict with the therapist (**deferential**).

Disclose internal experience versus acknowledge contribution

- Whenever the therapist acknowledges how they may be contributing to a rupture, code **acknowledge contribution**.

- If the therapist also shares how they experience the rupture with the patient—the therapist's thoughts and feelings about their interaction, about how they work together—then also code **disclose internal experience**.

Invite thoughts/feelings versus redirect/refocus

- If the therapist is trying to explore the patient's feelings about a rupture—to expand the discussion—then code **invite thoughts/feelings**.

- The therapist is trying to stop a patient who is withdrawing from the task of therapy, perhaps by telling avoidant stories—to rein in the discussion—code **redirect/refocus**.

REFERENCES

Abrams, D. (2015). Social identity and intergroup relations. In M. Mikulincer, P. R. Shaver, J. F. Dovidio, & J. A. Simpson (Eds.), *APA handbook of personality and social psychology* (Vol. 2, pp. 203–228). Washington, DC: American Psychological Association. http://dx.doi.org/10.1037/14342-008

Ægisdóttir, S., White, M. J., Spengler, P. M., Maugherman, A. S., Anderson, L. A., Cook, R. S., . . . Rush, J. D. (2006). The Meta-Analysis of Clinical Judgment project: Fifty-six years of accumulated research on clinical versus statistical prediction. *The Counseling Psychologist, 34,* 341–382. http://dx.doi.org/10.1177/0011000005285875

Agnew, R. M., Harper, H., Shapiro, D. A., & Barkham, M. (1994). Resolving a challenge to the therapeutic relationship: A single-case study. *British Journal of Medical Psychology, 67,* 155–170. http://dx.doi.org/10.1111/j.2044-8341.1994.tb01783.x

Aldao, A., Gee, D. G., De Los Reyes, A., & Seager, I. (2016). Emotion regulation as a transdiagnostic factor in the development of internalizing and externalizing psychopathology: Current and future directions. *Development and Psychopathology, 28,* 927–946. http://dx.doi.org/10.1017/S0954579416000638

Aldao, A., Nolen-Hoeksema, S., & Schweizer, S. (2010). Emotion-regulation strategies across psychopathology: A meta-analytic review. *Clinical Psychology Review, 30,* 217–237. http://dx.doi.org/10.1016/j.cpr.2009.11.004

Alexander, F., & French, T. M. (1946). The principle of corrective emotional experience. In *Psychoanalytic therapy: Principles and application* (pp. 66–70). New York, NY: Ronald Press.

Anderson, T., Crowley, M. E. J., Himawan, L., Holmberg, J. K., & Uhlin, B. D. (2016). Therapist facilitative interpersonal skills and training status: A randomized clinical trial on alliance and outcome. *Psychotherapy Research, 26,* 511–529. http://dx.doi.org/10.1080/10503307.2015.1049671

Anderson, T., McClintock, A. S., Himawan, L., Song, X., & Patterson, C. L. (2016). A prospective study of therapist facilitative interpersonal skills as a predictor of treatment outcome. *Journal of Consulting and Clinical Psychology, 84,* 57–66. http://dx.doi.org/10.1037/ccp0000060

Anderson, T., Ogles, B. M., Patterson, C. L., Lambert, M. J., & Vermeersch, D. A. (2009). Therapist effects: Facilitative interpersonal skills as a predictor of therapist success. *Journal of Clinical Psychology, 65,* 755–768. http://dx.doi.org/10.1002/jclp.20583

Anderson, T., Patterson, C. L., & Weis, A. C. (2007). *Facilitative Interpersonal Skills Performance Analysis rating method.* Unpublished coding manual, Department of Psychology, Ohio University, Athens.

Andrade, E. B., & Ariely, D. (2009). The enduring impact of transient emotions on decision making. *Organizational Behavior and Human Decision Processes, 109,* 1–8. http://dx.doi.org/10.1016/j.obhdp.2009.02.003

Ariely, D. (2011). *The upside of irrationality.* New York, NY: HarperCollins. http://dx.doi.org/10.1109/AERO.2011.5747214

Aron, L. (1996). *A meeting of minds: Mutuality in psychoanalysis.* Hillsdale, NJ: The Analytic Press.

Aron, L. (1999). Clinical choices and the relational matrix. *Psychoanalytic Dialogues, 9,* 1–29. http://dx.doi.org/10.1080/10481889909539301

Aspland, H., Llewelyn, S., Hardy, G. E., Barkham, M., & Stiles, W. (2008). Alliance ruptures and rupture resolution in cognitive-behavior therapy: A preliminary task analysis. *Psychotherapy Research, 18,* 699–710. http://dx.doi.org/10.1080/10503300802291463

Atzil-Slonim, D., Bar-Kalifa, E., Rafaeli, E., Lutz, W., Rubel, J., Schiefele, A.-K., & Peri, T. (2015). Therapeutic bond judgments: Congruence and incongruence. *Journal of Consulting and Clinical Psychology, 83,* 773–784. http://dx.doi.org/10.1037/ccp0000015

Auszra, L., Greenberg, L. S., & Herrmann, I. (2013). Client emotional productivity-optimal client in-session emotional processing in experiential therapy. *Psychotherapy Research, 23,* 732–746. http://dx.doi.org/10.1080/10503307.2013.816882

Awkward, M. (1995). *Negotiating difference: Race, gender, and the politics of positionality.* Chicago, IL: University of Chicago Press.

Ayduk, O., & Kross, E. (2010). From a distance: Implications of spontaneous self-distancing for adaptive self-reflection. *Journal of Personality and Social Psychology, 98,* 809–829. http://dx.doi.org/10.1037/a0019205

Baddeley, A., Eysenck, A. W., & Anderson, M. C. (2009). *Memory: Motivated forgetting.* New York, NY: Psychology Press.

Bakan, D. (1966). *The duality of human existence.* Boston, MA: Beacon Press.

Baldwin, S. A., & Imel, Z. E. (2013). Therapist effects: Findings and methods. In M. J. Lambert (Ed.), *Bergin and Garfield's handbook of psychotherapy and behavior change* (6th ed., pp. 258–297). Hoboken, NJ: Wiley.

Baldwin, S. A., Wampold, B. E., & Imel, Z. E. (2007). Untangling the alliance-outcome correlation: Exploring the relative importance of therapist and patient variability in the alliance. *Journal of Consulting and Clinical Psychology, 75,* 842–852. http://dx.doi.org/10.1037/0022-006X.75.6.842

Bambling, M., King, R., Raue, P., Schweitzer, R., & Lambert, W. (2006). Clinical supervision: Its influence on client-rated working alliance and client symptom reduction in the brief treatment of major depression. *Psychotherapy Research, 16,* 317–331.

Banaji, M. R., & Greenwald, A. G. (2013). *Blindspot: Hidden biases of good people.* New York, NY: Delacorte Press.

Bancroft, M. (1987). *The effect of experience on anchoring errors in clinical judgment.* Unpublished dissertation, University of Iowa, Ames.

Barlow, D. H. (1988). *Anxiety and its disorders: The nature and treatment of anxiety and panic.* New York, NY: Guilford Press.

Barlow, D. H., Bullis, J. R., Comer, J. S., & Ametaj, A. A. (2013). Evidence-based psychological treatments: An update and a way forward. *Annual Review of Clinical Psychology, 9,* 1–27. http://dx.doi.org/10.1146/annurev-clinpsy-050212-185629

Barlow, D. H., Farchione, T. J., Bullis, J. R., Gallagher, M. W., Murray-Latin, H., Sauer-Zavala, S., . . . Cassiello-Robbins, C. (2017). The unified protocol for trans-diagnostic treatment of emotional disorders compared with diagnosis-specific protocols for anxiety disorders: A randomized clinical trial. *JAMA Psychiatry, 74,* 875–884. http://dx.doi.org/10.1001/jamapsychiatry.2017.2164

Barnett, J. E., Baker, E. K., Elman, N. S., & Schoener, G. R. (2007). In pursuit of wellness: The self-care imperative. *Professional Psychology: Research and Practice, 38,* 603–612. http://dx.doi.org/10.1037/0735-7028.38.6.603

Barnett, J. E., & Cooper, N. (2009). Creating a culture of self-care. *Clinical Psychology: Science and Practice, 16,* 16–20. http://dx.doi.org/10.1111/j.1468-2850.2009.01138.x

Barrett, L. F. (2017). *How emotions are made: The secret life of the brain.* New York, NY: Houghton Mifflin Harcourt.

Barrett, L. F., Lewis, M., & Haviland-Jones, J. M. (Eds.). (2016). *Handbook of emotions* (4th ed.). New York, NY: Guilford Press.

Barrett, L. F., & Russell, J. A. (Eds.). (2015). *The psychological construction of emotion.* New York, NY: Guilford Press.

Basescu, S. (2009). *Selected papers on human nature and psychoanalysis.* New York, NY: Routledge.

Bateman, A., & Fonagy, P. (2006). Mentalizing and borderline personality disorder. In J. G. Allen & P. Fonagy (Eds.), *Handbook of mentalization-based treatment* (pp. 185–200). Chichester, England: Wiley.

Batson, C. D. (2011). *Altruism in humans.* Oxford, England: Oxford University Press.

Baumeister, R. F. (1984). Choking under pressure: Self-consciousness and paradoxical effects of incentives on skillful performance. *Journal of Personality and Social Psychology, 46,* 610–620. http://dx.doi.org/10.1037/0022-3514.46.3.610

Baumeister, R. F., Bratslavsky, E., Finkenauer, C., & Vohs, K. D. (2001). Bad is stronger than good. *Review of General Psychology, 5,* 323–370. http://dx.doi.org/10.1037/1089-2680.5.4.323

Baumeister, R. F., & Showers, C. J. (1986). A review of paradoxical performance effects: Choking under pressure in sports and mental tests. *European Journal of Social Psychology, 16,* 361–383. http://dx.doi.org/10.1002/ejsp.2420160405

Baumeister, R. F., Stillwell, A. M., & Heatherton, T. F. (1994). Guilt: An inter-personal approach. *Psychological Bulletin, 115,* 243–267. http://dx.doi.org/10.1037/0033-2909.115.2.243

Beck, A. T. (1967). *Depression: Clinical, experimental, and theoretical aspects.* Philadelphia: University of Pennsylvania Press.

Beck, A. T. (1976). *Cognitive therapy and the emotional disorders.* New York, NY: Penguin Press.

Beck, J. S. (2011). *Cognitive behavior therapy: Basics and beyond* (2nd ed.). New York, NY: Guilford Press.

Beebe, B., & Lachmann, F. M. (2002). *Infant research and adult treatment: Co-constructing interactions*. New York, NY: The Analytic Press.

Beebe, B., & Lachmann, F. M. (2015). The expanding world of Edward Tronick. *Psychoanalytic Inquiry, 35*, 328–336.

Beebe, B., Messinger, D., Bahrick, L. E., Margolis, A., Buck, K. A., & Chen, H. (2016). A systems view of mother–infant face-to-face communication. *Developmental Psychology, 52*, 556–571. http://dx.doi.org/10.1037/a0040085

Beilock, S. L. (2010). *Choke: What the secrets of the brain reveal about getting it right when you have to*. New York, NY: Simon & Schuster.

Beilock, S. L., & Carr, T. H. (2001). On the fragility of skilled performance: What governs choking under pressure? *Journal of Experimental Psychology: General, 130*, 701–725. http://dx.doi.org/10.1037/0096-3445.130.4.701

Beilock, S. L., & Carr, T. H. (2005). When high-powered people fail: Working memory and "choking under pressure" in math. *Psychological Science, 16*, 101–105. http://dx.doi.org/10.1111/j.0956-7976.2005.00789.x

Beilock, S. L., & DeCaro, M. S. (2007). From poor performance to success under stress: Working memory, strategy selection, and mathematical problem solving under pressure. *Journal of Experimental Psychology: Learning, Memory, and Cognition, 33*, 983–998. http://dx.doi.org/10.1037/0278-7393.33.6.983

Beilock, S. L., & Gray, R. (2007). Why do athletes choke under pressure? In G. Tenenbaum & R. C. Eklund (Eds.), *Handbook of sport psychology* (pp. 425–444). Hoboken, NJ: Wiley & Sons.

Bein, E., Anderson, T., Strupp, H., Henry, W. P., Schacht, T. E., Binder, J., & Butler, S. (2000). The effects of training in time-limited dynamic psychotherapy: Changes in therapeutic outcome. *Psychotherapy Research, 10*, 119–132.

Benjamin, J. (1988). *The bonds of love*. New York, NY: Pantheon Books.

Benjamin, J. (1990). An outline of intersubjectivity: The development of recognition. *Psychoanalytic Psychology, 7*(Suppl.), 33–46. http://dx.doi.org/10.1037/h0085258

Benjamin, J. (1995). *Like subjects, love objects*. New Haven, CT: Yale University Press.

Benjamin, L. S. (1974). Structural analysis of social behavior. *Psychological Review, 81*, 392–425. http://dx.doi.org/10.1037/h0037024

Benjamin, L. S. (1993). *Interpersonal diagnosis and treatment of personality disorders*. New York, NY: Guilford Press.

Bennett, D., Parry, G., & Ryle, A. (2006). Resolving threats to the therapeutic alliance in cognitive analytic therapy of borderline personality disorder: A task analysis. *Psychology and Psychotherapy, 79*, 395–418. http://dx.doi.org/10.1348/147608305X58355

Bennett-Levy, J. (2019). Why therapists should walk the talk: The theoretical and empirical case for personal practice in therapist training and professional development. *Journal of Behavior Therapy and Experimental Psychiatry, 62*, 133–145. http://dx.doi.org/10.1016/j.jbtep.2018.08.004

Bernard, J. M., & Goodyear, R. K. (2019). *Fundamentals of clinical supervision* (6th ed.). New York, NY: Pearson.

Black, S., Hardy, G., Turpin, G., & Parry, G. (2005). Self-reported attachment styles and therapeutic orientation of therapists and their relationship with reported general alliance quality and problems in therapy. *Psychology and Psychotherapy, 78*, 363–377. http://dx.doi.org/10.1348/147608305X43784

Blair, I. V. (2002). The malleability of automatic stereotypes and prejudice. *Personality and Social Psychology Review, 6*, 242–261. http://dx.doi.org/10.1207/S15327957PSPR0603_8

Bohart, A. C., & Greenberg, L. S. (Eds.). (1997). *Empathy reconsidered: New directions in psychotherapy.* Washington, DC: American Psychological Association. http://dx.doi.org/10.1037/10226-000

Bonanno, G. A. (2004). Loss, trauma, and human resilience: Have we underestimated the human capacity to thrive after extremely aversive events? *American Psychologist, 59,* 20–28. http://dx.doi.org/10.1037/0003-066X.59.1.20

Bonanno, G. A., Papa, A., Lalande, K., Westphal, M., & Coifman, K. (2004). The importance of being flexible: The ability to both enhance and suppress emotional expression predicts long-term adjustment. *Psychological Science, 15,* 482–487. http://dx.doi.org/10.1111/j.0956-7976.2004.00705.x

Bordin, E. S. (1979). The generalizability of the psychoanalytic concept of the working alliance. *Psychotherapy: Theory, Research, & Practice, 16,* 252–260. http://dx.doi.org/10.1037/h0085885

Boston Change Process Study Group. (2010). *Change in psychotherapy: A unifying paradigm.* New York, NY: Norton.

Bowlby, J. (1969). *Attachment and loss: Vol. 1. Attachment.* New York, NY: Basic Books.

Bowlby, J. (1988). *A secure base: Parent-child attachment and healthy human development.* New York, NY: Basic Books.

Brattland, H., Koksvik, J. M., Burkeland, O., Gråwe, R. W., Klöckner, C., Linaker, O. M., . . . Iversen, V. C. (2018). The effects of routine outcome monitoring (ROM) on therapy outcomes in the course of an implementation process: A randomized clinical trial. *Journal of Counseling Psychology, 65,* 641–652. http://dx.doi.org/10.1037/cou0000286

Bröder, A. (2000). A methodological comment on behavioral decision research. *Psychologische Beiträge, 42,* 645–662.

Bröder, A. (2003). Decision making with the "adaptive toolbox": Influence of environmental structure, intelligence, and working memory load. *Journal of Experimental Psychology: Learning, Memory, and Cognition, 29,* 611–625. http://dx.doi.org/10.1037/0278-7393.29.4.611

Bromberg, P. M. (1998). *Standing in the space.* Hillsdale, NJ: The Analytic Press.

Bromberg, P. M. (2006). *Awakening the dreamer: Clinical journeys.* Mahwah, NJ: The Analytic Press.

Buber, M. (1958). *I and thou* (2nd rev. ed., R. G. Smith, Trans.). New York, NY: Scribner's. (Original work published 1923)

Burke, W. (1992). Countertransference disclosure and the asymmetry/mutuality dilemma. *Psychoanalytic Dialogues, 2,* 241–271. http://dx.doi.org/10.1080/10481889209538931

Burns, D. D. (1989). *The feeling good handbook.* New York, NY: William Morrow.

Butler, E. A., & Randall, A. K. (2013). Emotional coregulation in close relationships. *Emotion Review, 5,* 202–210. http://dx.doi.org/10.1177/1754073912451630

Button, M. L., Westra, H. A., Hara, K. M., & Aviram, A. (2015). Disentangling the impact of resistance and ambivalence on therapy outcomes in cognitive behavioural therapy for generalized anxiety disorder. *Cognitive Behaviour Therapy, 44,* 44–53. http://dx.doi.org/10.1080/16506073.2014.959038

Cannon-Bowers, J. A., & Salas, E. (1998). Individual and team decision making under stress: Theoretical underpinnings. In J. A. Cannon-Bowers & E. Salas (Eds.), *Making decisions under stress: Implications for individual and team training* (pp. 17–38). Washington, DC: American Psychological Association. http://dx.doi.org/10.1037/10278-001

Carey, T. A., & Mullan, R. J. (2004). What is Socratic questioning? *Psychotherapy, 41,* 217–226.

Cash, S. K., Hardy, G. E., Kellett, S., & Parry, G. (2014). Alliance ruptures and resolution during cognitive behaviour therapy with patients with borderline personality disorder. *Psychotherapy Research, 24,* 132–145. http://dx.doi.org/10.1080/10503307.2013.838652

Caspar, F. (1995). Hypothesis-generation in intake interviews. In B. Boothe, R. Hirsig, A. Helminger, B. Meier, & R. Volkart (Eds.), *Perception—evaluation—interpretation* (pp. 3–11). Ashland, OH: Hogrefe & Huber.

Caspar, F. (2017). Professional expertise in psychotherapy. In L. G. Castonguay & C. E. Hill (Eds.), *How and why are some therapists better than others? Understanding therapist effects* (pp. 193–214). Washington, DC: American Psychological Association.

Castonguay, L. G. (1996). *Integrative cognitive therapy for depression treatment manual.* Unpublished manuscript, The Pennsylvania State University, State College.

Castonguay, L. G., Eubanks, C. F., Goldfried, M. R., Muran, J. C., & Lutz, W. (2015). Research on psychotherapy integration: Building on the past, looking to the future. *Psychotherapy Research, 25,* 365–382. http://dx.doi.org/10.1080/10503307.2015.1014010

Castonguay, L. G., Goldfried, M. R., Wiser, S., Raue, P. J., & Hayes, A. M. (1996). Predicting the effect of cognitive therapy for depression: A study of unique and common factors. *Journal of Consulting and Clinical Psychology, 64,* 497–504. http://dx.doi.org/10.1037/0022-006X.64.3.497

Castonguay, L. G., & Hill, C. E. (Eds.). (2017). *How and why are some therapists better than others? Understanding therapist effects.* Washington, DC: American Psychological Association. http://dx.doi.org/10.1037/0000034-000

Castonguay, L. G., Nelson, D. L., Boswell, J. F., Nordberg, S. S., McAleavey, A. A., Newman, M. G., & Borkovec, T. D. (2012). Corrective experiences in cognitive behavior and interpersonal–emotional processing therapies: A qualitative analysis of a single case. In L. G. Castonguay & C. E. Hill (Eds.), *Transformation in psychotherapy: Corrective experiences across cognitive behavioral, humanistic, and psychodynamic approaches* (pp. 245–279). Washington, DC: American Psychological Association. http://dx.doi.org/10.1037/13747-013

Castonguay, L. G., Schut, A. J., Aikins, D., Constantino, M. J., Lawrenceau, J. P., Bologh, L., & Burns, D. D. (2004). Integrative cognitive therapy for depression: A preliminary investigation. *Journal of Psychotherapy Integration, 14,* 4–20. http://dx.doi.org/10.1037/1053-0479.14.1.4

Chang, D. F., & Berk, A. (2009). Making cross-racial therapy work: A phenomenological study of clients' experiences of cross-racial therapy. *Journal of Counseling Psychology, 56,* 521–536. http://dx.doi.org/10.1037/a0016905

Chase, W. G., & Simon, H. A. (1973). Perception in chess. *Cognitive Psychology, 4,* 55–81. http://dx.doi.org/10.1016/0010-0285(73)90004-2

Chawla, N., & Ostafin, B. (2007). Experiential avoidance as a functional dimensional approach to psychopathology: An empirical review. *Journal of Clinical Psychology, 63,* 871–890. http://dx.doi.org/10.1002/jclp.20400

Chen, R., Atzil-Slonim, D., Bar-Kalifa, E., Hasson-Ohayon, I., & Refaeli, E. (2018). Therapists' recognition of alliance ruptures as a moderator of change in alliance and symptoms. *Psychotherapy Research, 28,* 560–570. http://dx.doi.org/10.1080/10503307.2016.1227104

Chow, D. L., Miller, S. D., Seidel, J. A., Kane, R. T., Thornton, J. A., & Andrews, W. P. (2015). The role of deliberate practice in the development of highly effective psychotherapists. *Psychotherapy, 52,* 337–345. http://dx.doi.org/10.1037/pst0000015

Christian, C., Safran, J. D., & Muran, J. C. (2012). The corrective emotional experience: A relational perspective and critique. In L. G. Castonguay & C. E. Hill (Eds.), *Transformation in psychotherapy: Corrective experiences across cognitive behavioral, humanistic, and psychodynamic approaches* (pp. 51–67). Washington, DC: American Psychological Association. http://dx.doi.org/10.1037/13747-004

Cilliers, P. (1998). *Complexity and postmodernism: Understanding complex systems.* New York, NY: Routledge.

Coan, J. A. (2011). The social regulation of emotion. In J. Decety & J. T. Cacioppo (Eds.), *The Oxford handbook of social neuroscience* (pp. 614–623). Oxford, England: Oxford University Press.

Coan, J. A., Schaefer, H. S., & Davidson, R. J. (2006). Lending a hand: Social regulation of the neural response to threat. *Psychological Science, 17,* 1032–1039. http://dx.doi.org/10.1111/j.1467-9280.2006.01832.x

Colli, A., & Lingiardi, V. (2009). The Collaborative Interactions Scale: A new transcript-based method for the assessment of therapeutic alliance ruptures and resolutions in psychotherapy. *Psychotherapy Research, 19,* 718–734. http://dx.doi.org/10.1080/10503300903121098

Collyer, S. C., & Malecki, G. S. (1998). Tactical decision making under stress: History and overview. In J. A. Cannon-Bowers & E. Salas (Eds.), *Making decisions under stress: Implications for individual and team training* (pp. 3–15). Washington, DC: American Psychological Association. http://dx.doi.org/10.1037/10278-016

Colombo, P. J., & Gold, P. E. (2004). Multiple memory systems. *Neurobiology of Learning and Memory, 82,* 169–170. http://dx.doi.org/10.1016/j.nlm.2004.07.008

Constantino, M. J. (2000). Interpersonal process in psychotherapy through the lens of the structural analysis of social behavior. *Applied & Preventive Psychology, 9,* 153–172. http://dx.doi.org/10.1016/S0962-1849(05)80002-2

Constantino, M. J., Marnell, M. E., Haile, A. J., Kanther-Sista, S. N., Wolman, K., Zappert, L., & Arnow, B. A. (2008). Integrative cognitive therapy for depression: A randomized pilot comparison. *Psychotherapy, 45,* 122–134. http://dx.doi.org/10.1037/0033-3204.45.2.122

Crandall, B., & Getchell-Reiter, K. (1993). Critical decision method: A technique for eliciting concrete assessment indicators from the intuition of NICU nurses. *Advances in Nursing Science, 16,* 42–51. http://dx.doi.org/10.1097/00012272-199309000-00006

Credé, M., Tynan, M. C., & Harms, P. D. (2017). Much ado about grit: A meta-analytic synthesis of the grit literature. *Journal of Personality and Social Psychology, 113,* 492–511. http://dx.doi.org/10.1037/pspp0000102

Crenshaw, K. W. (2019). *On intersectionality: Essential writings.* New York, NY: New Press.

Crits-Christoph, P., Connolly Gibbons, M. B., Crits-Christoph, K., Narducci, J., Schamberger, M., & Gallop, R. (2006). Can therapists be trained to improve their alliances? A preliminary study of alliance-fostering psychotherapy. *Psychotherapy Research, 16,* 268–281. http://dx.doi.org/10.1080/10503300500268557

Dalenberg, C. J. (2004). Maintaining the safe and effective therapeutic relationship in the context of distrust and anger. *Psychotherapy, 41,* 438–447. http://dx.doi.org/10.1037/0033-3204.41.4.438

Daley, R. (Producer), & Post, T. (Director). (1973). *Magnum force* [Motion picture]. United States: Warner Brothers.

Daly, A.-M., Llewelyn, S., McDougall, E., & Chanen, A. M. (2010). Rupture resolution in cognitive analytic therapy for adolescents with borderline personality disorder. *Psychology & Psychotherapy: Theory, Research & Practice, 83*, 273–288. http://dx.doi.org/10.1348/147608309X481036

Darwin, C. (2002). *The expression of the emotions in man and animal*. New York, NY: Oxford University Press. (Original work published 1892)

Davies, J. M., & Frawley, M. (1994). *Treating the adult survivor of childhood sexual abuse: Psychoanalytic perspectives*. New York, NY: Basic Books.

Dawes, R. M. (1986). Representative thinking in clinical judgment. *Clinical Psychology Review, 6*, 425–441. http://dx.doi.org/10.1016/0272-7358(86)90030-9

Dawes, R. M., Faust, D., & Meehl, P. E. (1989). Clinical versus actuarial judgment. *Science, 243*, 1668–1674. http://dx.doi.org/10.1126/science.2648573

de Beauvoir, S. (2010). *The second sex* (C. Borde & S. Malovany-Chevallier, Trans.). New York, NY: Random House. (Original work published 1949)

DeCaro, M. S., Thomas, R. D., Albert, N. B., & Beilock, S. L. (2011). Choking under pressure: Multiple routes to skill failure. *Journal of Experimental Psychology: General, 140*, 390–406. http://dx.doi.org/10.1037/a0023466

de Groot, A. D. (1978). *Thought and choice in chess* (2nd ed.). Hague, the Netherlands: Morton. (Original work published 1946)

Delgadillo, J., Saxon, D., & Barkham, M. (2018). Associations between therapists' occupational burnout and their patients' depression and anxiety treatment outcomes. *Depression and Anxiety, 35*, 844–850. Advance online publication. http://dx.doi.org/10.1002/da.22766

Del Re, A. C., Flückiger, C., Horvath, A. O., Symonds, D., & Wampold, B. E. (2012). Therapist effects in the therapeutic alliance-outcome relationship: A restricted-maximum likelihood meta-analysis. *Clinical Psychology Review, 32*, 642–649. http://dx.doi.org/10.1016/j.cpr.2012.07.002

DePue, M. K., Lambie, G. W., Liu, R., & Gonzalez, J. (2016). Investigating supervisory relationships and therapeutic alliances using structural equation modeling. *Counselor Education and Supervision, 55*, 263–277. http://dx.doi.org/10.1002/ceas.12053

Derrida, J. (1978). *Writing and difference* (A. Bass, Trans.). Chicago, IL: University of Chicago.

Dewey, J. (1998). *How we think: A restatement of the relation of reflective thinking to the educative process*. Boston, MA: Houghton Mifflin. (Original work published 1933)

Diamond, L. M., & Aspinwall, L. G. (2003). Emotion regulation across the life span: An integrative perspective emphasizing self-regulation, positive affect, and dyadic processes. *Motivation and Emotion, 27*, 125–156. http://dx.doi.org/10.1023/A:1024521920068

Diehl, M., Owen, S. K., & Youngblade, L. M. (2004). Agency and communion attributes in adults' spontaneous self-representations. *International Journal of Behavioral Development, 28*, 1–15. http://dx.doi.org/10.1080/01650250344000226

Dinger, U., Strack, M., Leichsenring, F., Wilmers, F., & Schauenburg, H. (2008). Therapist effects on outcome and alliance in inpatient psychotherapy. *Journal of Clinical Psychology, 64*, 344–354. http://dx.doi.org/10.1002/jclp.20443

Dinger, U., Strack, M., Sachsse, T., & Schauenburg, H. (2009). Therapists' attachment, patients' interpersonal problems and alliance development over time in inpatient psychotherapy. *Psychotherapy, 46*, 277–290. http://dx.doi.org/10.1037/a0016913

Dinnerstein, D. (1976). *The mermaid and the minotaur*. New York, NY: Harper & Row.

Dougherty, M. R., & Hunter, J. E. (2003). Hypothesis generation, probability judgment, and individual differences in working memory capacity. *Acta Psychologica, 113*, 263–282. http://dx.doi.org/10.1016/S0001-6918(03)00033-7

Driskell, J., & Salas, E. (1996). *Stress and human performance*. Mahwah, NJ: Erlbaum.

Duckworth, A. (2016). *Grit: The power of passion and perseverance* (Vol. 124). New York, NY: Scribner's.

Duckworth, A. L., Peterson, C., Matthews, M. D., & Kelly, D. R. (2007). Grit: Perseverance and passion for long-term goals. *Journal of Personality and Social Psychology, 92*, 1087–1101. http://dx.doi.org/10.1037/0022-3514.92.6.1087

Dunn, R., Callahan, J. L., Swift, J. K., & Ivanovic, M. (2013). Effects of pre-session centering for therapists on session presence and effectiveness. *Psychotherapy Research, 23*, 78–85. http://dx.doi.org/10.1080/10503307.2012.731713

Eby, M. A. (2000). Understanding professional development. In A. Brechin, H. Brown, & M. A. Eby (Eds.), *Clinical practice in health and social care* (pp. 48–69). London, England: Sage.

Ehrenberg, D. B. (1992). *The intimate edge: Extending the reach of psychoanalytic interaction*. New York, NY: Norton.

Ekman, P. (1972). Universal and cultural differences in facial expression of emotions. In J. Cole (Ed.), *Nebraska Symposium on motivation* (pp. 207–283). Lincoln: University of Nebraska Press.

Elliott, R., Bohart, A. C., Watson, J. C., & Murphy, D. (2018). Therapist empathy and client outcome: An updated meta-analysis. *Psychotherapy, 55*, 399–410. http://dx.doi.org/10.1037/pst0000175

Ellis, A. (1962). *Reason and emotion in psychotherapy*. Oxford, England: Lyle Stuart.

Ellison, R. (1952). *Invisible man*. New York, NY: Modern Library.

Emerick, L., & Hatten, J. (1974). *Diagnosis and evaluation in speech pathology*. Englewood Cliffs, NJ: Prentice-Hall.

Epstein, D. (2014). *The sports gene: Talent, practice and the truth about success*. New York, NY: Random House.

Epstein, L. (1984). An interpersonal-object relations perspective on working with destructive aggression. *Contemporary Psychoanalysis, 20*, 651–662. http://dx.doi.org/10.1080/00107530.1984.10745761

Epstein, M. (1995). *Thoughts without a thinker*. New York, NY: Basic Books.

Ericsson, K. A., Krampe, R. T., & Tesch-Römer, C. (1993). The role of deliberate practice in the acquisition of expert performance. *Psychological Review, 100*, 363–406. http://dx.doi.org/10.1037/0033-295X.100.3.363

Ericsson, K. A., & Lehmann, A. C. (1996). Expert and exceptional performance: Evidence of maximal adaptation to task constraints. *Annual Review of Psychology, 47*, 273–305. http://dx.doi.org/10.1146/annurev.psych.47.1.273

Ericsson, K. A., & Pool, R. (2016). *Peak: Secrets from the new science of expertise*. New York, NY: Houghton Mifflin Harcourt.

Ericsson, K. A., Roring, R. W., & Nandagopal, K. (2007). Giftedness and evidence for reproducibly superior performance: An account based on the expert performance framework. *High Ability Studies, 18*, 3–56. http://dx.doi.org/10.1080/13598130701350593

Eriksson, T., Germundsjö, L., Åström, E., & Rönnlund, M. (2018). Mindful self-compassion training reduces stress and burnout symptoms among practicing psychologists: A randomized controlled trial of a brief web-based intervention. *Frontiers in Psychology, 9*, Article 2340.

Eubanks, C. F. (2019). Alliance-focused formulation: A work in process. In U. Kramer (Ed.), *Case formulation for personality disorders: Tailoring psychotherapy to the individual client* (pp. 337–354). Cambridge, MA: Academic Press. http://dx.doi.org/10.1016/B978-0-12-813521-1.00017-5

Eubanks, C. F., Lubitz, J., Muran, J. C., & Safran, J. D. (2019). Rupture Resolution Rating System (3RS): Development and validation. *Psychotherapy Research, 29*, 306–319. http://dx.doi.org/10.1080/10503307.2018.1552034

Eubanks, C. F., Muran, J. C., Dreher, D., Sergi, J., Silberstein, E., & Wasserman, M. (2019). Trainees' experiences in alliance-focused training: The risks and rewards of learning to negotiate ruptures. *Psychoanalytic Psychology, 36*, 122–131. http://dx.doi.org/10.1037/pap0000233

Eubanks, C. F., Muran, J. C., & Safran, J. D. (2015). *Rupture resolution rating system (3RS): Manual*. Unpublished manuscript, Mount Sinai Beth Israel, New York, NY.

Eubanks, C. F., Muran, J. C., & Safran, J. D. (2018). Alliance rupture repair: A meta-analysis. *Psychotherapy, 55*, 508–519. http://dx.doi.org/10.1037/pst0000185

Eubanks, C. F., Muran, J. C., & Safran, J. D. (2019). Alliance rupture repair. In J. C. Norcross & M. J. Lambert (Eds.), *Psychotherapy relationships that work* (3rd ed., pp. 549–579). New York, NY: Oxford University Press. http://dx.doi.org/10.1093/med-psych/9780190843953.003.0016

Eubanks-Carter, C., Muran, J. C., & Safran, J. D. (2015). Alliance-focused training. *Psychotherapy, 52*, 169–173. http://dx.doi.org/10.1037/a0037596

Fairbairn, W. R. D. (1952). *Psychoanalytic studies of the personality*. Oxford, England: Routledge & Kegan Paul.

Falender, C. A., & Shafranske, E. P. (2017). *Supervision essentials for the practice of competency-based supervision*. Washington, DC: American Psychological Association. http://dx.doi.org/10.1037/15962-000

Faust, D. (1986). Research on human judgment and its application to clinical practice. *Professional Psychology, Research and Practice, 17*, 420–430. http://dx.doi.org/10.1037/0735-7028.17.5.420

Ferenczi, S. (1988). *The clinical diary of Sandor Ferenczi* (M. B. N. Z. Jackson, Trans.). Cambridge, MA: Harvard University Press. (Original work published 1932)

Finlay, L. (2002). Negotiating the swamp: The opportunity and challenge of reflexivity in research practice. *Qualitative Research, 2*, 209–230. http://dx.doi.org/10.1177/146879410200200205

Finlay, L. (2003). The reflexive journey: Mapping multiple routes. In L. Finlay & B. Gough (Eds.), *Reflexivity: A practical guide for researchers in health and social sciences* (pp. 3–20). Oxford, England: Blackwell. http://dx.doi.org/10.1002/9780470776094.ch1

Finlay, L. (2008). *Reflecting on 'reflective practice'* (Tech. rep. PBPL 52). Practice-based Professional Learning Centre, The Open University, Milton Keynes, England.

Fisher, C. D. (1993). Boredom at work: A neglected concept. *Human Relations, 46*, 395–417.

FitzGerald, C., & Hurst, S. (2017). Implicit bias in healthcare professionals: A systematic review. *BMC Medical Ethics, 18*, 1–18.

Fleming, A. S., O'Day, D. H., & Kraemer, G. W. (1999). Neurobiology of mother–infant interactions: Experience and central nervous system plasticity across development and generations. *Neuroscience and Biobehavioral Reviews, 23*, 673–685. http://dx.doi.org/10.1016/S0149-7634(99)00011-1

Fletcher, G., Simpson, J. A., Campbell, L., & Overall, N. C. (2013). *The science of intimate relationships*. Oxford, England: Wiley-Blackwell.

Flückiger, C., Del Re, A. C., Wampold, B. E., & Horvath, A. O. (2018). The alliance in adult psychotherapy: A meta-analytic synthesis. *Psychotherapy, 55*, 316–340. http://dx.doi.org/10.1037/pst0000172

Flückiger, C., Del Re, A. C., Wampold, B. E., & Horvath, A. O. (2019). Alliance in adult psychotherapy. In J. C. Norcross & M. J. Lambert (Eds.), *Psychotherapy relationships that work, Volume I* (3rd ed., pp. 24–78). New York, NY: Oxford University Press.

Fogarty, W. M. (1988). *Formal investigation into the circumstances surrounding the downing of a commercial airliner by the U.S.S. Vincennes (CG 49) on 3 July 1988. Unclassified Letter Ser. 1320 of 28 July 1988, to Commander in Chief*. Tampa, FL: U.S. Central Command.

Fonagy, P., Gergely, G., Jurist, E., & Target, M. (2002). *Affect regulation, mentalization, and the development of the self*. London, England: Routledge.

Foucault, M. (1972). *The archaeology of knowledge* (A. M. Sheridan Smith, Trans.). New York, NY: Pantheon.

Frattaroli, J. (2006). Experimental disclosure and its moderators: A meta-analysis. *Psychological Bulletin, 132,* 823–865. http://dx.doi.org/10.1037/0033-2909.132.6.823

Freud, S. (1937). Analysis terminable and interminable. In J. Strachey (Trans. & Ed.), *The standard edition of the complete psychological works of Sigmund Freud* (Vol. 23, pp. 211–254). London, England: Hogarth.

Freud, S., & Breuer, J. (1895). *Studies on hysteria*. London, England: Hogarth.

Frevert, U. (2016). The history of emotions. In L. Feldman Barrett, M. Lewis, & J. M. Haviland-Jones (Eds.), *Handbook of emotions* (4th ed., pp. 49–65). New York, NY: Guilford Press.

Friedlander, M. L. (2015). Use of relational strategies to repair alliance ruptures: How responsive supervisors train responsive psychotherapists. *Psychotherapy, 52,* 174–179. http://dx.doi.org/10.1037/a0037044

Friedlander, M. L., Escudero, V., Horvath, A. O., Heatherington, L., Cabero, A., & Martens, M. P. (2006). System for observing family therapy alliances: A tool for research and practice. *Journal of Counseling Psychology, 53,* 214–225. http://dx.doi.org/10.1037/0022-0167.53.2.214

Fuller, F., & Hill, C. E. (1985). Counselor and helpee perceptions of counselor intentions in relation to outcome in a single counseling session. *Journal of Counseling Psychology, 32,* 329–338. http://dx.doi.org/10.1037/0022-0167.32.3.329

Gadamer, H.-G. (1975). *Truth and method* (G. Barden & J. Cumming, Trans. & Eds.). New York, NY: Seabury Press. (Original work published 1960)

Garb, H. N., & Boyle, P. A. (2015). Understanding why some clinicians use pseudoscientific methods: Findings from research on clinical judgment. In S. O. Lilienfeld, S. J. Lynn, & J. M. Lohr (Eds.), *Science and pseudoscience in clinical psychology* (pp. 19–41). New York, NY: Guilford Press.

Geertz, C. (1973). *The interpretation of cultures* (Vol. 5043). New York, NY: Basic Books.

Geertz, C. (1983). *Local knowledge: Further essays in interpretive anthropology*. New York, NY: Basic Books.

Geller, S. M. (2017). *A practical guide to cultivating therapeutic presence*. Washington, DC: American Psychological Association. http://dx.doi.org/10.1037/0000025-000

Geller, S. M. (2019). Therapeutic presence: The foundation for effective emotion-focused therapy. In L. S. Greenberg & R. N. Goldman (Eds.), *Clinical handbook of emotion-focused therapy* (pp. 129–145). Washington, DC: American Psychological Association. http://dx.doi.org/10.1037/0000112-006

Geller, S. M., Greenberg, L. S., & Watson, J. C. (2010). Therapist and client perceptions of therapeutic presence: The development of a measure. *Psychotherapy Research, 20,* 599–610. http://dx.doi.org/10.1080/10503307.2010.495957

Gendlin, E. T. (1962). *Experiencing and the creation of meaning.* New York, NY: Free Press.

Gendlin, E. T. (1982). *Focusing* (2nd ed.). New York, NY: Bantam Books.

Gendlin, E. T. (1996). *Focusing-oriented psychotherapy.* New York, NY: Guilford Press.

Gergen, K. J. (1991). *The saturated self: Dilemmas of identity in community life.* New York, NY: Basic Books.

Gergen, K. J. (1994). *Realities and relationships: Soundings in social construction.* Cambridge, MA: Harvard University Press.

Gergen, K. J. (2009). *Relational being: Beyond self and community.* New York, NY: Oxford University Press.

Gibbs, G. (1988). *Learning by doing: A guide to teaching and learning methods.* London, England: Further Education Unit.

Gigerenzer, G. (1996). On narrow norms and vague heuristics: A reply to Kahneman and Tversky. *Psychological Review, 103,* 592–596. http://dx.doi.org/10.1037/0033-295X.103.3.592

Gilbert, P. (1998). What is shame? Some core issues and controversies. In P. Gilbert & B. Andrews (Eds.), *Shame: Interpersonal behavior, psychopathology and culture* (pp. 3–38). New York, NY: Oxford University Press.

Gilbert, P. (2005). Introduction and outline. In P. Gilbert (Ed.), *Compassion: Conceptualisations, research and use in psychotherapy* (pp. 1–16). New York, NY: Routledge.

Gladwell, M. (2008). *Outliers: The story of success.* New York, NY: Little, Brown.

Goetz, J. L., Keltner, D., & Simon-Thomas, E. (2010). Compassion: An evolutionary analysis and empirical review. *Psychological Bulletin, 136,* 351–374. http://dx.doi.org/10.1037/a0018807

Goldberg, C. (1992). *The seasoned psychotherapist—Triumph over adversity.* New York, NY: Norton.

Goldberg, S. B., Rousmaniere, T., Miller, S. D., Whipple, J., Nielsen, S. L., Hoyt, W. T., & Wampold, B. E. (2016). Do psychotherapists improve with time and experience? A longitudinal analysis of outcomes in a clinical setting. *Journal of Counseling Psychology, 63,* 1–11. http://dx.doi.org/10.1037/cou0000131

Goldin, P. R., McRae, K., Ramel, W., & Gross, J. J. (2008). The neural bases of emotion regulation. *Biological Psychiatry, 63,* 577–586. http://dx.doi.org/10.1016/j.biopsych.2007.05.031

Grecucci, A., & Sanfey, A. G. (2014). Emotion regulation and decision making. In J. J. Gross (Ed.), *Handbook of emotion regulation* (pp. 140–153). New York, NY: Guilford Press.

Green, A. R., Carney, D. R., Pallin, D. J., Ngo, L. H., Raymond, K. L., Iezzoni, L. I., & Banaji, M. R. (2007). Implicit bias among physicians and its prediction of thrombolysis decisions for black and white patients. *Journal of General Internal Medicine, 22,* 1231–1238. http://dx.doi.org/10.1007/s11606-007-0258-5

Greenberg, J. (1995). Psychoanalytic technique and the interactive matrix. *The Psychoanalytic Quarterly, 64,* 1–22. http://dx.doi.org/10.1080/21674086.1995.11927441

Greenberg, L. S. (2011). *Emotion-focused therapy.* Washington, DC: American Psychological Association.

Greenberg, L. S. (2016). The clinical application of emotion in psychotherapy. In M. Lewis, J. M. Haviland-Jones, & L. F. Barrett (Eds.), *Handbook of emotions* (4th ed., pp. 670–684). New York, NY: Guilford Press.

Greenberg, L. S., & Paivio, S. C. (1997). *Working with emotions in psychotherapy.* New York, NY: Guilford Press.

Greenberg, L. S., & Pascual-Leone, J. (1995). A dialectical constructivist approach to experiential change. In R. A. Neimeyer & M. J. Mahoney (Eds.), *Constructivism in psychotherapy* (pp. 169–191). Washington, DC: American Psychological Association. http://dx.doi.org/10.1037/10170-008

Greenberg, L. S., & Pascual-Leone, J. (2001). A dialectical constructivist view of the creation of personal meaning. *Journal of Constructivist Psychology, 14,* 165–186. http://dx.doi.org/10.1080/10720530151143539

Greenberg, L. S., Rice, L. N., & Elliott, R. (1995). *Process-experiential therapy: Facilitating emotional change.* New York, NY: Guilford Press.

Greenberg, L. S., & Safran, J. D. (1987). *Emotion in psychotherapy: Affect, cognition, and the process of change.* New York, NY: Guilford Press.

Greenwald, A. G., & Banaji, M. R. (1995). Implicit social cognition: Attitudes, self-esteem, and stereotypes. *Psychological Review, 102,* 4–27. http://dx.doi.org/10.1037/0033-295X.102.1.4

Greenwald, A. G., & Banaji, M. R. (2017). The implicit revolution: Reconceiving the relation between conscious and unconscious. *American Psychologist, 72,* 861–871. http://dx.doi.org/10.1037/amp0000238

Greenwald, A. G., Banaji, M. R., & Nosek, B. A. (2015). Statistically small effects of the Implicit Association Test can have societally large effects. *Journal of Personality and Social Psychology, 108,* 553–561. http://dx.doi.org/10.1037/pspa0000016

Greenwald, A. G., McGhee, D. E., & Schwartz, J. L. (1998). Measuring individual differences in implicit cognition: The Implicit Association Test. *Journal of Personality and Social Psychology, 74,* 1464–1480. http://dx.doi.org/10.1037/0022-3514.74.6.1464

Greenwald, A. G., Poehlman, T. A., Uhlmann, E. L., & Banaji, M. R. (2009). Understanding and using the Implicit Association Test: III. Meta-analysis of predictive validity. *Journal of Personality and Social Psychology, 97,* 17–41. http://dx.doi.org/10.1037/a0015575

Grepmair, L., Mitterlehner, F., Loew, T., Bachler, E., Rother, W., & Nickel, M. (2007). Promoting mindfulness in psychotherapists in training influences the treatment results of their patients: A randomized, double-blind, controlled study. *Psychotherapy and Psychosomatics, 76,* 332–338. http://dx.doi.org/10.1159/000107560

Griffiths, P. E., & Scarantino, A. (2005). Emotions in the wild: The situated perspective on emotion. In P. Robbins & M. Aydede (Eds.), *The Cambridge handbook of situated cognition* (pp. 437–453). Cambridge, England: Cambridge University Press.

Gross, J. J. (1998). The emerging field of emotion regulation: An integrative review. *Review of General Psychology, 2,* 271–299. http://dx.doi.org/10.1037/1089-2680.2.3.271

Gross, J. J. (2014a). Emotion regulation: Conceptual and empirical foundations. In J. J. Gross (Ed.), *Handbook of emotion regulation* (pp. 3–20). New York, NY: Guilford Press.

Gross, J. J. (Ed.). (2014b). *Handbook of emotion regulation* (2nd ed.). New York, NY: Guilford Press.

Gross, J. J., & John, O. P. (2003). Individual differences in two emotion regulation processes: Implications for affect, relationships, and well-being. *Journal of Personality and Social Psychology, 85,* 348–362. http://dx.doi.org/10.1037/0022-3514.85.2.348

Gross, J. J., & Thompson, R. A. (2007). Emotion regulation: Conceptual foundations. In J. J. Gross (Ed.), *Handbook of emotion regulation* (pp. 3–24). New York, NY: Guilford Press.

Grove, W. M., Zald, D. H., Lebow, B. S., Snitz, B. E., & Nelson, C. (2000). Clinical versus mechanical prediction: A meta-analysis. *Psychological Assessment, 12,* 19–30. http://dx.doi.org/10.1037/1040-3590.12.1.19

Guidano, V. F., & Liotti, G. (1983). *Cognitive processes and emotional disorders: A structural approach to psychotherapy.* New York, NY: Guilford Press.

Guisinger, S., & Blatt, S. J. (1994). Individuality and relatedness: Evolution of a fundamental dialectic. *American Psychologist, 49,* 104–111. http://dx.doi.org/10.1037/0003-066X.49.2.104

Habermas, J. (1971). *Knowledge and human interests* (J. Shapiro, Trans.). Boston, MA: Beacon.

Habermas, J. (1979). *Communication & the evolution of society* (T. McCarthy, Trans.). London, England: Heinemann.

Hara, K. M., Westra, H. A., Aviram, A., Button, M. L., Constantino, M. J., & Antony, M. M. (2015). Therapist awareness of client resistance in cognitive-behavioral therapy for generalized anxiety disorder. *Cognitive Behaviour Therapy, 44,* 162–174. http://dx.doi.org/10.1080/16506073.2014.998705

Harmon-Jones, E., & Harmon-Jones, C. (2016). Anger. In L. F. Barrett, M. Lewis, & J. Haviland-Jones (Eds.), *Handbook of emotions* (4th ed., pp. 774–791). New York, NY: Guilford Press.

Hatcher, R. L. (2015). Interpersonal competencies: Responsiveness, technique, and training in psychotherapy. *American Psychologist, 70,* 747–757. http://dx.doi.org/10.1037/a0039803

Hatfield, E., Cacioppo, J. T., & Rapson, R. L. (1994). *Emotional contagion.* Paris, France, and Cambridge, England: Editions de la Maison des Sciences de l'Homme and Cambridge University Press.

Hayes, J. A., Gelso, C. J., Goldberg, S., & Kivlighan, D. M. (2018). Countertransference management and effective psychotherapy: Meta-analytic findings. *Psychotherapy, 55,* 496–507. http://dx.doi.org/10.1037/pst0000189

Hayes, J. A., & Vinca, M. (2017). Therapist presence, absence, and extraordinary presence. In L. G. Castonguay & C. E. Hill (Eds.), *How and why are some therapists better than others? Understanding therapist effects* (pp. 85–99). Washington, DC: American Psychological Association. http://dx.doi.org/10.1037/0000034-006

Hayes, S. C. (Ed.). (2015). *The ACT in context: The canonical papers of Steven C. Hayes.* New York, NY: Routledge.

Hayes, S. C., Wilson, K. G., Gifford, E. V., Follette, V. M., & Strosahl, K. (1996). Experimental avoidance and behavioral disorders: A functional dimensional approach to diagnosis and treatment. *Journal of Consulting and Clinical Psychology, 64,* 1152–1168. http://dx.doi.org/10.1037/0022-006X.64.6.1152

Heaton, H. W., & Sigall, H. (1991). Self-consciousness, self-presentation, and performance under pressure: Who chokes, and when? *Journal of Applied Social Psychology, 21,* 175–188. http://dx.doi.org/10.1111/j.1559-1816.1991.tb02721.x

Hegel, G. W. F. (1969). *Phenomenology of spirit.* New York, NY: Oxford University. (Original work published 1807)

Heidegger, M. (1962). *Being and time* (J. Macquarrie & E. Robinson, Trans.). New York, NY: Harper. (Original work published 1927)

Henry, W. P., Schacht, T. E., Strupp, H. H., Butler, S. F., & Binder, J. L. (1993). Effects of training in time-limited dynamic psychotherapy: Mediators of therapists' responses to training. *Journal of Consulting and Clinical Psychology, 61,* 441–447. http://dx.doi.org/10.1037/0022-006X.61.3.441

Henry, W. P., Strupp, H. H., Butler, S. F., Schacht, T. E., & Binder, J. L. (1993). Effects of training in time-limited dynamic psychotherapy: Changes in therapist behavior. *Journal of Consulting and Clinical Psychology, 61,* 434–440. http://dx.doi.org/10.1037/0022-006X.61.3.434

Hill, C. E. (Ed.). (2004). *Dream work in therapy: Facilitating exploration, insight, and action* (pp. 283–297). Washington, DC: American Psychological Association. http://dx.doi.org/10.1037/10624-000

Hill, C. E. (2010). Qualitative studies of negative experiences in psychotherapy. In J. C. Muran & J. P. Barber (Eds.), *The therapeutic alliance: An evidence-based guide to practice* (pp. 63–73). New York, NY: Guilford Press.

Hill, C. E. (2020). *Helping skills: Facilitating exploration, insight, and action* (5th ed.). Washington, DC: American Psychological Association.

Hill, C. E., & Kellems, I. S. (2002). Development and use of the helping skills measure to assess client perceptions of the effects of training and of helping skills in sessions. *Journal of Counseling Psychology, 49,* 264–272. http://dx.doi.org/10.1037/0022-0167.49.2.264

Hill, C. E., Kellems, I. S., Kolchakian, M. R., Wonnell, T. L., Davis, T. L., & Nakayama, E. Y. (2003). The therapist experience of being the target of hostile versus suspected-unasserted client anger: Factors associated with resolution. *Psychotherapy Research, 13,* 475–491.

Hill, C. E., & Knox, S. (2013). Training and supervision in psychotherapy. In M. J. Lambert (Ed.), *Bergin and Garfield's handbook of psychotherapy and behavior change* (pp. 775–813). New York, NY: Wiley & Sons.

Hill, C. E., Roffman, M., Stahl, J., Friedman, S., Hummel, A., & Wallace, C. (2008). Helping skills training for undergraduates: Outcomes and prediction of outcomes. *Journal of Counseling Psychology, 55,* 359–370. http://dx.doi.org/10.1037/0022-0167.55.3.359

Hill, C. E., Thompson, B. J., Cogar, M. C., & Denman, D. W. (1993). Beneath the surface of long-term therapy: Therapist and client report of their own and each other's covert processes. *Journal of Counseling Psychology, 40,* 278–287. http://dx.doi.org/10.1037/0022-0167.40.3.278

Hoffman, I. Z. (1998). *Ritual and spontaneity in the psychoanalytic process: A dialectical-constructivist view.* Hillsdale, NJ: The Analytic Press.

Hook, J. N., Davis, D., Owen, J., & DeBlaere, C. (2017). *Cultural humility: Engaging diverse identities in therapy.* Washington, DC: American Psychological Association. http://dx.doi.org/10.1037/0000037-000

Horney, K. (1991). *Neurosis and human growth: The struggle toward self-realization.* New York, NY: Norton. (Original work published 1950)

Horowitz, L. M., & Strack, S. (Eds.). (2010). *Handbook of interpersonal psychology: Theory, research, assessment and therapeutic interventions.* New York, NY: Wiley & Sons. http://dx.doi.org/10.1002/9781118001868

Husserl, E. (1931). *Méditations cartésiennes: Introduction à la phénoménologie* [Cartisian meditations: An introduction to phenomenology] (G. Peiffer & E. Lévinas, Trans.). Paris, France: Armand Colin.

Hutton, R. J., Thordsen, M. L., & Mogford, R. (1997). Recognition-primed decision model in air traffic controller error analysis. In R. S. Jensen & L. A. Rakovan (Eds.), *Proceedings of the Ninth International Symposium on Aviation Psychology* (pp. 721–726). Columbus: Ohio State University.

Izard, C. E. (1971). *The face of emotion.* East Norwalk, CT: Appleton-Century-Crofts.

Jakubowski, P., & Lange, A. (1978). *The assertive option: Your rights and responsibilities*. Champaign, IL: Research Press.

James, W. (1884). What is an emotion? *Mind, 9*, 188–205. http://dx.doi.org/10.1093/mind/os-IX.34.188

James, W. (1981). *Principles of psychology*. Cambridge, MA: Harvard University Press. (Original work published 1890)

Janis, I., Defares, P., & Grossman, P. (1983). Hypervigilant reactions to threat. In H. Seyle (Ed.), *Selye's guide to stress research* (Vol. 3, pp. 1–42). New York, NY: Van Nostrand Reinhold.

Janis, I. L., & Mann, L. (1977). Emergency decision making: A theoretical analysis of responses to disaster warnings. *Journal of Human Stress, 3*, 35–45. http://dx.doi.org/10.1080/0097840X.1977.9936085

Johns, C. (1995). The value of reflective practice for nursing. *Journal of Clinical Nursing, 4*, 23–30. http://dx.doi.org/10.1111/j.1365-2702.1995.tb00006.x

Johnson, G. (2009). Theories of emotion. In J. Fieser & B. Dowden (Eds.), *The Internet encyclopedia of philosophy*. Available from https://www.iep.utm.edu/emotion/

Johnson, W. B., Barnett, J. E., Elman, N. S., Forrest, L., & Kaslow, N. J. (2012). The competent community: Toward a vital reformulation of professional ethics. *American Psychologist, 67*, 557–569. http://dx.doi.org/10.1037/a0027206

Johnston, E., & Olson, L. (2015). *The feeling brain: The biology and psychology of emotions*. New York, NY: Norton.

Jurist, E. (2018). *Minding emotions: Cultivating mentalization in psychotherapy*. New York, NY: Guilford Press.

Kabat-Zinn, J. (2013). *Full catastrophe living: Using the wisdom of your body and mind to face stress, pain, and illness*. New York, NY: Bantam Books. (Original work published 1991)

Kahneman, D. (2011). *Thinking, fast and slow*. New York, NY: Farrar, Straus and Giroux.

Kanske, P., Heissler, J., Schonfelder, S., Bongers, A., & Wessa, M. (2011). How to regulate emotion: Neural networks for reappraisal and distraction. *Cerebral Cortex, 21*, 1379–1388.

Kant, I. (1996). *The metaphysics of morals*. Cambridge, England: Cambridge University Press. (Original work published 1797) http://dx.doi.org/10.1017/CBO9780511809644

Karasu, T. B. (2001). *The psychotherapist as healer*. New York, NY: Aronson.

Keinan, G. (1987). Decision making under stress: Scanning of alternatives under controllable and uncontrollable threats. *Journal of Personality and Social Psychology, 52*, 639–644. http://dx.doi.org/10.1037/0022-3514.52.3.639

Kelley, F. A. (2015). The therapy relationship with lesbian and gay clients. *Psychotherapy, 52*, 113–118. http://dx.doi.org/10.1037/a0037958

Kiesler, D. J. (1966). Some myths of psychotherapy research and the search for a paradigm. *Psychological Bulletin, 65*, 110–136. http://dx.doi.org/10.1037/h0022911

Kiesler, D. J. (1988). *Therapeutic metacommunication: Therapist impact disclosure as feedback in psychotherapy*. Palo Alto, CA: Consulting Psychologists Press.

Kiesler, D. J. (1996). *Contemporary interpersonal theory and research: Personality, psychopathology, and psychotherapy*. New York, NY: Wiley & Sons.

Killingsworth, M. A., & Gilbert, D. T. (2010). A wandering mind is an unhappy mind. *Science, 330*, 932–932. http://dx.doi.org/10.1126/science.1192439

King, B. J. (2008). *Pressure is a privilege*. New York, NY: LifeTime Media.

Kircanski, K., Lieberman, M. D., & Craske, M. G. (2012). Feelings into words: Contributions of language to exposure therapy. *Psychological Science, 23*, 1086–1091. http://dx.doi.org/10.1177/0956797612443830

Klein, G. A. (1993). *A recognition-primed decision (RPD) model of rapid decision making.* New York, NY: Ablex.

Klein, G. A. (1998). *Sources of power: How people make decisions.* Cambridge, MA: MIT Press.

Klein, G. A., Calderwood, R., & Clinton-Cirocco, A. (1986, September). Rapid decision making on the fire ground. In *Proceedings of the Human Factors Society Annual Meeting* (Vol. 30, No. 6, pp. 576–580). Los Angeles, CA: Sage.

Klein, G. A., & Thordsen, M. L. (1991, January 1). Representing cockpit crew decision making (SEE A92-44901). Moffett Field, CA: NASA Ames Research Center.

Klein, M. H., Mathieu, P. L., Gendlin, E. T., & Kiesler, D. J. (1969). *The experiencing scale: Vol. 1. A research and training manual.* Madison: Wisconsin Psychiatric Institute.

Klein, M. H., Mathieu-Coughlan, P., & Kiesler, D. J. (1986). The Experiencing Scales. In L. S. Greenberg & W. M. Pinsof (Eds.), *The psychotherapeutic process: A research handbook* (pp. 21–72). New York, NY: Guilford Press.

Kline, K. V., Hill, C. E., Morris, T., O'Connor, S., Sappington, R., Vernay, C., . . . Okuno, H. (2019). Ruptures in psychotherapy: Experiences of therapist trainees. *Psychotherapy Research, 29*, 1086–1098. http://dx.doi.org/10.1080/10503307.2018.1492164

Kohut, H. (1984). *How does analysis cure?* Chicago, IL: University of Chicago Press. http://dx.doi.org/10.7208/chicago/9780226006147.001.0001

Kristeva, J. (1991). *Strangers to ourselves.* New York, NY: Columbia University Press.

Kross, E., & Ayduk, O. (2008). Facilitating adaptive emotional analysis: Distinguishing distanced-analysis of depressive experiences from immersed-analysis and distraction. *Personality and Social Psychology Bulletin, 34*, 924–938. http://dx.doi.org/10.1177/0146167208315938

Ladany, N., Friedlander, M. L., & Nelson, M. L. (2016). *Clinical supervision essentials series. Supervision essentials for the critical events in psychotherapy supervision model.* Washington, DC: American Psychological Association. http://dx.doi.org/10.1037/14916-000

Ladany, N., Hill, C. E., Corbett, M. M., & Nutt, E. A. (1996). Nature, extent, and importance of what psychotherapy trainees do not disclose to their supervisors. *Journal of Counseling Psychology, 43*, 10–24. http://dx.doi.org/10.1037/0022-0167.43.1.10

Laing, R. D. (1972). *The politics of family.* New York, NY: Vintage.

Lambert, M. J. (2010). *Prevention of treatment failure: The use of measuring, monitoring, and feedback in clinical practice.* Washington, DC: American Psychological Association.

Lambert, M. J. (2013). The efficacy and effectiveness of psychotherapy. In M. J. Lambert (Ed.), *Bergin and Garfield's handbook of psychotherapy and behavior change* (6th ed., pp. 169–218). New York, NY: Wiley.

Laneri, R. (2016, March 10). How to figure out which therapy is right for you. *New York Post.* Available at https://nypost.com/

Langton, R. (2009). *Sexual solipsism: Philosophical essays on pornography and objectification.* Oxford, England: Oxford University Press. http://dx.doi.org/10.1093/acprof:oso/9780199247066.001.0001

Larson, R. W., & Almeida, D. M. (1999). Emotional transmission in the daily lives of families: A new paradigm for studying family process. *Journal of Marriage and the Family, 61,* 5–20. http://dx.doi.org/10.2307/353879

Leahy, R. L. (2009). Emotional schemas in treatment-resistant anxiety. In D. Sookman & R. L. Leahy (Eds.), *Treatment resistant anxiety disorders: Resolving impasses to symptom remission* (pp. 135–164). New York, NY: Routledge.

Lee, H. (1960). *To kill a mockingbird.* Philadelphia, PA: Lippincott.

Lee, J., Lim, N., Yang, E., & Lee, S. M. (2011). Antecedents and consequences of three dimensions of burnout in psychotherapists: A meta-analysis. *Professional Psychology: Research and Practice, 42,* 252–258. http://dx.doi.org/10.1037/a0023319

Lehner, P., Seyed-Solorforough, M. M., O'Connor, M. F., Sak, S., & Mullin, T. (1997). Cognitive biases and time stress in team decision making. *IEEE Transactions on Systems, Man, and Cybernetics. Part A, Systems and Humans, 27,* 698–703. http://dx.doi.org/10.1109/3468.618269

Levenson, E. A. (1991). *The purloined self: Interpersonal perspectives in psychoanalysis.* New York, NY: Contemporary Psychoanalysis Books.

Levenson, E. A. (2005). *The fallacy of understanding and the ambiguity of change.* New York, NY: Routledge.

Levenson, R. W. (2011). Basic emotion questions. *Emotion Review, 3,* 379–386. http://dx.doi.org/10.1177/1754073911410743

Leventhal, H. (1984). A perceptual-motor theory of emotion. In L. Berkowitz (Ed.), *Advances in experimental social psychology* (Vol. 17, pp. 117–182). New York, NY: Academic Press.

Lewis, M. (2016). Self-conscious emotions: Embarrassment, pride, shame, guilt, and hubris. In L. Feldman Barrett, M. Lewis, & J. M. Haviland-Jones (Eds.), *Handbook of emotions* (4th ed., pp. 792–814). New York, NY: Guilford Press.

Lewis, M., & Rosenblum, L. A. (1974). *The effect of the infant on its caregiver.* New York, NY: Wiley-Interscience.

Lieberman, M. D. (2009). The brain's braking system (and how to 'use your words' to tap into it). *NeuroLeadership Journal, 2,* 9–14.

Lieberman, M. D., Eisenberger, N. I., Crockett, M. J., Tom, S. M., Pfeifer, J. H., & Way, B. M. (2007). Putting feelings into words. *Psychological Science, 18,* 421–428. http://dx.doi.org/10.1111/j.1467-9280.2007.01916.x

Ligiéro, D. P., & Gelso, C. J. (2002). Countertransference, attachment, and the working alliance: The therapist's contribution. *Psychotherapy, 39,* 3–11. http://dx.doi.org/10.1037/0033-3204.39.1.3

Lilienfeld, S. O., Ritschel, L. A., Lynn, S. J., Cautin, R. L., & Latzman, R. D. (2014). Why ineffective psychotherapies appear to work: A taxonomy of causes of spurious therapeutic effectiveness. *Perspectives on Psychological Science, 9,* 355–387. http://dx.doi.org/10.1177/1745691614535216

Lindquist, K., & Barrett, L. F. (2008). Emotional complexity. In M. Lewis, J. M. Haviland-Jones, & L. F. Barrett (Eds.), *Handbook of emotions* (3rd ed., pp. 513–530). New York, NY: Guilford Press.

Linehan, M. M. (1993a). *Cognitive-behavioral treatment of borderline personality disorder.* New York, NY: Guilford Press.

Linehan, M. M. (1993b). Dialectical behavior therapy for treatment of borderline personality disorder: Implications for the treatment of substance abuse. *NIDA Research Monograph, 137,* 201–216.

Lipshitz, R. (1993). Converging themes in the study of decision making in realistic settings. In G. A. Klein, J. Orasanu, R. Calderwood, & C. E. Zsambok (Eds.), *Decision making in action: Models and methods* (pp. 103–137). Westport, CT: Ablex.

Littlejohn, S. W. (2002). *Theories of human communication*. Belmont, CA: Wadsworth/Thomson Learning.

Lovlie, L. (1992). Postmodernism and subjectivity. In S. Kvale (Ed.), *Psychology and postmodernism* (pp. 119–134). London, England: Sage.

Mackie, D. M., & Smith, E. R. (2015). Intergroup emotions. In M. Mikulincer, P. R. Shaver, J. F. Dovidio, & J. A. Simpson (Eds.), *APA handbook of personality and social psychology* (Vol. 2, pp. 263–293). Washington, DC: American Psychological Association. http://dx.doi.org/10.1037/14342-010

Maranzan, K. A., Kowatch, K. R., Mascioli, B. A., McGeown, L., Popowich, A. D., & Spiroiu, F. (2018). Self-care and the Canadian Code of Ethics: Implications for training in professional psychology. *Canadian Psychology, 59*, 361–368. http://dx.doi.org/10.1037/cap0000153

Markman, A. B., Maddox, W. T., & Worthy, D. A. (2006). Choking and excelling under pressure. *Psychological Science, 17*, 944–948. http://dx.doi.org/10.1111/j.1467-9280.2006.01809.x

Martin, A., Buchheim, A., Berger, E., & Strauss, B. (2007). The impact of attachment organization on potential countertransference reactions. *Psychotherapy Research, 17*, 46–58. http://dx.doi.org/10.1080/10503300500485565

Martin, J., Martin, W., Meyer, M., & Slemon, A. (1986). Empirical investigation of the cognitive mediational paradigm for research on counseling. *Journal of Counseling Psychology, 33*, 115–123.

Martin, J., Martin, W., & Slemon, A. G. (1987). Cognitive mediation in person-centered and rational-emotive therapy. *Journal of Counseling Psychology, 34*, 251–260.

Maslach, C., & Jackson, S. E. (1981). *Maslach Burnout Inventory: Manual* (2nd ed.). Palo Alto, CA: Consulting Psychologists Press.

Maslach, C., Schaufeli, W. B., & Leiter, M. P. (2001). Job burnout. *Annual Review of Psychology, 52*, 397–422. http://dx.doi.org/10.1146/annurev.psych.52.1.397

Masten, A., Best, K., & Garmezy, N. (1990). Resilience and development: Contributions from the study of children who overcome adversity. *Development and Psychopathology, 2*, 425–444. http://dx.doi.org/10.1017/S0954579400005812

McCullough, L. (2003). *Treating affect phobia: A manual for short-term dynamic psychotherapy*. New York, NY: Guilford Press.

McGrath, J. E. (1970). A conceptual formulation for research on stress. In J. E. McGrath (Ed.), *Social & psychological factors in stress* (pp. 10–21). New York, NY: Rinehart & Winston.

McRae, K., Hughes, B., Chopra, S., Gabrieli, J. D., Gross, J. J., & Ochsner, K. N. (2010). The neural bases of distraction and reappraisal. *Journal of Cognitive Neuroscience, 22*, 248–262. http://dx.doi.org/10.1162/jocn.2009.21243

Mead, G. H. (1934). *Mind self and society from the standpoint of a social behaviorist* (C. W. Morris, Ed.). Chicago, IL: University of Chicago.

Meador, B., & Rogers, C. (1979). Person-centered therapy. In R. Corsini (Ed.), *Current psychotherapies* (pp. 131–184). Itasca, IL: Peacock.

Meehl, P. E. (1954). *Clinical versus statistical prediction: A theoretical analysis and a review of the evidence*. Minneapolis: University of Minnesota Press. http://dx.doi.org/10.1037/11281-000

Meehl, P. (1960). The cognitive activity of the clinician. *American Psychologist, 15,* 19–27. http://dx.doi.org/10.1037/h0041744

Mehr, K. E., Ladany, N., & Caskie, G. I. L. (2015). Factors influencing trainee willingness to disclose in supervision. *Training and Education in Professional Psychology, 9,* 44–51. http://dx.doi.org/10.1037/tep0000028

Mennin, D. S., & Fresco, D. M. (2013). What, me worry and ruminate about *DSM-5* and RDoC? The importance of targeting negative self-referential processing. *Clinical Psychology: Science and Practice, 20,* 258–267. http://dx.doi.org/10.1111/cpsp.12038

Metzinger, T. (2009). *The ego tunnel: The science of the mind and the myth of the self.* New York, NY: Basic Books.

Miller, K. (2005). *Communication theories: Perspectives, processes, and contexts.* New York, NY: McGraw-Hill.

Miller, N. K. (1991). *Getting personal: Feminist occasions and other autobiographical acts.* New York, NY: Routledge.

Mitchell, S. A. (1988). The intrapsychic and the interpersonal: Different theories, different domains, or historical artifacts? *Psychoanalytic Inquiry, 8,* 472–496. http://dx.doi.org/10.1080/07351698809533738

Mitchell, S. A. (1992). Commentary on Trop and Stolorow's "Defense Analysis in Self Psychology." *Psychoanalytic Dialogues, 2,* 455–465. http://dx.doi.org/10.1080/10481889209538944

Mitchell, S. A. (1993). *Hope and dread in psychoanalysis.* New York, NY: Basic Books.

Mohr, J. J., Gelso, C. J., & Hill, C. E. (2005). Client and counselor trainee attachment as predictors of session evaluation and countertransference behavior in first counseling sessions. *Journal of Counseling Psychology, 52,* 298–309. http://dx.doi.org/10.1037/0022-0167.52.3.298

Muran, J. C. (2001a). Contemporary constructions & contexts. In J. C. Muran (Ed.), *Self-relations in the psychotherapy process* (pp. 3–44). Washington, DC: American Psychological Association. http://dx.doi.org/10.1037/10391-001

Muran, J. C. (2001b). Meditations on both/and. In J. C. Muran (Ed.), *Self-relations in the psychotherapy process* (pp. 347–372). Washington, DC: American Psychological Association. http://dx.doi.org/10.1037/10391-014

Muran, J. C. (Ed.). (2001c). *Self-relations in the psychotherapy process.* Washington, DC: American Psychological Association. http://dx.doi.org/10.1037/10391-000

Muran, J. C. (2002). A relational approach to understanding change: Plurality and contextualism in a psychotherapy research program. *Psychotherapy Research, 12,* 113–138. http://dx.doi.org/10.1080/713664276

Muran, J. C. (Ed.). (2007a). *Dialogues on difference: Studies of diversity in the therapeutic relationship.* Washington, DC: American Psychological Association. http://dx.doi.org/10.1037/11500-000

Muran, J. C. (2007b). A relational turn on thick description. In J. C. Muran (Ed.), *Dialogues on difference: Studies of diversity in the therapeutic relationship* (pp. 257–274). Washington, DC: American Psychological Association. http://dx.doi.org/10.1037/11500-029

Muran, J. C. (2007c). Reply: The power of/in language. In J. C. Muran (Ed.), *Dialogues on difference: Studies of diversity in the therapeutic relationship* (pp. 285–288). Washington, DC: American Psychological Association. http://dx.doi.org/10.1037/11500-032

Muran, J. C. (2019). Confessions of a New York rupture researcher: An insider's guide and critique. *Psychotherapy Research, 29*, 1–14. http://dx.doi.org/10.1080/10503307.2017.1413261

Muran, J. C., & Barber, J. P. (Eds.). (2010). *Therapeutic alliance: An evidence-based guide to practice*. New York, NY: Guilford Press.

Muran, J. C., & Hungr, C. (2013). Power plays, negotiation, & mutual recognition in the therapeutic alliance. In A. W. Wolf, M. R. Goldfried, & J. C. Muran (Eds.), *Transforming negative reactions to clients: From frustration to compassion* (pp. 23–44). Washington, DC: American Psychological Association. http://dx.doi.org/10.1037/13940-001

Muran, J. C., & Safran, J. D. (2002). Resolving ruptures in the therapeutic alliance: A relational approach. In J. Magnavita (Ed.), *Handbook of psychotherapy* (Vol. 1, pp. 253–282). New York, NY: Wiley & Sons.

Muran, J. C., Safran, J. D., Eubanks, C. F., & Gorman, B. S. (2018). The effect of alliance-focused training on a cognitive-behavioral therapy for personality disorders. *Journal of Consulting and Clinical Psychology, 86*, 384–397. http://dx.doi.org/10.1037/ccp0000284

Muran, J. C., Safran, J. D., & Eubanks-Carter, C. (2010). Developing therapist abilities to negotiate the therapeutic alliance: Beth Israel Psychotherapy Research Program. In J. C. Muran & J. P. Barber (Eds.), *Therapeutic alliance: An evidence-based guide to practice* (pp. 320–340). New York, NY: Guilford Press.

Muran, J. C., Safran, J. D., Gorman, B. S., Samstag, L. W., Eubanks-Carter, C., & Winston, A. (2009). The relationship of early alliance ruptures and their resolution to process and outcome in three time-limited psychotherapies for personality disorders. *Psychotherapy, 46*, 233–248.

Muran, J. C., Safran, J. D., Samstag, L. W., & Winston, A. (2005). Evaluating an alliance-focused treatment for personality disorders. *Psychotherapy, 42*, 532–545. http://dx.doi.org/10.1037/0033-3204.42.4.532

Najavits, L. M., & Strupp, H. H. (1994). Differences in the effectiveness of psychodynamic therapists: A process-outcome study. *Psychotherapy, 31*, 114–123. http://dx.doi.org/10.1037/0033-3204.31.1.114

Newell, B. R., Lagnado, D. A., & Shanks, D. R. (2007). *Straight choices: The psychology of decision making*. New York, NY: Psychology Press.

Newman, M. G., Castonguay, L. G., Borkovec, T. D., Fisher, A. J., Boswell, J. F., Szkodny, L. E., & Nordberg, S. S. (2011). A randomized controlled trial of cognitive-behavioral therapy for generalized anxiety disorder with integrated techniques from emotion-focused and interpersonal therapies. *Journal of Consulting and Clinical Psychology, 79*, 171–181. http://dx.doi.org/10.1037/a0022489

Newman, M. G., Castonguay, L. G., Jacobson, N. C., & Moore, G. A. (2015). Adult attachment as a moderator of treatment outcome for generalized anxiety disorder: Comparison between cognitive-behavioral therapy (CBT) plus supportive listening and CBT plus interpersonal and emotional processing therapy. *Journal of Consulting and Clinical Psychology, 83*, 915–925. http://dx.doi.org/10.1037/a0039359

Nietzsche, E. (1968). *The will to power* (W Kaufmann, Trans.). New York, NY: Vintage Books. (Original work published 1888)

Nissen-Lie, H. A., Havik, O. E., Høglend, P. A., Monsen, J. T., & Rønnestad, M. H. (2013). The contribution of the quality of therapists' personal lives to the development of the working alliance. *Journal of Counseling Psychology, 60,* 483–495. http://dx.doi.org/10.1037/a0033643

Niven, K., Totterdell, P., & Holman, D. (2009). A classification of controlled interpersonal affect regulation strategies. *Emotion, 9,* 498–509. http://dx.doi.org/10.1037/a0015962

Norcross, J. C., & Lambert, M. J. (Eds.). (2019a). *Psychotherapy relationships that work: Vol. 1. Evidence-based therapist contributions.* New York, NY: Oxford University Press.

Norcross, J. C., & Lambert, M. J. (2019b). What works in the psychotherapy relationship: Results, conclusions, and practices. In J. C. Norcross & M. J. Lambert (Eds.), *Psychotherapy relationships that work: Vol. 1 Evidence-based therapist contributions* (3rd ed., pp. 631–646). New York, NY: Oxford University Press.

Norcross, J. C., & VandenBos, G. R. (2018). *Leaving it at the office: A guide to psychotherapist self-care* (2nd ed.). New York, NY: Guilford Press.

Nosek, B. A., Greenwald, A. G., & Banaji, M. R. (2007). The Implicit Association Test at age 7: A methodological and conceptual review. In J. A. Bargh (Ed.), *Automatic processes in social thinking and behavior* (pp. 265–292). London, England: Psychology Press.

Nussbaum, M. C. (1995). Objectification. *Philosophy & Public Affairs, 24,* 249–291. http://dx.doi.org/10.1111/j.1088-4963.1995.tb00032.x

Ochsner, K. N. (2004). Current directions in social cognitive neuroscience. *Current Opinion in Neurobiology, 14,* 254–258. http://dx.doi.org/10.1016/j.conb.2004.03.011

Ochsner, K. N., Bunge, S. A., Gross, J. J., & Gabrieli, J. D. (2002). Rethinking feelings: An fMRI study of the cognitive regulation of emotion. *Journal of Cognitive Neuroscience, 14,* 1215–1229. http://dx.doi.org/10.1162/089892902760807212

Ochsner, K. N., & Gross, J. J. (2005). The cognitive control of emotion. *Trends in Cognitive Sciences, 9,* 242–249. http://dx.doi.org/10.1016/j.tics.2005.03.010

Ochsner, K. N., & Gross, J. J. (2008). Cognitive emotion regulation: Insights from social cognitive and affective neuroscience. *Current Directions in Psychological Science, 17,* 153–158. http://dx.doi.org/10.1111/j.1467-8721.2008.00566.x

Ochsner, K. N., Silvers, J. A., & Buhle, J. T. (2012). Functional imaging studies of emotion regulation: A synthetic review and evolving model of the cognitive control of emotion. *Annals of the New York Academy of Sciences, 1251,* E1–E24. http://dx.doi.org/10.1111/j.1749-6632.2012.06751.x

Ogden, T. H. (1994). The concept of interpretive action. *The Psychoanalytic Quarterly, 63,* 219–245. http://dx.doi.org/10.1080/21674086.1994.11927413

Ogden, T. H. (1997). Reverie and interpretation. *The Psychoanalytic Quarterly, 66,* 567–595. http://dx.doi.org/10.1080/21674086.1997.11927546

Olson, M. A., & Fazio, R. H. (2003). Relations between implicit measures of prejudice: What are we measuring? *Psychological Science, 14,* 636–639. http://dx.doi.org/10.1046/j.0956-7976.2003.psci_1477.x

Oskamp, S. (1965). Overconfidence in case-study judgments. *Journal of Consulting Psychology, 29,* 261–265. http://dx.doi.org/10.1037/h0022125

Oswald, F. L., Mitchell, G., Blanton, H., Jaccard, J., & Tetlock, P. E. (2013). Predicting ethnic and racial discrimination: A meta-analysis of IAT criterion studies. *Journal of Personality and Social Psychology, 105,* 171–192. http://dx.doi.org/10.1037/a0032734

Otten, M. (2009). Choking vs. clutch performance: A study of sport perfor-mance under pressure. *Journal of Sport & Exercise Psychology, 31*, 583–601. http://dx.doi.org/10.1123/jsep.31.5.583

Oudejans, R. R. D. (2008). Reality-based practice under pressure improves hand-gun shooting performance of police officers. *Ergonomics, 51*, 261–273. http://dx.doi.org/10.1080/00140130701577435

Oudejans, R. R. D., & Pijpers, J. R. (2009). Training with anxiety has a positive effect on expert perceptual-motor performance under pressure. *Quarterly Journal of Experimental Psychology, 62*, 1631–1647. http://dx.doi.org/10.1080/17470210802557702

Overholser, J. C. (2011). Collaborative empiricism, guided discovery, and the Socratic method: Core processes for effective cognitive therapy. *Clinical Psychology: Science and Practice, 18*, 62–66. http://dx.doi.org/10.1111/j.1468-2850.2011.01235.x

Owen, J., Tao, K. W., Imel, Z. E., Wampold, B. E., & Rodolfa, E. (2014). Address-ing racial and ethnic microaggressions in therapy. *Professional Psychology: Research and Practice, 45*, 283–290. http://dx.doi.org/10.1037/a0037420

Owen, J., Tao, K., & Rodolfa, E. (2010). Microaggressions and women in short-term psychotherapy: Initial evidence. *The Counseling Psychologist, 38*, 923–946. http://dx.doi.org/10.1177/0011000010376093

Paas, F. G. W. C., & van Merriënboer, J. J. G. (1993). The efficiency of instruc-tional conditions: An approach to combine mental effort and performance measures. *Human Factors, 35*, 737–743. http://dx.doi.org/10.1177/001872089303500412

Pascual-Leone, A., & Yeryomenko, N. (2017). The client "experiencing" scale as a predictor of treatment outcomes: A meta-analysis on psychotherapy process. *Psychotherapy Research, 27*, 653–665. http://dx.doi.org/10.1080/10503307.2016.1152409

Peluso, P. R., & Freund, R. R. (2018). Therapist and client emotional expression and psychotherapy outcomes: A meta-analysis. *Psychotherapy, 55*, 461–472. http://dx.doi.org/10.1037/pst0000165

Pennebaker, J. W. (1997). Writing about emotional experiences as a therapeu-tic process. *Psychological Science, 8*, 162–166. http://dx.doi.org/10.1111/j.1467-9280.1997.tb00403.x

Pennebaker, J. W., & Smyth, J. (2016). *Opening up by writing it down: The healing power of expressive writing* (3rd ed.). New York, NY: Guilford Press.

Perez Foster, R., Moskowitz, M., & Javier, R. (Eds.). (1996). *Reaching across bound-aries of culture and class: Widening the scope of psychotherapy.* Northvale, NJ: Aronson.

Petrowski, K., Pokorny, D., Nowacki, K., & Buchheim, A. (2013). The therapist's attachment representation and the patient's attachment to the therapist. *Psycho-therapy Research, 23*, 25–34. http://dx.doi.org/10.1080/10503307.2012.717307

Piaget, J. (1970). Piaget's theory. In P. H. Mussen (Ed.) & G. Gellerier & J. Langer (Trans.), *Carmichael's manual of child psychology* (3rd ed., Vol. 1, pp. 703–732). New York, NY: Wiley.

Pinderhughes, E. (1989). *Understanding race, ethnicity, and power: The key to efficacy in clinical practice.* New York, NY: Simon and Schuster.

Piper, M. (1979). Practical aspects of psychometric testing in the elderly. *Age and Ageing, 8*, 299–302. http://dx.doi.org/10.1093/ageing/8.4.299

Piper, W. E., Azim, H. F., Joyce, A. S., & McCallum, M. (1991). Transference inter-pretations, therapeutic alliance, and outcome in short-term individual psycho-therapy. *Archives of General Psychiatry, 48*, 946–953. http://dx.doi.org/10.1001/archpsyc.1991.01810340078010

Piper, W. E., Ogrodniczuk, J. S., Joyce, A. S., McCallum, M., Rosie, J. S., O'Kelly, J. G., & Steinberg, P. I. (1999). Prediction of dropping out in time-limited, interpretive individual psychotherapy. *Psychotherapy, 36*, 114–122. http://dx.doi.org/10.1037/h0087787

Pizer, S. A. (1998). *Building bridges: The negotiation of paradox in psychoanalysis.* Hillsdale, NJ: The Analytic Press.

Politser, P. (1981). Decision analysis and clinical judgment. A re-evaluation. *Medical Decision Making, 1*, 361–389. http://dx.doi.org/10.1177/0272989X8100100406

Pope, K. S., Sonne, J. L., & Greene, B. (2006). *What therapists don't talk about and why: Understanding taboos that hurt us and our clients.* Washington, DC: American Psychological Association. http://dx.doi.org/10.1037/11413-000

Pope, K. S., & Tabachnick, B. G. (1993). Therapists' anger, hate, fear, and sexual feelings: National survey of therapist responses, client characteristics, critical events, formal complaints, and training. *Professional Psychology: Research and Practice, 24*, 142–152. http://dx.doi.org/10.1037/0735-7028.24.2.142

Pos, A. E., Greenberg, L. S., Goldman, R. N., & Korman, L. M. (2003). Emotional processing during experiential treatment of depression. *Journal of Consulting and Clinical Psychology, 71*, 1007–1016. http://dx.doi.org/10.1037/0022-006X.71.6.1007

Randall, A. K., & Bodenmann, G. (2009). The role of stress on close relation-ships and marital satisfaction. *Clinical Psychology Review, 29*, 105–115. http://dx.doi.org/10.1016/j.cpr.2008.10.004

Records, N. L., & Weiss, A. L. (1990). Clinical judgment: An overview. *Journal of Childhood Communication Disorders, 13*, 153–165.

Redelmeier, D. A., & Cialdini, R. B. (2002). Problems for clinical judgement: 5. Principles of influence in medical practice. *Canadian Medical Association Journal, 166*, 1680–1684.

Redelmeier, D. A., Ferris, L. E., Tu, J. V., Hux, J. E., & Schull, M. J. (2001). Prob-lems for clinical judgement: Introducing cognitive psychology as one more basic science. *Canadian Medical Association Journal, 164*, 358–360.

Regan, A. M., & Hill, C. E. (1992). Investigation of what clients and counselors do not say in brief therapy. *Journal of Counseling Psychology, 39*, 168–174. http://dx.doi.org/10.1037/0022-0167.39.2.168

Rennie, D. L. (1994). Clients' deference in psychotherapy. *Journal of Counseling Psychology, 41*, 427–437. http://dx.doi.org/10.1037/0022-0167.41.4.427

Rhodes, R., Hill, C., Thompson, B., & Elliott, R. (1994). Client retrospective recall of resolved and unresolved misunderstanding events. *Journal of Counseling Psychologist, 41*, 473–483. http://dx.doi.org/10.1037/0022-0167.41.4.473

Rice, L. N., & Kerr, G. P. (1986). Measures of client and therapist vocal quality. In L. S. Greenberg & W. M. Pinsof (Eds.), *The psychotherapeutic process: A research handbook* (pp. 73–105). New York, NY: Guilford Press.

Rimé, B. (2009). Emotion elicits the social sharing of emotion: Theory and empirical review. *Emotion Review, 1*, 60–85. http://dx.doi.org/10.1177/1754073908097189

Roberts, L. J., Jackson, M. S., & Grundy, I. H. (2019). Choking under pressure: Illuminating the role of distraction and self-focus. *International Review of*

Sport and Exercise Psychology, *12*, 49–69. http://dx.doi.org/10.1080/ 1750984X.2017.1374432

Roese, N. J. (1997). Counterfactual thinking. *Psychological Bulletin*, *121*, 133–148. http://dx.doi.org/10.1037/0033-2909.121.1.133

Rogers, C. R. (1951). *Client-centered therapy: Its current practice, implications, and theory*. Oxford, England: Houghton Mifflin.

Rogers, C. R. (1957). The necessary and sufficient conditions of therapeutic personality change. *Journal of Consulting Psychology*, *21*, 95–103. http://dx.doi.org/ 10.1037/h0045357

Rousmaniere, T. (2017). *Deliberate practice for psychotherapists: A guide to improving clinical effectiveness*. New York, NY: Routledge/Taylor & Francis Group.

Rousmaniere, T. (2019). *Mastering the inner skills of psychotherapy: A deliberate practice manual*. Seattle, WA: Gold Lantern Books.

Rousmaniere, T., Goodyear, R. K., Miller, S. D., & Wampold, B. E. (Eds.). (2017). *The cycle of excellence: Using deliberate practice to improve supervision and training*. Hoboken, NJ: Wiley-Blackwell. http://dx.doi.org/10.1002/ 9781119165590

Rousmaniere, T. G., Swift, J. K., Babins-Wagner, R., Whipple, J. L., & Berzins, S. (2016). Supervisor variance in psychotherapy outcome in routine practice. *Psychotherapy Research*, *26*, 196–205. http://dx.doi.org/10.1080/10503307. 2014.963730

Rubel, J. A., Zilcha-Mano, S., Feils-Klaus, V., & Lutz, W. (2018). Session-to-session effects of alliance ruptures in outpatient CBT: Within- and between-patient associations. *Journal of Consulting and Clinical Psychology*, *86*, 354–366. http://dx.doi.org/10.1037/ccp0000286

Rubino, G., Barker, C., Roth, T., & Fearon, P. (2000). Therapist empathy and depth of interpretation in response to potential alliance ruptures: The role of therapist and patient attachment styles. *Psychotherapy Research*, *10*, 408–420. http:// dx.doi.org/10.1093/ptr/10.4.408

Rumelhart, D. E., Smolensky, P., McClelland, J. L., & Hinton, G. (1986). Sequential thought processes in PDP models. *Parallel Distributed Processing: Explorations in the Microstructures of Cognition*, *2*, 3–57.

Russell, J. A. (2015). My psychological constructionist perspective. In L. F. Barrett & J. A. Russell (Eds.), *The psychological construction of emotion* (pp. 183–208). New York, NY: Guilford Press.

Ryle, G. (1980). *The concept of mind*. New York, NY: Penguin Books. (Original work published 1949)

Safran, J. D. (1998). *Widening the scope of cognitive therapy: The therapeutic relationship, emotion, and the process of change*. Northvale, NJ: Aronson.

Safran, J. D., Crocker, P., McMain, S., & Murray, P. (1990). The therapeutic alliance rupture as a therapy event for empirical investigation. *Psychotherapy: Theory, Research and Practice*, *27*, 154–165.

Safran, J. D., & Greenberg, L. S. (Eds.). (1991). *Emotion, psychotherapy, and change*. New York, NY: Guilford Press.

Safran, J. D., & Muran, J. C. (1996). The resolution of ruptures in the therapeutic alliance. *Journal of Consulting and Clinical Psychology*, *64*, 447–458. http://dx.doi.org/10.1037/0022-006X.64.3.447

Safran, J. D., & Muran, J. C. (2000). *Negotiating the therapeutic alliance: A relational treatment guide*. New York, NY: Guilford Press.

Safran, J. D., & Muran, J. C. (2006). Has the concept of the therapeutic alliance outlived its usefulness? *Psychotherapy, 43,* 286–291. http://dx.doi.org/10.1037/0033-3204.43.3.286

Safran, J. D., Muran, J. C., & Samstag, L. W. (1994). Resolving therapeutic alliance ruptures: A task analytic investigation. In A. O. Horvath & L. S. Greenberg (Eds.), *The working alliance: Theory, research, and practice* (pp. 225–255). New York, NY: Wiley.

Safran, J. D., Muran, J. C., Samstag, L. W., & Winston, A. (2005). Evaluating alliance-focused intervention for potential treatment failures: A feasibility study and descriptive analysis. *Psychotherapy, 42,* 512–531. http://dx.doi.org/10.1037/0033-3204.42.4.512

Safran, J. D., & Segal, Z. V. (1990). *Cognitive therapy: An interpersonal process perspective.* New York, NY: Basic Books.

Salovey, P., Detweiler-Bedell, B. T., Detweiler-Bedell, J. B., & Mayer, J. D. (2008). Emotional intelligence. In M. Lewis, J. M. Haviland-Jones, & L. F. Barrett (Eds.), *Handbook of emotions* (3rd ed., pp. 533–547). New York, NY: Guilford Press.

Samstag, L. W., Muran, J. C., & Safran, J. D. (2004). Defining and identifying alliance ruptures. In D. P. Charman (Ed.), *Core processes in brief psychodynamic psychotherapy: Advancing effective practice* (pp. 187–214). Mahwah, NJ: Erlbaum.

Sandler, J. (1976). Countertransference and role responsiveness. *International Journal of Psycho-Analysis, 3,* 33–42.

Saxon, D., & Barkham, M. (2012). Patterns of therapist variability: Therapist effects and the contribution of patient severity and risk. *Journal of Consulting and Clinical Psychology, 80,* 535–546. http://dx.doi.org/10.1037/a0028898

Sayer, N. A., Noorbaloochi, S., Frazier, P. A., Pennebaker, J. W., Orazem, R. J., Schnurr, P. P., . . . Litz, B. T. (2015). Randomized controlled trial of online expressive writing to address readjustment difficulties among U.S. Afghanistan and Iraq war veterans. *Journal of Traumatic Stress, 28,* 381–390. http://dx.doi.org/10.1002/jts.22047

Scarantino, A. (2015). Basic emotions, psychological construction, and the problem of variability. In L. F. Barrett & J. A. Russell (Eds.), *The psychological construction of emotion* (pp. 334–376). New York, NY: Guilford Press.

Schachtel, E. G. (1959). *Metamorphosis: On the development of affect, perception, attention, and memory.* New York, NY: Basic Books.

Schafer, R. (1983). *The analytic attitude.* New York, NY: Basic Books.

Schauenburg, H., Buchheim, A., Beckh, K., Nolte, T., Brenk-Franz, K., Leichsenring, F., . . . Dinger, U. (2010). The influence of psychodynamically oriented therapists' attachment representations on outcome and alliance in inpatient psychotherapy [corrected]. *Psychotherapy Research, 20,* 193–202. http://dx.doi.org/10.1080/10503300903204043

Scherer, K. R. (2005). What are emotions? And how can they be measured? *Social Sciences Information, 44,* 695–729. http://dx.doi.org/10.1177/0539018405058216

Schön, D. A. (1983). *The reflective practitioner: How professionals think in action.* New York, NY: Basic Books.

Schöttke, H., Flückiger, C., Goldberg, S. B., Eversmann, J., & Lange, J. (2017). Predicting psychotherapy outcome based on therapist interpersonal skills: A five-year longitudinal study of a therapist assessment protocol. *Psychotherapy Research, 27,* 642–652. http://dx.doi.org/10.1080/10503307.2015.1125546

Schut, A. J., Castonguay, L. G., Flanagan, K. M., Yamasaki, A. S., Barber, J. P., Bedics, J. D., & Smith, T. L. (2005). Therapist interpretation, patient–therapist interpersonal process, and outcome in psychodynamic psychotherapy for avoidant personality disorder. *Psychotherapy, 42,* 494–511. http://dx.doi.org/10.1037/0033-3204.42.4.494

Schwarz, N. (2010). Meaning in context: Metacognitive experiences. In L. F. Barrett, B. Mesquita, & E. Smith (Eds.), *The mind in context* (pp. 105–125). New York, NY: Guilford Press.

Seligman, M. E. (2000, February). Optimism, pessimism, and mortality. *Mayo Clinic Proceedings, 75,* 133–134. http://dx.doi.org/10.1016/S0025-6196(11)64182-7

Seligman, M. E. (2002). Positive psychology, positive prevention, and positive therapy. In C. R. Snyder & S. J. Lopez (Eds.), *Handbook of positive psychology* (pp. 3–12). New York, NY: Oxford University Press.

Seligman, M. E., & Csikszentmihalyi, M. (2000). Positive psychology: An introduction. *American Psychologist, 55,* 5–14. http://dx.doi.org/10.1037/0003-066X.55.1.5

Seligman, M. E., & Csikszentmihalyi, M. (2014). Positive psychology: An introduction. In M. Csikszentmihalyi & R. Larson (Eds.), *Flow and the foundations of positive psychology* (pp. 279–298). New York, NY: Springer.

Seligman, M. E., Steen, T. A., Park, N., & Peterson, C. (2005). Positive psychology progress: Empirical validation of interventions. *American Psychologist, 60,* 410–421. http://dx.doi.org/10.1037/0003-066X.60.5.410

Selye, H. (1975). Confusion and controversy in the stress field. *Journal of Human Stress, 1,* 37–44. http://dx.doi.org/10.1080/0097840X.1975.9940406

Shimokawa, K., Lambert, M. J., & Smart, D. W. (2010). Enhancing treatment outcome of patients at risk of treatment failure: Meta-analytic and mega-analytic review of a psychotherapy quality assurance system. *Journal of Consulting and Clinical Psychology, 78,* 298–311. http://dx.doi.org/10.1037/a0019247

Silberschatz, G. (Ed.). (2013). *Transformative relationships: The control mastery theory of psychotherapy.* New York, NY: Routledge. http://dx.doi.org/10.4324/9780203955963

Simon, H. A. (1957). *Models of man: Social and rational.* Oxford, England: Wiley & Sons.

Singer, E. (1965). *Key concepts in psychotherapy.* New York, NY: Random House.

Singer, J. L. (1966). *Daydreaming: An introduction to the experimental study of inner experience.* New York, NY: Crown/Random House.

Sloan, E., Hall, K., Moulding, R., Bryce, S., Mildred, H., & Staiger, P. K. (2017). Emotion regulation as a transdiagnostic treatment construct across anxiety, depression, substance, eating and borderline personality disorders: A systematic review. *Clinical Psychology Review, 57,* 141–163. http://dx.doi.org/10.1016/j.cpr.2017.09.002

Slochower, J. (1996). Holding and the fate of the analyst's subjectivity. *Psychoanalytic Dialogues, 6,* 323–353. http://dx.doi.org/10.1080/10481889609539123

Slovic, P., Finucane, M. L., Peters, E., & MacGregor, D. G. (2002a). The affect heuristic. In T. Gilovich, D. Griffin, & D. Kahneman (Eds.), *Heuristics and biases: The psychology of intuitive judgment* (pp. 397–420). Cambridge, England: Cambridge University Press. http://dx.doi.org/10.1017/CBO9780511808098.025

Slovic, P., Finucane, M., Peters, E., & MacGregor, D. G. (2002b). Rational actors or rational fools: Implications of the affect heuristic for behavioral economics. *Journal of Socio-Economics, 31,* 329–342. http://dx.doi.org/10.1016/S1053-5357(02)00174-9

Slovic, P., & Peters, E. (2006). Risk perception and affect. *Current Directions in Psychological Science, 15*, 322–325. http://dx.doi.org/10.1111/j.1467-8721.2006.00461.x

Smith, P. L., & Moss, S. B. (2009). Psychologist impairment: What is it, how can it be prevented, and what can be done to address it? *Clinical Psychology: Science and Practice, 16*, 1–15. http://dx.doi.org/10.1111/j.1468-2850.2009.01137.x

Spence, D. P. (1982). *Narrative truth and historical truth: Meaning and interpretation in psychoanalysis*. New York, NY: Norton.

Spielberger, C. D., Krasner, S. S., & Solomon, E. P. (1988). The experience, expression, and control of anger. In M. P. Janisse (Ed.), *Individual differences, stress, and health psychology* (pp. 89–108). New York, NY: Springer. http://dx.doi.org/10.1007/978-1-4612-3824-9_5

Staal, M. A. (2004). *Stress, cognition, and human performance: A literature review and conceptual framework* (NASA Technical Memorandum 212824). Moffett Field, CA: NASA Ames Research Center.

Staw, B. M., Sandelands, L. E., & Dutton, J. E. (1981). Threat rigidity effects in organizational behavior: A multilevel analysis. *Administrative Science Quarterly, 26*, 501–524. http://dx.doi.org/10.2307/2392337

Stern, D. B. (1997). *Unformulated experience*. Hillsdale, NJ: The Analytic Press.

Stern, D. B. (2015). *Relational freedom*. New York, NY: Routledge. http://dx.doi.org/10.4324/9781315765570

Stern, D. N. (1985). *The interpersonal world of the infant: A view from psychoanalysis and developmental psychology*. New York, NY: Basic Books.

Stern, D. N. (2000). Putting time back into our considerations of infant experience: A microdiachronic view. *Infant Mental Health Journal, 21*, 21–28. http://dx.doi.org/10.1002/(SICI)1097-0355(200001/04)21:1/2<21::AID-IMHJ3>3.0.CO;2-Z

Sternberg, R. J. (1986). A triangular theory of love. *Psychological Review, 93*, 119–135. http://dx.doi.org/10.1037/0033-295X.93.2.119

Stiles, W. B., Glick, M. J., Osatuke, K., Hardy, G. E., Shapiro, D. A., Agnew-Davies, R., Rees, A., & Barkham, M. (2004). Patterns of alliance development and the rupture-repair hypothesis: Are productive relationships U-shaped or V-shaped? *Journal of Counseling Psychology, 51*, 81–92. http://dx.doi.org/10.1037/0022-0167.51.1.81

Stiles, W. B., Honos-Webb, L., & Surko, M. (1998). Responsiveness in psychotherapy. *Clinical Psychology: Science and Practice, 5*, 439–458. http://dx.doi.org/10.1111/j.1468-2850.1998.tb00166.x

Stokes, A. F., Kemper, K. L., & Marsh, R. (1992). *Time-stressed flight decision making: A study of expert and novice aviators* (TR ARL-93-1/INTEL-93-1). Urbana-Champaign, IL: Institute of Aviation.

Stone, M., Friedlander, M. L., & Moeyaert, M. (2018). Illustrating novel techniques for analyzing single-case experiments: Effects of pre-session mindfulness practice. *Journal of Counseling Psychology, 65*, 690–702. http://dx.doi.org/10.1037/cou0000291

Strauss, B. M., & Petrowski, K. (2017). The role of the therapist's attachment in the process and outcome of psychotherapy. In L. G. Castonguay & C. E. Hill (Eds.), *How and why are some therapists better than others? Understanding therapist effects* (pp. 117–138). Washington, DC: American Psychological Association. http://dx.doi.org/10.1037/0000034-008

Streufert, S., & Streufert, S. C. (1981). *Stress and information search in complex decision making: Effects of load and time urgency* (Tech. Rep. No. TR-4). Department of Behavioral Science, Milton's Hershey Medical Center, Hershey, PA.

Strupp, H. H. (1980a). Success and failure in time-limited psychotherapy. A systematic comparison of two cases: Comparison 1. *Archives of General Psychiatry, 37*, 595–603. http://dx.doi.org/10.1001/archpsyc.1980.01780180109014

Strupp, H. H. (1980b). Success and failure in time-limited psychotherapy. A systematic comparison of two cases: Comparison 2. *Archives of General Psychiatry, 37*, 708–716. http://dx.doi.org/10.1001/archpsyc.1980.01780190106013

Strupp, H. H. (1980c). Success and failure in time-limited psychotherapy: With special reference to the performance of a lay counselor. *Archives of General Psychiatry, 37*, 831–841. http://dx.doi.org/10.1001/archpsyc.1980.01780200109014

Strupp, H. H. (1980d). Success and failure in time-limited psychotherapy: Further evidence (comparison 4). *Archives of General Psychiatry, 37*, 947–954. http://dx.doi.org/10.1001/archpsyc.1980.01780210105011

Strupp, H. H. (1993). The Vanderbilt Psychotherapy studies: Synopsis. *Journal of Consulting and Clinical Psychology, 61*, 431–433.

Strupp, H. H. (1998). The Vanderbilt I Study revisited. *Psychotherapy Research, 8*, 17–29. http://dx.doi.org/10.1080/10503309812331332167

Strupp, H. H., & Binder, J. L. (1984). *Psychotherapy in a new key: A guide to time-limited dynamic psychotherapy*. New York, NY: Basic Books.

Strupp, H. H., & Hadley, S. W. (1979). Specific vs nonspecific factors in psychotherapy. A controlled study of outcome. *Archives of General Psychiatry, 36*, 1125–1136. http://dx.doi.org/10.1001/archpsyc.1979.01780100095009

Sue, D. W. (2010). *Microaggressions in everyday life: Race, gender, and sexual orientation*. New York, NY: Wiley & Sons.

Sullivan, H. S. (1953). *The interpersonal theory of psychiatry*. New York, NY: Norton.

Sullivan, H. S. (1964). *The fusion of psychiatry and the social sciences*. New York, NY: Norton.

Suzuki, D. T. (1991). *An introduction to Zen Buddhism*. New York, NY: Grove Press.

Suzuki, S. (1970). *Zen mind, beginner's mind*. New York, NY: Walker/Weatherhill.

Swank, L. E., & Wittenborn, A. K. (2013). Repairing alliance ruptures in emotionally focused couple therapy: A preliminary task analysis. *American Journal of Family Therapy, 41*, 389–402. http://dx.doi.org/10.1080/01926187.2012.726595

Sweller, J. (1988). Cognitive load during problem solving: Effects on learning. *Cognitive Science, 12*, 257–285. http://dx.doi.org/10.1207/s15516709cog1202_4

Symington, N. (1983). The analyst's act of freedom as agent of therapeutic change. *International Review of Psycho-Analysis, 10*, 283–291.

Talia, A., Muzi, L., Lingiardi, V., & Taubner, S. (2018). How to be a secure base: Therapists' attachment representations and their link to attunement in psychotherapy. *Attachment & Human Development*. Advance online publication. http://dx.doi.org/10.1080/14616734.2018.1534247

Tangney, J. P. (1999). The self-conscious emotions: Shame, guilt, embarrassment and pride. In T. Dalgleish & M. J. Power (Eds.), *Handbook of cognition and emotion* (pp. 541–568). New York, NY: Wiley & Sons. http://dx.doi.org/10.1002/0470013494.ch26

Tangney, J. P., & Dearing, R. L. (2003). *Shame and guilt*. New York, NY: Guilford Press.

Tee, J., & Kazantzis, N. (2011). Collaborative empiricism in cognitive therapy: A definition and theory for the relationship construct. *Clinical Psychology: Science and Practice, 18*, 47–61. http://dx.doi.org/10.1111/j.1468-2850.2010.01234.x

Tepas, D. I., & Price, J. M. (2001). What is stress and what is fatigue? In P. A. Hancock & P. A. Desmond (Eds.), *Stress, workload, and fatigue* (pp. 607–622). Mahwah, NJ: Erlbaum.

Tompkins, S. S. (1962). *Affect, imagery, consciousness: The positive affects*. New York, NY: Springer.

Tracey, T. J., Wampold, B. E., Lichtenberg, J. W., & Goodyear, R. K. (2014). Expertise in psychotherapy: An elusive goal? *American Psychologist, 69*, 218–229. http://dx.doi.org/10.1037/a0035099

Tracy, J. L., & Robins, R. W. (2014). Conceptual and empirical strengths of the authentic/hubristic model of pride. *Emotion, 14*, 33–37. http://dx.doi.org/10.1037/a0034490

Tronick, E. (2007). *The neurobehavioral and social-emotional development of infants and children*. New York, NY: Norton.

Tuohy, W. (2011, June 20). Disarming Dylan Moran. *Herald Sun*. Retrieved from https://www.heraldsun.com.au/entertainment/arts/disarming-dylan/news-story/a73a863c5e15b9f0cdc2d8c063693a3b?sv=264e367eedce3bdce7c9d4ddb3ee5e1

Tversky, A., & Kahneman, D. (1974). Judgment under uncertainty: Heuristics and biases. *Science, 185*, 1124–1131. http://dx.doi.org/10.1126/science.185.4157.1124

Uchino, B. N. (2004). *Social support and physical health: Understanding the health consequences of relationships*. New Haven, CT: Yale University Press. http://dx.doi.org/10.12987/yale/9780300102185.001.0001

Uchino, B. N., Cacioppo, J. T., & Kiecolt-Glaser, J. K. (1996). The relationship between social support and physiological processes: A review with emphasis on underlying mechanisms and implications for health. *Psychological Bulletin, 119*, 488–531. http://dx.doi.org/10.1037/0033-2909.119.3.488

U.S. Army Field Manual on Command and Control FM 101-5. (1997, May 31). Washington, DC: Department of the Army.

U.S. Department of Defense. (2002, February 12). DoD news briefing—Secretary Rumsfeld and General Myers. https://archive.defense.gov/Transcripts/Transcript.aspx?TranscriptID=2636

Van Wagoner, S. L., Gelso, C. J., Hayes, J. A., & Diemer, R. A. (1991). Countertransference and the reputedly excellent therapist. *Psychotherapy, 28*, 411–421. http://dx.doi.org/10.1037/0033-3204.28.3.411

Vohs, K. D., Baumeister, R. F., & Loewenstein, G. (Eds.). (2007). *Do emotions help or hurt decision-making? A Hedgefoxian perspective*. New York, NY: Russell Sage Foundation.

Vrieze, S. I., & Grove, W. M. (2009). Survey on the use of clinical and mechanical prediction methods in clinical psychology. *Professional Psychology: Research and Practice, 40*, 525–531. http://dx.doi.org/10.1037/a0014693

Vygotsky, L. S. (1980). *Mind in society: The development of higher psychological processes*. Cambridge, MA: Harvard University Press. (Original work published 1930)

Wachtel, P. L. (1982). Vicious circles: The self and the rhetoric of emerging and unfolding. *Contemporary Psychoanalysis, 18*, 259–273. http://dx.doi.org/10.1080/00107530.1982.10746582

Wachtel, P. L. (2008). *Relational theory and the practice of psychotherapy*. New York, NY: Guilford Press.

Wachtel, P. L. (2014). *Cyclical psychodynamics and the contextual self*. New York, NY: Routledge. http://dx.doi.org/10.4324/9781315794037

Walfish, S., McAlister, B., O'Donnell, P., & Lambert, M. J. (2012). An investigation of self-assessment bias in mental health providers. *Psychological Reports, 110*, 639–644. http://dx.doi.org/10.2466/02.07.17.PR0.110.2.639-644

Wallace, H. M., Baumeister, R. F., & Vohs, K. D. (2005). Audience support and choking under pressure: A home disadvantage? *Journal of Sports Sciences, 23,* 429–438. http://dx.doi.org/10.1080/02640410400021666

Walton, R. E., & McKersie, R. B. (1965). *A behavioral theory of labor negotiations: An analysis of a social interaction system.* New York, NY: McGraw-Hill.

Wampold, B. E., & Imel, Z. E. (2015). *The great psychotherapy debate: The evidence for what makes psychotherapy work.* New York, NY: Routledge. http://dx.doi.org/10.4324/9780203582015

Wass, R., & Golding, C. (2014). Sharpening a tool for teaching: The zone of proximal development. *Teaching in Higher Education, 19,* 671–684. http://dx.doi.org/10.1080/13562517.2014.901958

Watkins, C. E., Hook, J. N., Mosher, D. K., & Callahan, J. L. (2019). Humility in clinical supervision: Fundamental, foundational, and transformational. *The Clinical Supervisor, 38,* 58–78.

Watkins, C. E., Jr., & Riggs, S. (2012). Psychotherapy supervision and attachment theory: Review, reflections, and recommendations. *The Clinical Supervisor, 31,* 256–289. http://dx.doi.org/10.1080/07325223.2012.743319

Watzlawick, P., Bavelas, J. B., & Jackson, D. D. (1967). *Pragmatics of human communication.* New York, NY: Norton.

Webb, T. L., Schweiger Gallo, I., Miles, E., Gollwitzer, P. M., & Sheeran, P. (2012). Effective regulation of affect: An action control perspective on emotion regulation. *European Review of Social Psychology, 23,* 143–186. http://dx.doi.org/10.1080/10463283.2012.718134

Weisinger, H., & Pawliw-Fry, J. P. (2015). *Performing under pressure: The science of doing your best when it matters most.* New York, NY: Crown.

Weiss, J., Sampson, H., & the Mount Zion Psychotherapy Research Group. (Eds.). (1986). *The psychoanalytic process: Theory, clinical observation, and empirical research.* New York, NY: Guilford Press.

Werner, E. E. (1989). *Vulnerable but invincible: A longitudinal study of resilient children and youth.* New York, NY: McGraw-Hill.

Westra, H. A., Aviram, A., Connors, L., Kertes, A., & Ahmed, M. (2012). Therapist emotional reactions and client resistance in cognitive behavioral therapy. *Psychotherapy, 49,* 163–172. http://dx.doi.org/10.1037/a0023200

Whelton, W. J. (2004). Emotional processes in psychotherapy: Evidence across therapeutic modalities. *Clinical Psychology & Psychotherapy, 11,* 58–71. http://dx.doi.org/10.1002/cpp.392

Whitman, W. (1950). *Leaves of grass and selected poems.* New York, NY: Random House. (Original work published 1855)

Williams, E. N., Hayes, J. A., & Fauth, J. (2008). Therapist self-awareness: Interdisciplinary connections and future directions. In S. D. Brown & R. W. Lent (Eds.), *Handbook of counseling psychology* (pp. 303–319). New York, NY: Guilford Press.

Winnicott, D. W. (1965). *The maturational process and the facilitating environment.* New York, NY: International Universities.

Winnicott, D. W. (1971). *Playing and reality.* London, England: Penguin Books.

Wolf, A. W., Goldfried, M. R., & Muran, J. C. (2017). Therapist negative reactions: How to transform toxic experiences. In L. G. Castonguay & C. E. Hill (Eds.), *How and why are some therapists better than others? Understanding therapist effects* (pp. 175–192). Washington, DC: American Psychological Association. http://dx.doi.org/10.1037/0000034-011

Wonderlich, S. A., Peterson, C. B., & Smith, T. L. (2015). *Integrative cognitive-affective therapy for bulimia nervosa: A treatment manual.* New York, NY: Guilford Press.

Wood, D., Bruner, J. S., & Ross, G. (1976). The role of tutoring in problem solving. *Journal of Child Psychology and Psychiatry, 17,* 89–100. http://dx.doi.org/10.1111/j.1469-7610.1976.tb00381.x

Wright, P. (1974). The harassed decision maker: Time pressures, distractions, and the use of evidence. *Journal of Applied Psychology, 59,* 555–561. http://dx.doi.org/10.1037/h0037186

Yerkes, R. M., & Dodson, J. D. (1908). The relation of strength of stimulus to rapidity of habit formation. *Journal of Comparative Neurology and Psychology, 18,* 459–482. http://dx.doi.org/10.1002/cne.920180503

Young, J. E., Klosko, J. S., & Weishaar, M. E. (2003). *Schema therapy: A practitioner's guide.* New York, NY: Guilford Press.

Zaki, J., & Ochsner, K. (2016). Empathy. In L. Feldman-Barrett, M. Lewis, & J. M. Haviland-Jones (Eds.), *The handbook of emotion* (4th ed., pp. 871–884). New York, NY: Guilford Press.

Zaki, J., & Williams, W. C. (2013). Interpersonal emotion regulation. *Emotion, 13,* 803–810. http://dx.doi.org/10.1037/a0033839

Zilcha-Mano, S., Snyder, J., & Silberschatz, G. (2017). The effect of congruence in patient and therapist alliance on patient's symptomatic levels. *Psychotherapy Research, 27,* 371–380. http://dx.doi.org/10.1080/10503307.2015.1126682

INDEX

A

Academic performance, 25
Acceptance strategies, 55
Adaptive emotions, 54
Addiction, 29
Affect effect, 17–18
Affect heuristic, 17–18
Affective attunement, 67, 70
Affect labeling, 7, 23, 55
AFT. *See* Alliance-focused training
Agency
   and emotion, 67, 71
   and metacommunication, 77
   and objectification of others, 98
   and rupture repair, 42, 49
   and self-schemas, 57
   and types of rupture, 37–38
Aggression, 38
Ahmed, M., 34
Alexander, F., 66
Alliance-focused training (AFT), 106–126
   goal of, 103–104
   key principles of, 109–114
   and practicing under pressure, 140–141
   research support for, 106–109, 127,
      145–146
   strategies for implementation of,
      114–117
   structure of, 117
   use of video recordings in, 138–139
Allocentricity, 7
Altruism, 56
Ambivalence, 29

American Psychological Association
   (APA), 5
Amygdala activity, 22, 23
Analysis, 15
Anchoring (counterfactual thinking),
   15–16
Anchoring effect, 16
Anderson, T., 36
Andrade, E., 18
Anger
   aggressive, 25
   assertive, 86
   controlled expressions of, 86
   defined, 85
   function of, 53
   and metacommunication, 85–88
   passive, 86
   toward patients, 29
   and training, 106
Antistatistics bias, 16
Anxiety
   in alliance-focused training, 111
   defined, 83
   management of, 32
   and metacommunication, 83–85
   optimal range of, 105
   practicing under, 25
   responding to, 154
   and Rupture Resolution Rating System,
      149
   toward patients, 29
APA (American Psychological Association), 5

Ariely, D., 18
Aron, L., 64
Assertion, 86
Athletes, 129
Attachment, 32, 49, 76
Attention
    in alliance-focused training, 110
    and emotion, 56
Attentional distraction, 22, 55
Attunement, 55, 67, 70
Automatic thoughts, 58
Availability (counterfactual thinking), 15
Aviation personnel, 14
Aviram, A., 34
Awareness in relation, 79

B

Balance, 130, 134–135
Bambling, M., 107
Banaji, M., 17
Barkham, M., 30–31
Barlow, D. H., 86
Barnett, J. E., 141–142
Barrett, L. F., 53–54
Baumeister, R. F., 18, 21
Bavelas, J. B., 74
Beginner's mind, 7, 75–76, 133
Beilock, S. L., 20, 25
Benjamin, J., 62, 64–65
Bernard, J. M., 105
Biases
    antistatistics, 16
    confirmation, 16, 139–140
    and counterfactual thinking, 15–16
    and critical inquiry, 139
    cultural, 19
    curiosity as guard against, 133
    hindsight, 16, 140
    implicit, 17, 63
    research on, 26, 145
    and therapist self-care, 130, 139–140
Bisexual patients, 33
Bodily experiences
    and alliance-focused training, 111
    and emotions, 51, 54
Bonanno, G. A., 23
Borderline personality disorder, 44,
    149–150
Bordin, E. S., 37, 67, 70, 154
Boredom
    defined, 96
    and metacommunication, 96–97
Bowlby, J., 32
Brain activity, 53
Bratslavsky, E., 18
Breathing exercises, 136
Brief relational therapy (BRT), 107–108
Bromberg, P., 62

Bruner, J., 24
Buber, M., 3
Burnout
    as impediment to therapeutic alliance,
        30–31
    and therapist self-care, 129, 131, 141
Butler, E. A., 55
Button, M. L., 34

C

Callahan, J. L., 105, 136
Carlyle, T., 29
Carr, T. H., 20
Case conceptualization
    bias in, 140
    and therapeutic alliance, 29
    therapist ability for, 32
Caskie, G. I. L., 106
Castonguay, L. G., 108
CBT. *See* Cognitive behavior therapy
CFI (Countertransference Factors
    Inventory), 31–32
Chow, D. L., 138
Clarity, 36
Clinical judgment
    overview, 18–19
    research on, 145–146
    and therapist self-care, 129–130, 140
Cognitive appraisal, 20, 134
Cognitive behavior therapy (CBT)
    and alliance-focused training, 107–109,
        127
    conceptualization of change in, 59
    conceptualizations of emotion in, 51
    research on, 34, 35
    in research on rupture resolution, 41
    and Rupture Resolution Rating System,
        149
    studies of rupture repair in, 44
Cognitive challenges, 82
Cognitive error, 145
Cognitive load, 20
Cognitive processing, 54
Cognitive reappraisal, 22, 55
Cognitive therapy, 35–36. *See also* Cognitive
    behavior therapy
Coifman, K., 23
Collaboration, 154
Collaborative inquiry, 74, 75
Collaborative Interactions Scale, 41
Commitment, 98
Communication
    and emotion, 53, 67
    meta-. *See* Metacommunication
Communion. *See also* Relatedness
    and emotion, 71
    and metacommunication, 77
    and rupture repair, 42, 49

and self-schemas, 57
and types of rupture, 37–38
Compassion, 56, 99, 130, 132–133
Competence constellation, 141–142
Competency-based supervision, 104
Competitor neglect, 16
Confirmation bias, 16, 139–140
Conflict splits, 59
Confrontation ruptures
    and emotion, 68
    markers of, 38, 40
    overview, 37–38
    in Rupture Resolution Rating System,
        154, 157, 169–177
    steps in repairing of, 42
    in supervision, 113
Connors, L., 34
Constantino, M. J., 108
Construction (self experience), 65–67
Consultation, 29, 137, 141
Control, 86
Coordination (mother–infant research),
    55
Core competencies, 5
Coregulation, 55
Counterfactual thinking, 15–16
Countertransference
    as factor in therapeutic alliance, 31–32,
        49
    and therapist uniformity, 5
    and training, 104
Countertransference Factors Inventory
    (CFI), 31–32
Courting surprise, 7
Court-mandated treatment, 29, 132
Critical events in supervision model,
    104–105
Critical inquiry, 139–140
Critical thinking, 25
Crits-Cristoph, P., 107
Cultural background, 64
Cultural biases, 19
Cultural competence, 7
Cultural humility, 7
Curiosity, 44, 111, 130, 133, 136
Cynicism, 30

D

Dalenberg, C. J., 29
Darwin, C., 51–52
Decision making, 129–130, 145
Deconstruction (post-modernist method),
    66
De Beauvoir, S., 51
De Groot, A., 14
Delgadillo, J., 31
Deliberate practice, 24–25, 138, 143, 146
Depersonalization, 131

Depression
    and alliance-focused training, 107, 108
    in research on rupture resolution, 41,
        44
    and Rupture Resolution Rating System,
        149–150
    and sadness, 88
Dewey, J., 25
Diagnostic categories, 148
Dialectical behavior therapy, 141
Dialectical-constructivist perspective on
    emotions, 54
Dialectical tension, 68
Dialogic epistemologies, 73
Dialogic model of understanding, 63
Didactic training, 114–115
Differences between self and other, 58, 63
Disconfirmatory approaches, 140
Discovery (self-awareness), 65–67
Dissociation
    and alliance-focused training, 115
    and rupture repair, 70
    and ruptures, 67, 71
    and self states, 58–59
Distancing strategies, 55
Distraction theory, 21
Distress, 20
Duckworth, A., 23–24
Dunn, R., 136
Dysregulatory disorders, 7

E

Ehrenberg, D., 77
Ellison, R., 63
Elman, N. S., 141–142
Embarrassment
    defined, 91
    and metacommunication, 91–93
Emotion, 51–71. *See also specific headings*
    and affect effect, 17–18
    and balancing with positivity, 134
    complexity of, 50–52
    generation and regulation of, 52–56
    metacommunication about, 82–100
    and multiplicity of selves, 56–67
    research on, 145
    in ruptures, 67–70
    and therapist self-care, 130
Emotional communication, 6
Emotional modulation, 56
Emotional transmission, 56
Emotion journals, 136–137
Emotion labeling, 7, 23, 55
Emotion regulation
    and alliance-focused training, 110, 114,
        115
    defined, 7, 54
    development of skills for, 7, 27

future directions for research on,
147–148
with metacommunication, 75
overview, 21–23
range of perspectives on, 51–52
research on, 145
for therapist self-care, 130
Empathic failure, 67
Empathic reciprocity, 6
Empathy
components of, 99
for creation of therapeutic alliance, 44
defined, 99
measurement of therapist, 32
and therapeutic alliance, 36
Empty-chair exercises, 116
Enactments, 71
Ericsson, K. A., 24, 138
Ethnicity, 33
Eustress, 20
Eversmann, J., 36
Evolution, 51–52
Existential frameworks, 61, 144
Experience sharing, 99
Experiencing (therapy concept), 76
Experiencing Scale, 76, 115
Experiential avoidance, 59–60, 67, 115
Experiential interventions, 109, 111
Experiential training, 115
Exploration approaches, 109
Exploratory rupture resolution strategies,
45, 46
Exposure therapy, 137
*The Expression of the Emotions in Man and
Animals* (Darwin), 51–52
Expressive behaviors, 54
Expressive suppression, 22, 55

F

Facial affect, 56
Facilitative Interpersonal Skills task
(Anderson), 36
Fear, 53, 83. *See also* Anxiety
Feedback
and therapeutic alliance, 29
for therapists, 131
Felt sense, 69, 70
Feminism
and intersubjectivity, 62
and shifts in psychotherapy, 6
Ferenczi, S., 6, 66–67
Ferris, L. E., 130
Finkenauer, C., 18
Finlay, L., 25
Fire commanders, 14
Fisher, C. D., 96
Flückiger, C., 36

fMRI (functional magnetic resonance
imaging) research, 53
Focusing (therapy concept), 76
Forrest, L., 141–142
Foucault, M., 64, 65
Frattaroli, J., 136–137
Friedlander, M. L., 105, 136

G

Gadamer, H.-G., 63, 64
Garmezy, N., 23
Gay patients, 33
Geertz, C., 76
Gender, 33
Gendlin, E., 76
Generalized anxiety disorder
and alliance-focused training, 108
research on therapy outcomes and, 34,
35
Gibbs, G., 25
Goldberg, S. B., 36
Good-enough parenting, 132–133
Goodyear, R. K., 105, 130
Granularity. *See also* Affect labeling
defined, 23
movement toward, 71
and orientation to emotional experience,
60
research on, 55
Greenberg, J., 61
Greenberg, L., 54
Greenwald, A., 17
Griffiths, P. E., 53
Grit, 23–24
Gross, J. J., 22, 55
Guilt, 93–94

H

Habermas, J., 64, 65
Handbook of Emotion (Barrett, Lewis, &
Haviland-Jones), 51
Handbook of Emotion Regulation (Gross), 51
Hara, K. M., 34
Hate, 85–88
Hayes, J. A., 133
Hegel, G. W. F., 64, 144
Helping skills training program (Hill), 104
Here-and-now, 78–79
Heuristics, 15–16, 19, 26, 130, 145. *See also*
Biases
Hill, C. E., 33, 74, 103
Hindsight bias, 16, 140
Hoffman, I., 64, 65
Hook, J. N., 105
Horney, K., 154

Hostility, 34
Hubris, 94–96
Humanistic psychotherapies, 51
Humility
    and asking for help, 144
    and clinical judgment, 19
    importance of, 26
    and metacommunication, 94
    of supervisors, 105
    and therapist self-care, 130–131
Hux, J. E., 130
Hyperreflexivity, 21

I

IAT (Implicit Association Test), 17
Identity politics, 67
Illusion of understanding, 16
Immediacy, 74
Immediate rupture resolution strategies,
    45, 46
Implicit Association Test (IAT), 17
Implicit bias
    and emotion, 63
    overview, 17
Individual differences
    foundation for, 58
    of therapists, 6
Insecure attachment, 32, 49
Instrumental behaviors, 54
Integrative cognitive therapy, 108
Interpersonal complementarity, 6
Interpersonal pulls, 67–68, 70, 71
Interpersonal theory, 66
Interruptive splits, 59
Intersectionality, 58
Intersubjective negotiation
    overview, 65
    ruptures as breakdowns in, 67
Intersubjective reflection, 25
Intersubjectivity
    and emotion, 62–65, 71
    overview, 6
Intimacy, 6, 98
Introspection, 25
Intuition, 15–16, 18, 139
Invisible Man (Ellison), 63
Ironic deconstruction, 25
I–Thou relationship, 77, 101
Ivanovic, M., 136

J

Jackson, D. D., 74
Jakubowski, P., 82
James, W., 51, 56–57
John, O. P., 22
Johns, C., 25

Johnson, W. B., 141–142
Journaling, 136–137
Jurist, E., 77

K

Kahneman, D.
    and affect effect, 18
    and clinical judgment, 19
    and counterfactual thinking, 15, 16
    and therapist self-care, 139, 140
Kaslow, N. J., 141–142
Kertes, A., 34
Kiesler, D., 5, 13, 61, 74
King, B. J., 143
King, R., 107
Klein, M., 76
Knox, S., 103

L

Ladany, N., 106
Lalande, K., 23
Lambert, W., 107
Laneri, R., 5
Lange, A., 82
Lange, J., 36
Langton, R., 98
Law of small numbers, 16
Learning
    continuous, 27
    and scaffolding, 24–25
Lee, B., 13
Lehmann, A. C., 138
Lesbian, gay, and bisexual (LGB) patients,
    33
Levenson, E., 61, 74, 100
Lichtenberg, J. W., 130
Love, 98–99

M

Magnum Force (movie), 94
Maladaptive emotions, 54
Managed care, 29
Manualized therapy, 5
Master–slave dialectic, 64–65
Matrical enactments, 68
Mechanical judgment, 18–19
Meehl, P., 18
Mehr, K. E., 106
Memory
    and emotion, 53
    procedural, 20
    and self schemas, 58
    working, 20, 21
Mentalization, 77, 99
Mentalized affectivity, 76–77

Mental representation (rupture resolution), 42
Mental simulation, 15
Metacommunication, 73–101
  in alliance-focused training, 109, 121
  and basic negative emotions, 82–91
  and challenging emotional states, 96–100
  collaborative frame for, 78
  early ruptures with, 81–82
  effect of, 7–8
  finding balance for, 82
  here-and-now focus of, 78–79
  overview, 73–78
  as process, 80–81
  relatedness and responsiveness in, 80
  and self-conscious emotions, 91–96
  and therapist self-care, 132
  therapist subjectivity in, 79–80
Metacompetence, 104
Microaggressions
  patient ratings of, 33
  and ruptures, 7, 68
Military officers, 14
Mindfulness
  in alliance-focused training, 115
  and curiosity, 133
  for emotion regulation, 7, 55
  in interaction, 75. *See also*
    Metacommunication
  for therapist self-care, 135–136
Misempathy, 99–100
Mitchell, S., 61, 66
Moeyaert, M., 136
Moran, D., 73
Mosher, D. K., 105
Mother–infant research, 55
Mount Zion Psychotherapy Research
  Group, 66
Multicultural awareness, 104
Multiplicity of selves, 56–67
Muran, J. C.
  and alliance-focused training, 107, 108
  stage-process model of rupture
    resolution developed by, 41–42, 46
Mutual collaboration, 25
Mutual influence, 55
Mutuality, 6, 64
Mutual recognition
  importance of, 8
  and intersubjectivity, 62
  and metacommunication, 77
  and power, 64
  and rupture repair, 70
Mutual regulation model, 55

N

Naïve realism, 139
Narcissism, 130–131

National Aeronautics and Space
  Administration (NASA), 15
Naturalistic decision making, 14–15
Negations (ruptures), 68, 71
Neglect, 96–97
Neurological changes, 54, 56, 150
Neuroticism, 61
Newman, M. G., 108
Nonjudgmental awareness, 129, 136
Norcross, J. C., 30, 129
Nussbaum, M., 98

O

Objectification
  and metacommunication, 77, 98
  and ruptures, 68, 70
Object use, 65
Ochsner, K., 24
O'Connor, F., 137
Ourdejans, R., 25
Overconfidence effect, 16, 130–131
Overidentification, 99–100
Overoptimism, 16
Oxytocin, 150

P

Panic, 83–85
Papa, A., 23
Pascual-Leone, J., 54
Passion, 98
Passive anger, 86
Patience, 130, 134
Pattern matching, 15
Patterson, C. L., 36
Peer review, 141, 142
Pennebaker, J. W., 136
Performance under pressure, 13–27.
  See also specific headings
  affect effect in, 17–18
  and clinical judgment, 18–19
  and counterfactual thinking, 15–16
  and deliberate practice, 24–25
  emotion regulation for, 21–23
  and implicit bias, 17
  and naturalistic decision making, 14–15
  and reflective practice, 25–26
  resilience for, 23–24
  and self-focus, 21
  and stress response, 20–21
Performers, 129
Personality disorders
  and alliance-focused training, 107–109
  and emotion regulation, 7
  and Rupture Resolution Rating System, 149
Phenomenological experiences, 54
Pizer, S., 62, 65, 77
Politser, P., 19

Pope, K. S., 29
Positionality, 67
Positive regard, 132
Positivity, 134–135, 143
Power
  and emotion, 62–65, 71
  plays in, 68
Practice under pressure, 140–141
Prefrontal cortex, 22
Prejudice, 62–65
Pressure, 14. *See also specific headings*
Pressure Is a Privilege (King), 143
Pride
  defined, 94
  and metacommunication, 94–96
Primary emotions, 53, 54
Probability theory, 140
Procedural memory, 20
Progressive deepening, 14
Projective identification, 115
Prosocial motivation, 99
Psychoanalysis
  conceptualizations of emotion in, 51
  and identity of analyst, 5
Psychodynamic-interpersonal therapy
  and alliance-focused training, 107
  in research on rupture resolution, 41
  and struggle to know oneself, 144
  studies of rupture repair in, 44
Psychodynamic therapy, 35–36
Psychotherapy research, 13

R

Race, 33
Randall, A. K., 55
Raue, P., 107
Reciprocal emotion, 6
Reciprocity
  and emotion, 61
  in mother–infant research, 55
Recognition-primed decision (RPD) model,
  15
Redelmeier, D. A., 19, 130, 140, 141
Reflection-in-action, 25
Reflection-on-action, 25
Reflective practice, 25–26
Reflexivity, 25
Reinforcement pattern, 115
Relatedness. *See also* Communion
  defined, 57
  monitoring of, 79
Relational matrices, 115
Relational movement in psychotherapy
  effects of, 5–6
  multiplicity of selves in, 59
Reparation (mother–infant research), 55
Representativeness (counterfactual
  thinking), 15

Resilience
  development of, 27
  overview, 23–24
  and positivity, 134–135
  promotion of, 144, 145
Resistance
  and alliance-focused training, 115
  as predictor of poor treatment outcome,
    34–35
Respect, 36
Responsiveness
  in alliance-focused training, 105–106,
    112, 126
  monitoring of, 79
Rimé, B., 55
Rivera, M., 12
Rogers, C. R., 76, 132
Role conflicts, 104
Role plays, 116–117, 119–120, 140–142
Ross, G., 24
Rousmaniere, T., 138
RPD (recognition-primed decision) model,
  15
Rumsfeld, D., 144–145
Rupture resolution, 41–49
  as change event, 101
  change opportunities with, 70
  components of, 41–42
  immediate and exploratory strategies for,
    45, 46
  in Rupture Resolution Rating System,
    178–187
  strategies for, 155
Rupture Resolution Rating System (3RS),
  149–190
  future directions for research with, 150
  overview, 4
  research applications of, 149–150
  training in, 115
  types of ruptures in, 38–41
Ruptures
  in alliance-focused training. *See*
    Alliance-focused training
  and competence, 142
  and emotion, 67–70
  as emotional challenges, 101
  future directions for research on, 146–147
  management of, 7–8
  with metacommunication, 81–82
  outcomes with, 6–7
  overview, 37–41, 144, 146
  and therapist self-care, 135

S

Sachs, H., 144
Sadness
  function of, 53
  and metacommunication, 88–91

Safran, J. D.
  and alliance-focused training, 107, 108
  stage-process model of rupture
    resolution developed by, 41–42, 46
Samstag, L. W., 108
SASB (Structural Analysis of Social
    Behavior), 115
Satisficing options, 14
Saxon, D., 30–31
Scaffolding, 24–25, 111–112, 126
Scarantino, A., 53
Schön, D. A., 25, 139
Schöttke, H., 36
Schull, M. J., 130
Schweitzer, R., 107
Secondary emotions, 54
Secure attachment, 32, 106
Seduction, 98–99
Self-analysis, 141
Self-approval, 130
Self-awareness
  discovery of, 65–66
  and reflective practice, 25
Self-care. *See* Therapist self-care
Self-compassion, 132, 136
Self-conscious emotions, 91–96
Self-definition, 57
Self-disclosure, 75, 77, 80
Self-doubt, 93–94
Self-efficacy, 106
Self-exploration, 110–111
Self-focus, 21
Self-harm, 29, 31
Self-insight, 32
Self-integration, 32
Self-regulation theory, 137
Self relations, 61–62
Self schemas, 57–58
Self-splits
  and ruptures, 67, 71
  types of, 59
Self states
  and alliance-focused training, 115
  and metacommunication, 77
  overview, 58–61
Seligman, M., 24
Selye, H., 20
Sexual attraction, 105
Shame, 91–93
Short-term dynamic psychotherapy
    (STDP), 107, 108
Simon, H., 14
Skill execution, 20
"Skillful tentativeness," 44
Skin conductance research, 23
Social categorization, 131
Social constructionism, 6, 73
Social critique, 25
Social sharing of emotion, 55

Social support, 56
Socratic method, 75
Spontaneous distancing, 22–23
Stage-process model of rupture resolution
  exploratory strategies in, 46
  overview, 7–8, 41–43
STDP (short-term dynamic psychotherapy),
    107, 108
Stern, D. B., 55–56, 75, 77
Sternberg, R., 98
Stone, M., 136
Stress. *See also specific headings*
  definitions of, 14
  as impediment to therapeutic alliance,
    30
Stress, Cognition, and Human Performance
    (report), 15
Stress buffering, 56
Stress response, 20–21
Structural Analysis of Social Behavior
    (SASB), 115
Strupp, H., 33–35
Subjectification, 68, 70, 77
Subjective experiences
  and emotion, 54
  and love, 98
  and metacommunication, 79–80
Substitution (affect effect), 18
Suicidality, 29
Sullivan, H. S., 6, 57, 58, 100, 105
Supervision
  effects of, 103. *See also* Training
  and therapeutic alliance, 29
  and therapist self-care, 141
Supervision groups, 141
Supervisory alliance, 104
Swift, J. K., 136
Symington, N., 81
Sympathy, 99
Synchrony, 55
System 1 thinking, 16
System 2 thinking, 16
System for Observing Family Therapy
    Alliances, 41

T

Tabachnick, B. G., 29
Tactical Decision Making Under Stress
    Project, 15
Task fixation, 15
Tension, 106
Therapeutic alliance, 29–49
  case example, 47–49
  effects of supervisory alliance on, 106
  impediments to, 30–31
  importance of, 30
  research on, 145–146
  ruptures in. *See* Ruptures

and therapist contributions to negative
process, 33–36
and therapist personal difficulties, 31–33
therapist proclivity for development of, 13
Therapeutic presence, 133
Therapeutic relationship. *See also Therapeutic
alliance*
research on, 145–146
shift in importance of, 5–6
Therapist identity, 5
Therapist self-care, 129–142
basic attitudes for, 129–135, 142
strategies for, 135–142
Thick description, 76
Thinking, Fast and Slow (Kahneman), 16
3RS. *See* Rupture Resolution Rating System
To Kill a Mockingbird (Lee), 99
Tracey, T. J., 130
Training, 103–127
alliance-focused, 103–104, 106–126
case example, 118–126
models in, 104–105
and supervisors as models, 105–106
Transference interpretations, 82
Trauma, 23, 29, 59, 134
Tronick, E., 55
Tu, J. V., 130
Tversky, A., 15, 16, 19, 140
Two-chair exercises, 116

U

Unawareness, 130
Uncertainty-identity theory, 131
"Uniformity myth," 5, 13
Unknown knowns, 16
U.S. Army, 15
U.S. Navy, 15
USS *Vincennes* incident, 15

V

Validation, 44
VandenBos, G. R., 30, 129
Vanderbilt studies, 33, 35, 106
"Vicious circles" (psychotherapy process),
68, 70, 71, 115

Video recordings of therapy sessions, 112,
115–117, 137–139
Vinca, M., 133
Vocal affect, 56
Vocal Quality measure, 115
Vohs, K. D., 18
Vygotsky, L., 24

W

Wachtel, P., 61
Wampold, B. E., 130
Warmth, 36
Watkins, C. E., 105
Watzlawick, P., 74
Weis, A. C., 36
Werner, E., 23
Westphal, M., 23
Westra, H. A., 34
"What you see is all there is" (WYSIATI), 16
Williams, C., 55
Winnicott, D., 65, 132–133
Winston, A., 108
Withdrawal ruptures
and emotion, 68
markers of, 38–40
overview, 37–38
in Rupture Resolution Rating System,
154, 157, 162–169
steps in repairing of, 42
Wood, D., 24
Working memory
defined, 20
and self-focus, 21
Writing exercises, 136–137
WYSIATI ("What you see is all there is"), 16

Y

Yerkes-Dodson curve, 20, 105

Z

Zaki, J., 55
Zone of proximal development (ZPD), 24,
105, 111–112

ABOUT THE AUTHORS

J. Christopher Muran, PhD, is associate dean and full professor at the Gordon F. Derner School of Psychology, Adelphi University, where he has served as training director for its doctoral program in clinical psychology (2009–present). He completed postdoctoral training in cognitive therapy (University of Toronto) and psychoanalysis (New York University). He is a fellow of the American Psychological Association (Divisions 12 and 29) and on its Advisory Steering Committee for the Development of Clinical Practice Guidelines. He is past president of the Society for Psychotherapy Research and past editor of its journal *Psychotherapy Research*; he is also on the editorial board for the *Journal of Consulting and Clinical Psychology* and *Clinical Psychology: Science and Practice*. Since 1990, Dr. Muran has directed the Psychotherapy Research Program at Beth Israel Medical Center (now Mount Sinai Beth Israel), which has been funded by grant awards from the National Institute of Mental Health. He was chief psychologist at Beth Israel for 15 years (1994–2009) and is on the faculty at Icahn School of Medicine at Mount Sinai. Dr. Muran has received several awards for his research and teaching; he has published more than 130 papers and nine books on change processes and the therapeutic relationship, including *Practice-Oriented Research in Psychotherapy: Building Partnerships Between Clinicians and Researchers* (2016; edited with Louis G. Castonguay), *Transforming Negative Reactions to Clients: From Frustration to Compassion* (2013; edited with Abraham W. Wolf and Marvin R. Goldfried), *The Therapeutic Alliance: An Evidence-Based Guide to Practice* (2010; edited with Jacques P. Barber), *Dialogues on Difference: Studies of Diversity in the Therapeutic Relationship* (2007; edited), *Self-Relations in the Psychotherapy Process* (2001; edited), and *Negotiating the Therapeutic Alliance: A Relational Treatment Guide* (2000; with Jeremy D. Safran).

Catherine F. Eubanks, PhD, is associate professor of clinical psychology at the Ferkauf Graduate School of Psychology of Yeshiva University. She also serves as associate director of the Mount Sinai-Beth Israel Brief Psychotherapy Research Program. Dr. Eubanks received the Early Career Award from the American Psychological Foundation Division 29 in 2018, the Outstanding Early Career Achievement Award from the Society for Psychotherapy Research in 2015, and the Dissertation Award from the Society for the Exploration of Psychotherapy Integration in 2007. She served as president of the Society for the Exploration of Psychotherapy Integration in 2019 and as executive officer of the North American chapter of the Society for Psychotherapy Research from 2013 to 2018. Dr. Eubanks has previously served as an associate editor for *Psychotherapy Research* and is currently an associate editor for the *Journal of Consulting and Clinical Psychology*. She is also on the editorial board of the *Journal of Psychotherapy Integration* and the *Journal of Clinical Psychology: In Session*.